THE MILLENNIAL'S GUIDE TO CHANGING THE WORLD

A NEW GENERATION'S HANDBOOK TO BEING YOURSELF & LIVING WITH PURPOSE

ALISON LEA SHER

Skyhorse Publishing

Skyhorse Publishing books may be purchased in bulk at special discounts for sales promotion, corporate gifts, fund-raising, or educational purposes. Special editions can also be created to specifications. For details, contact the Special Sales Department, Skyhorse Publishing, 307 West 36th Street, 11th Floor, New York, NY 10018 or info@skyhorsepublishing.com.

Skyhorse® and Skyhorse Publishing® are registered trademarks of Skyhorse Publishing, Inc.®, a Delaware corporation.

Visit our website at www.skyhorsepublishing.com.

10 9 8 7 6 5 4 3 2 1

Library of Congress Cataloging-in-Publication Data is available on file.

Cover design by Mason Greenewald

Print ISBN: 978-1-5107-3321-3
Ebook ISBN: 978-1-5107-3322-0

33614080639718

Printed in the United States of America

Table of Contents

Prologue

I'M A MILLENNIAL, AND THIS A BOOK ABOUT MILLENNIALS—THE (Next) Lost Generation, Generation WTF, Generation Frustrated, Generation Screwed. Some people have been hating on us up-and-comers because we're slicker. We're more sensitive. We've got the information, the attitude, and the energy needed to evolve this planet. But the question is, how can we harness it?

Millennials have a mixed reputation. Older generations think we're floundering—that we're only living up to a small sliver of our potential, that we're failing each other and future generations in the process. Is this accurate? Perhaps. But two truths can simultaneously exist.

From the millennial point of view, this is absurd. Because, from our perspective, we've inherited perhaps the most challenging social, political, and cultural milieu in human history, a myriad of problems that we have to somehow fix. It's been a tough road to adulthood, and many millennials feel resentment toward the expectations that we should do or be something other than what we are. And yet, we must tell ourselves that we *can* be more. This book is designed to help.

Love or hate the word *millennial,* you're stuck with it for a while. A millennial is someone born between 1980 and 2000. If this is you, this book is about you and for you; it's also for the baby boomers who want to get us, the Gen X'ers who might feel forgotten, and the Gen Z'ers who want to know what they'll have to face in the future.

We are a unique generation because we grew up during the technological revolution, in the sprawl of globalization, where a shrinking workforce, gobs of debt, high rents, and low wages are keeping us from graduating into the next phase of life as quickly as those who came before us did. We've witnessed 9/11 and the War on Terror, Occupy Wall Street, the emergence of climate change, mass shootings in public schools and public places, sociopathic corporate personhood, national surveillance, too-big-to-fail bank bailouts, and a gridlocked Congress. People act like this is business as usual, but these are the days that are trying the souls of a generation. We may be beaten down, but we're not broken. We may be scared, angry, and disappointed, but we are hopeful. We may have a reputation for leaving almost everything we start, but, in the larger picture, I believe we're not giving up.

We've got some rather large problems to face. By 2036, it's predicted that global warming will reach crisis levels. Scientists say the earth reached its sustainable capacity to support human life decades ago. Millennials are being handed down a system that's self-destructing: socially, economically, politically, psychologically, environmentally. Plus, what lies at the heart of these crises is a spiritual issue.

We haven't figured out how to become consciously aware of our impact on ourselves, each other, and the natural world. We have to devise a social system where life and all its elements are treated as sacred. To solve the problems we're inheriting, we must first figure out how to create a society where all life forms can thrive.

For all to be one, one must live for all. A culture of love that includes everyone. And it's up to millennials—the ones who value living consciously and pursuing purpose, who prize innovation, and who condemn inequality and consumerism. Our values have the power to restore this society to balance; we have to claim ourselves as stakeholders in it.

As this world continues to hurt, the calloused choir of elders yawns and disapproves. They say, *People have clubbed each other over the head since the dawn of civilization. The stock market and unemployment rates always go up and down. You can't stop war.* But this is an urgent time, and we can't keep listening to them.

A lot of people think the millennial struggle is not that unique. But hey, that's no fun to believe—and it's also not useful if we want to do something about all this. So, let's live our lives in a delusion of grandeur instead. Let's believe that every life matters. Let's live as if we can make a difference.

This book is a rallying cry. Because it just might be the millennial's destiny to become the generation that creates the critical mass to pioneer a new epoch in society, one defined by the conscious awareness of our human impact. It would be foolish for us to continue living in the conventional ways people have and expect a different result. Crisis is calling each of us to assume our role in the transformation of our communities and human civilization.

"Cynicism is our biggest problem—this very tragic idea that the world can't become a better place. I know people who say all of it is corrupt. I don't want to be a part of it. It takes a very strong person to go after changing it."
—Charlotte Clymer, twenty-seven,
social media influencer, writer, and activist

Chapter 1

What Are You Going to Do with Your Life?!

"MAKE YOUR LIFE INTO BRAND."

This was the advice of my graduation speaker at the mediocre liberal arts party school I attended. At the time, I wanted to vomit. Not because I had just popped and guzzled a bottle of champagne in the campus courtyard at 10 a.m., but because I was ready to go out and conquer the system, to offer it all my unique millennial gifts, and this woman was telling me to turn my life into a logo.

I had no idea that, in a few months, I'd be sobbing on a milk crate in the back room of a shitty food and beverage job, pleading to the cosmos to reveal to me the point of my existence.

I graduated in 2009. The economy had just crashed a year prior. Stock brokers were jumping out of the windows of Manhattan skyscrapers. Our own Great Depression was on. Mortgage-backed securities and collateralized debt obligations were not yet part of my vocabulary. All I knew was that something called the real estate bubble had burst. And so had my expectations. In typical, entitled millennial fashion, I had assumed the world was going to roll out a red carpet for me. And then I slowly began to realize that, in fact, the world disapproved of me, as a millennial.

I had no qualifications to do anything and just about zero life skills. I spent that summer pitching stories, working for free—thinking people were doing me a favor for giving me such wonderful opportunities—and binge drinking almost every night. And then I got my first job as a barista—the occupation de jour of millennial, misanthropic English majors. I worked three other side hustles, made roughly seven thousand dollars that year, and was lucky enough to be able to cash checks every month from my parents to pay the rent. I broke down twice from nervous exhaustion and contemplated becoming either a nun or a train hopper to avoid the responsibilities of a real world filled with mean people.

I wasn't alone in this impasse of identity. Millennials suffer from high rates of apocalyptic anxiety and existential doom. This was only amplified during the Great Recession. According to a study by the American Psychological Association, we have the highest perceived amount of stress of any living generation. Our stress is existential, interpersonal, and also financial. Millennials feel so depressed about the future that it's challenging for us to function day to day. We struggle with the idea that our entire value and worth are dependent on how well we perform in a toxic society. We're constantly comparing our lives to others. We've been taught to pretend that we're happy even when we're not. And we don't know what to do about the fact that we're unhappy.

It's a lot of work to build self-esteem, especially when you can't stop thinking about how your hands are stained with blood and how every footstep contributes to the problems that will cause the human race to destroy ourselves. Pretty much everything we buy contributes to the enslavement of someone on the other side of the planet. Every year, our tax dollars subsidize dirty fossil fuels and wars in the Middle East. We may love going to the beach, but those sea levels are starting to rise as ice caps melt. The worst part of it all is that while we're getting screwed over by a rigged system, we still need to write our authority figures thank you notes so can we use them on our resume as references in an increasingly competitive job market.

THE UNGLAMOROUS, PAINSTAKING PATH OF THE DREAMER

> "Not losing hope in humanity has been my greatest challenge. Not losing hope in the face of how man treats man, believing that we can all be good and genuinely want happiness for each other."
>
> —Peter Meli, twenty-six, screenwriter

Young people usually first attempt to solve our identity crises by hinging it entirely on what we do—and whether or not we're successful. But the truth is that many people succeed by failing—and failing a lot. I've had to learn that the strength of my sense of self relies more on my ability to fail and keep persevering than it does on the outcome of my efforts. Sometimes, allowing yourself to be average and to develop at your own timing is the healthiest approach if you want to succeed at anything in the world.

I've seen it with my peers time and again: so much of our self-image hangs on how powerful and influential we can be or whether we're able to fulfill our childhood dreams. And we're stressing ourselves out.

Like most creatively inclined millennials, Peter grew up dreaming of making a life in the arts. He was born with significant hearing loss, and his mother and speech therapists spent hundreds of hours teaching him how to speak. Unfortunately, we live in a world of ableism, where Peter's schoolmates would make fun of him for wearing a hearing aid and being different. He desperately searched for someone to believe in him so he could believe in himself, and soon he found his gift when an English teacher told him he had a writing ability. He also began to excel at sports.

Peter was accepted into Dickinson College on a football scholarship that he later walked away from to study film at New York University. He says he felt torn between the two worlds of athletics and the arts. When he graduated from Tisch, he threw himself into writing his first screenplay, "Magda's Last Words." It is based on the diary entries of an old, tattered journal of a Holocaust survivor that his father stumbled across. Peter was transported into this world of history, violence, and redemption of the human spirit. Writing this manuscript was a way to give his life purpose.

"I want to feel like my place in the world is worth something," he says. "Humans aren't organisms randomly wandering around. We have to have a sense of meaning, and it has come from within. We wouldn't be the most intelligent creatures on the planet if we weren't meant to communicate who we are with the world."

Years after completing "Magda's Last Words," Peter is still shopping it. Inside the pages are depictions of the Second World War. The narrative asks the kind of questions that tragedies like war bring up in the collective consciousness: Why are we here—to fight or to love? How do we deal with the aftermath of tragedy and brutality? Why do humans do horrendous things to each other?

For now, Peter makes his money working as a production assistant on movie and TV show sets in Los Angeles. He spends his time getting directors coffee and sweeping floors. He doesn't find this work meaningful, but he's positioning himself in the right kind of environments in order to make the connections so his voice can be heard. He knows he's capable of doing more than mopping floors. but he's grown content with working his way up. He sees companies chewing up young people and spitting them out, and he knows that he could become disposable like the others, but he's holding on to his purpose for dear life. Peter says he's following his dreams so he can one day teach his children to follow their own. It's what life's all about, he believes.

Peter has found something that he's passionate about. He knows that his parents made certain sacrifices so he could do what he's doing today—pursuing what he loves. Maybe the baby boomers "sold out" so millennials wouldn't have to—and perhaps it's not even about selling out; it's about "buying in."

IT'S OKAY . . . TO BE POOR, HORNY, AND CONFUSED

Your twenties just may be the most emotionally unstable period in your development. You may never be as poor as you are now; you may also never be hotter or hornier. You may never have to deal with more rejection in your life or be as simultaneously self-righteous and confused as you cobble together crumbs of personal achievement to form a veneer of competency to present to others. It's also a time when you can focus on doing the kind of inner work that will turn you into the kind of person who can change the world.

This decade of life, the one that falls between adolescence and adulthood, is what this book is largely about. Psychologists call this time period "emerging adulthood," which spans the ages eighteen to twenty-nine (and sometimes later). It is defined by the joys and perils of personal freedom. We're exploring identities and getting as many experiences as we can before we make big, committed choices about love and work. We're discovering our interests, lifestyle preferences, and the many options that exist for us in this big, wide world.

Millennials are not afraid of change—whether it be our partners, career paths, or living situations. In fact, we often seek out change during this time when we have less obligations to others. We're solo agents and can finally steer our own ships. We get to make our own decisions, and we also have to learn to meet our own needs. We get to envision what a worthy adult life might look like. And most of us believe that, one day, we will manifest it.

Jeffrey Jenson Arnett, PhD, a psychology professor at Clark University, was the first to propose that this demographic is unique from all other ages. He observed that young people are no longer quick to settle down. We aren't teenagers anymore, but we aren't acting like conventional adults either. We're burning through jobs and locations and lovers, delaying duty and obligation, valuing our own liberties instead and learning experientially. We are spending more time in school and accumulating more debt. We're loudly expressing ourselves through art, music, and other media. We are staying financially dependent on our parents for longer than ever. We are challenging the status quo. Arnett thinks that this prolonged adolescence is a natural evolutionary, adaptive response to social changes—increased demand for higher education, the advent of birth control, and economic competition.

This is a relatively new phenomenon. Young people didn't act out like this until the 1950s, with the emergence of social liberalism. First, there were the Beatniks. Then, rock and roll. The hippie movement started in the sixties. Music and messages of anti-war, revolt, and love spread through TV and the radio. People were beginning to talk about the existence of a benevolent universal consciousness, outside of the construct of religion, an energetic reality of unity. Then there was disco in the seventies, hip hop in the eighties, and grunge in the nineties. Throughout these last five or six decades, it has been a rite of passage for young people to scream, "Screw constrictive and oppressive traditions! I shall not do what you tell me!" We've created our own subcultures that push people to their emotional edges. For decades now, the youth has created different collectives of artistic and spiritual resistance to the historical period of oppression we're living in.

Arnett admits that his own emerging adulthood was filled with frowned-upon delays and fun-filled sidetracks such as hitchhiking, working as a musician, and traveling while earning his doctorate.

"I didn't want to assume conventional adult roles," Arnett says. "I knew the freedom I had was fleeting, and I was right. I think it's wise for people to make use of it."

His advice is to sow your wild oats before dropping anchor. Now Arnett has a family, a career, and a mortgage, but he got to it all in his own way, in his own divine timing. He can empathize with the subjects he studies.

Psychologists who study emerging adulthood say that this phase of life is characterized by instability, insecurity, a feeling of being in-between states, and extreme self-focus, all fueled by the ideation of multiple future possibilities. It's also a time when more than half of us will suffer from anxiety and about a third us will be clinically depressed. According to a study by the Substance Abuse and Mental Health Services Administration (SAMHSA), between the ages of eighteen and twenty-five is when most people suffer from thoughts of suicide and will make a suicide attempt. Almost 9 percent of young people wish they were dead. The society we live in doesn't prepare us well for life.

Then, a breakthrough happens. I've seen it. We find something—anything—and learn to take care of it. For Peter, it was a screenplay. For myself, it has been writing this book and, more important, learning how to take care of myself. To root down, so

I can bear fruit; and to commit to life, because I have something of great value to contribute.

GROWING UP DURING THE GREAT FALL

Getting older sucks. It looks like Lipitor, mailboxes filled with bills, and schedules with no wiggle room. It looks like the loss of spontaneity, creativity, and fun. It looks like settling with what's safe—a steady paycheck and finding someone to stay by your side until you die. Faced with this socially normative future, running off and joining the circus may seem like a more attractive idea than assuming traditional roles that'll rob you of your soul. The problem is, you need an income to exist.

The Great Recession in many ways defined millennials; it has at least defined my own coming-of-age experience. It made us emerging adults on steroids—Peter Pan Syndrome–styled, eternal children. A couple of external and internal variables kept us from progressing on traditional life trajectories.

If you graduated up to six years after that crash in 2008, you likely saw a lot of shut doors. Some of us didn't want to grow up and work right away, while others of us genuinely tried. Whether you chose to blow off your responsibilities and backpack in Guatemala or torture yourself by sending out resume after resume while hearing nothing back was up to you. Our parents were losing their jobs. The economy contracted. No one was hiring.

To complicate the problem, most millennials remain incredibly picky about the work we're willing to do. Out of the over two hundred millennials I've ever interviewed, almost every one expressed a deep desire to do good in the world on a professional level. We want to use our degrees to find paid work with companies that reflect our values. But let's get real—we can't all work for nonprofits, service organizations, or social enterprises.

For this reason, there exists a popular belief that millennials are entitled, narcissistic, and delusional. Look at most children: they're entitled, narcissistic, and delusional from the day they are born. But they are also the most pure. Perhaps we need to look at these attributes from another perspective. It would benefit others to try to understand what lies behind the so-called millennial condition that is often maligned. Our intentions are ultimately benevolent; it's our strategy that's often off. We're morbidly naïve, and perhaps we lack discipline. We've got potential, but potential is all we'll ever be if the systems of the world do not offer opportunities for the dreamers who wish to evolve it. This is why we're also called the lost generation. Our pure-hearted ambitions are lacking an outlet.

I, too, was just one member of a diaspora of young, bright-eyed, perpetually unemployed millennials, ready to change the world. But because we had few actual paid opportunities to do so, many of us ended up using our imaginations to make up jobs for ourselves to keep from rotting and spiraling into a state of depression. Social media platforms like Facebook allowed us to advertise the dream: you could promote yourself as a professional unicorn tamer, a cuddle coach, or even a hot sauce enthusiast. Millennials cooked up a bunch of pie-in-the-sky job titles for ourselves and ran around taking selfies—and tried to call that "making a living." We've created the culture of "funemployment"—taking happy advantage of the free time unemployment provided.

Just look at the stats. In 2010, 37 percent of eighteen to twenty-nine-years-olds were unemployed, the highest share in three decades, according to a PEW study. The Associated Press found that even in 2012, when the recession had ended, 53 percent of recent college graduates were unemployed or underemployed, the latter working a job that didn't require the degree they had. Thirty-four percent of millennial PhDs and 30 percent of MDs were underemployed in 2014, according to a study by PayScale—hundreds of thousands more than any previous generation. We have spent two decades at school, and ultimately we can't even use this investment to obtain gainful employment.

So, are we victims of a flawed mindset or of circumstance? The answer is a combination of both, but it becomes a problem when we choose to focus on either. Neither of these justifications for our current situation is empowering, and neither will help us get the job that needs to be done, done.

First, it's going to take more than just millennials, because the second largest generation in history, the baby boomers, wields all the power in our current society. Gatekeepers to our future success, they hoard the dollar bills. Historically, the boomers were compliant, doing whatever they were told was the right thing to do by culture. Those who retired from the peace-and-love revolution in the sixties got to a place of financial saliency by pulling themselves up by their bootstraps and making enough money to have families. As a result, many millennials grew up in middle class homes, and the boomers hoped their children would follow in their footsteps.

However, because of the bleak state of the economy upon our graduation (and our personality eccentricities that don't make us the best cog-in-a-machine-type employees), millennials are speculated to earn less than our parents. In 2015, we were earning less money than those who lived in the 1980s according to the US Census Bureau, even though we have more education.

It's important to note that our Great Recession looked nothing like our grandparents' Great Depression. Despite the recent extreme economic contraction, millennials are still privileged in comparison. We can buy brunch on credit and travel the world with cheap airfare. The refrigerator magnets at Whole Foods tell us to quit our day jobs, fall in love, and leave our nests. But that doesn't mean the problems we face today don't exist.

There you have it: concrete economic reasons that show why this generation's development is arrested. We're the largest generation in history, which means we have more competition. College costs six figures. The prices of daily living expenses continue to rise. The middle class is also shrinking. While our gross domestic product increases, our wages stagnate. Less and less US dollars are distributed among the majority of Americans. And the middle class is shrinking. In 1950, 61 percent of Americans were considered middle class. In 2015, the middle class contained only 50 percent of the population. It's no surprise that many of us come to the same conclusion.

Fuck it, let's find our own path instead of fighting to fit in a world that doesn't offer a safe space or path for us.

Most millennials will probably never become millionaires (major bummer). This may seem like a first world problem, but financial analysts now find that it costs the average American a million dollars to retire. It's absurd. After all the books we've buried our heads in and the debt we've accumulated, we're still not in a position to conventionally succeed in the same way as previous generations.

Millennials are the most highly educated generation in history. We're smart enough to see that not only is the system rigged against the average person, it's also completely unsustainable. In the midst of this madness, millennials have had to seriously consider the true indicators of self-worth—and if it's not the money, status, and power our culture promotes, what is it?

SELF-ACTUALIZATION OR BUST

Humans have both physical and emotional needs. It may seem a bit ridiculous that while three-quarters of the people in the world still don't have their physical needs met, millennials in the first world seem mainly concerned with our emotional ones. Shouldn't we just be happy that those of us living in developed economies have access to many luxuries, even if we are shouldering debt and if said economies are destroying the natural world? The answer is *no*. All of our needs are important, and when they're not met, humans can become murderously desperate.

Without food, shelter, and water, people will die or kill others for resources. But we'll also kill ourselves and others over less material reasons—the need to be emotionally safe, to be treated as an equal, and to have a sense of direction and belonging. We have a need to contribute, to be challenged, and to be seen and understood. Many of us question the purpose of our individual lives—*am I making the world worse, or better?* According to the American College Health Association (ACHA), the suicide rate among young adults aged fifteen to twenty-four has tripled since the 1950s. We have the highest levels of depression, stress, and anxiety compared to any other generation at the same age.

But we're not just stressed about our survival. We're stressed about how to thrive. How do I free myself from this existential angst? By devoting myself to volunteerism and charity? By sitting on an amethyst biomat for an hour every evening? By reading literature by marginalized members of society and signing online petitions? By drinking blue-green algae for breakfast? By meeting Elon Musk at Burning Man and funding my start-up? How does one thrive in this land?

It took me a while to surrender to the fact that even though I did not create this culture, I still contribute to its problems—until I start experimenting with solutions. I used to flush Monsanto tampons down the toilet until I bought a DivaCup; however, I still fill my car with gasoline and buy individually wrapped veggie burgers at Trader Joe's. I know that my need to consume is contributing to the giant tumor on the face of the Earth that is humanity. It is simply a fact that, in order for me to live, millions of other organisms have to die. My karma on this planet is checkered—like everyone else's—but it's getting lighter every day as I learn to change my ways to more consciously harness my human impact. I can still live a life of service.

I am one of the eight billion people on the planet playing out a history that keeps repeating, until we learn how to break the cycle. Even though we live with an abundance of consumer options, so many millennials are still miserable. Netflix and Pokemon Go can't solve our existential malaise. As far as my experience has shown, drifting is not a path; it can only last for so long until the inner demons take over.

The good news is that there is a way out of the fears that paralyze us. By honing our talents, staying informed, practicing tolerance for our own discomforts, picking a purpose, and pursuing goals despite the obstacles, we can break free and become who we've always wanted to be. The journey starts with a single step forward. And if you stay at it, you will make it in your own perfect time and pace.

In the face of an impending apocalypse, purpose is what millennials are searching for. We believe it is our birthright to thrive, come what may. We are questioning: Can we reverse the direction of all this? And even if no one knows the answer, many of us are still inspired to try. At the very least, we believe this pursuit will increase our quality of life.

Gandhi said, "First they ignore you, then they laugh at you, then they fight you, and then you win." The collapse of Western civilization will take a lot longer to happen than we imagine. The future is still unwritten. So, we've got to start integrating ourselves into the program so we can evolve it.

Can millennials correct the course of humanity? If our actions reach a critical mass at a conversion point, we might have a chance. If our arteries don't harden as we age and if we keep our values and imaginations intact, perhaps we can usher in a new epoch that reflects our true potential as galactic beings on a mission to create a heaven on earth—an enlightened society where every living thing's needs are met in harmony. But first, we need to expose the cause and effect of our individual and collective actions.

Nothing that is going on in our world right now is the fault of one generation, and these problems can't be solved by one generation alone. Millennials and everyone else have to accept certain realities if we want to shift them. Whatever new system we're hoping to birth is going to have to evolve out of this one. And it's going to start with facing a massive amount of shit. Awareness can do a lot.

SO WAIT, THERE'S HOPE?

"Where is everyone going to go when something bad goes down? I don't know how far along that will be, but I know that people are getting pushed closer and closer together. It seems like no one can almost stand each other."

—Midnight Sauzo, twenty-five, chef

The world is only getting more complex, volatile, fast-paced, densely populated, and chaotic. Our species is in crisis, "a turning point"—a dangerous moment of truth where events can unfold one way or another. We've got to open our hearts to all of it in order to transform it.

This is why I filled this book with stories. Without witnesses, what ails us will not go away. To write this book, I went out of my way to talk to people who were different than me: they had different backgrounds, ideologies, ethnicities, goals, and lifestyles. I've realized that despite our astonishing variance, humanity has much in common. We all came from a sperm and an egg. We call the same planet home. And we all struggle to feel safe in our own skin. I've recorded the voices from the widest cross-section of millennials I could find—from the ones working on Wall Street to those sleeping on it.

I knew there had to be another way to come of age that self-help books written by baby boomers fail to mention. The only advice they seem to proselytize is to not waste any time, to get your ass in graduate school, and, whatever you do, to not breed with someone from a bad gene pool. None of them talked about changing the world; instead, they were all about following "the plan"—whatever had worked in the past—to make it into the middle class.

After all my researching, I now declare that "growing up" and "changing our world" are similar, if not identical, processes—and neither can be done by subscribing to a dated, socially competitive formula to fly your flag on top of the social pyramid. They can only occur through what philosophers and political scientists call *praxis*.

Praxis is a combination of action and reflection. You self-realize, develop life skills, formulate theories, and apply them to life to solve problems by *doing*. Then you observe the feedback and find out what works and what doesn't. Right now, the earth is giving us enough feedback that the way we are going about our lives is not working. Let's listen and adapt.

Your body is going to get old—so don't worry about that. But will you, in the process of living, age your soul? Will you learn your lessons? Will you share your gifts with the world? Will you move beyond your inherited circumstance and liberate yourself into a space of love?

Millennials are big on self-actualization. It requires us to intentionally put one footstep in front of the other as we hone our conscious awareness of the ripple effect of our actions. To create the social conditions that cultivate internal and external peace for ourselves and others, we need to collectively develop our conscience and consciousness. Millennials may be taking a longer time to become traditional adults, but I believe that we're embarking on a unique journey.

And we are capable of so much. Eva Simone, twenty-eight, is the former manager of an orphanage in Nepal who reunited 95 percent of the trafficked children living there with their birth families.

"I might not have the most prestigious degrees or the pedigree to do what I've done, but I have grit," she says. "Humans are so adaptable. We're able to evolve and learn new skills. When you have that fire and are willing to put yourself at the feet of someone who can teach you something, so much is possible."

You don't have to be a perfect person or have specific skills to start moving mountains. Just look at Eva. She wasn't trained in child protection; she didn't know how to pass legislation. She didn't even how to run an orphanage. She initially moved to Nepal to teach women how to set up sustainable farming systems, and a series of chance connections led her to take a job at a children's home in Kathmandu. When she realized that the children living there were all missing paperwork, she asked them questions in Nepali, a language she could barely speak, and discovered that most of the children had been kidnapped from their families by child traffickers to be sold to wealthy Westerners wishing to adopt.

Eva had gone to Nepal looking for purpose, and her original plan was derailed when a huge call to action was laid out before her. She crusaded to create policies with Nepali orphanages and caseworkers to ensure that every child put into a home in the city arrives with a detailed profile so that no one could be smuggled into the center. The policies were passed, and Eva took it upon herself to walk each trafficked child home, reuniting them with their families.

Eva's story shows us that people can be fucking awesome when we believe in our own goodness. We are a generation that is being called to use everything we have and everything we've inherited to revise the status quo. Every generation has had to go through some kind of initiation, and it's our time to be in the spotlight. We're here, coming into ourselves at a unique time, and we have the potential to birth a new paradigm. To do this, we can't lead from fear or use force to control outcomes. It's not about aggression; it's about adaptation.

CREATING YOUR MISSION STATEMENT

STEP 1. What would you like to see be different in the world?
STEP 2. How can you use your gifts to contribute to this change?
STEP 3. Combine the two steps into an actionable item. Try writing a mission statement for both your personal and professional life.

Chapter 2

The Anatomy of an Adult

"When I was younger, everything was so clouded. Little things would drive me to hysteria. I used to be terrified. I wouldn't sleep at night due to existential questions. As I've gotten older, a part of me feels like there is good out there. There is beauty in enjoying the moment. Don't let fear consume you."

—Jimmy Shea, twenty-six,
YouTube influencer and digital storyteller

BECOMING AN ADULT IN MANY WAYS IS ABOUT COMING TO terms with the struggle to materially survive. For most of us, it boils down to a choice like that scene from *The Matrix* when Neo has to decide what color pill he's going to consume. What mental framework for reality will govern your life? Do you want falsehood, material security, and living in blissful ignorance? Or do you want knowledge and to taste the bitter truths of life for the sake of mental freedom?

Tony Dee, twenty-eight, is a musician and organic farmer.

He finds inspiration in Otis Redding, who dove into music and dedicated himself to his professional career. Somehow, Redding managed to make enough shit happen by his early twenties, and he was hailed as one of the greatest soul singers on the planet before he died in a plane crash at age twenty-six. At twenty-eight, Tony is still trying to figure out where he and his ideals fit into the world. He is still hovering around his options, battling with his own cognitive dissonance regarding what it takes to build a life in America and how that conflicts with the conclusions he's come to after spending a long time developing his own unique sense of morality.

"I'm getting old," Tony says. "I'm in my late twenties. I'm in a position where I need to make a decision about how to make money—grown-ass money."

Tony says he's back to being broke. His bank account is in the double digits. He works full-time for nine bucks an hour and can't afford health insurance. Tony knows he's privileged in many ways—he is a white man; he has clothes and shoes; he comes from an upper-middle-class background and would never consider himself poor. However, ironically, he currently lives at the poverty line.

These were the concerns that first compelled Tony to go back to school to become a nurse. He took out loans to take classes at the Medical University of South Carolina, only to suffer a nervous breakdown shortly after registering. He says his internal conflicts caught up to him. He didn't know if nursing was what he really wanted to do, when playing punk rock music and organizing people around social advocacy have always been his passions. He has devoted his life to these goals up until this point, just as he promised he would when he was a teen, and he's never known of a practical career that appeals to him outside of it.

After his anxiety attack, Tony decided to quit school. "I'm currently choosing to live with this debt," Tony says. "It's useless—except that it teaches me a valuable lesson, which is not to rush things. Don't make big decisions that you're not sure about."

Because few people can make a living as an activist or a musician, Tony works during the day as a sustainable farmer, a popular millennial answer to escaping the banes of the modern world. (Many of the socially-aware young people I interviewed have fantasized about becoming agrarians.) However, at the time of our meeting, Tony is about to retire from farming. It's mid-December in the Lowcountry. In a few weeks, there'll be nothing left grow. To top it off, Tony says he doesn't even like farming anymore.

Tony's idealistic pursuits have once again gone awry—he's found farming to be like any other capitalist form of labor. When he was first getting into farming, he thought it would be romantic—he would return to the Earth and become one with the land; he would immerse himself in simple traditions of the past, before society became so chaotic and complicated. But what he's found is that being a farmer for income is a really rough way to live. He's entirely alienated from what he produces and is ambivalent about its impact. He's not growing food to feed his family or teaching people about healthful ways of living. He works for a business that sells produce to high-end restaurants, where only the wealthy few can afford to dine.

"If you know anyone with a job opening, please hook me up," Tony says. He says this as a joke, although he's not kidding.

Millennials are spontaneous. Some might call us avoidant. Do we simply lack fortitude? Or are we unwilling to waste our one precious, wild life on things we don't believe in? It's maddening to older folks that millennials seem to treat work so trivially. At first glance, we appear to be living in an alternative universe, hooked into social media, stalking ourselves online, and obsessed with our image versus our substance. But maybe, just maybe, we've decided to swallow the red pill instead of the blue.

We are highly sensitive to the world around us, and we're beyond persnickety about how we spend our time in our professional pursuits. We do so because we want to know our potential and make a difference. Eight-six percent of us crave careers with meaning.

Many millennials were told that we could do anything we wanted with our lives, but we weren't equipped with the appropriate tools and skills. As a result, we're spending a lot of time searching for a dream that we can bring to fruition.

QUESTIONS ABOUT CLASS AND ADULTESCENCE

On the crux of adulthood, some of us are shocked into stepping up and facing the responsibilities of real life when faced with pregnancy, poverty, or dire family situations. There are plenty of people who don't have time for existential contemplation or the luxury to champion causes that don't directly impact them, the way Tony does. Some of us are forced to work immediately in order to sustain themselves, and there are people who don't get to spend two decades in school or out of work delaying adult stressors.

The issue of class plays a big role in determining who gets to indulge in a prolonged adolescence. According to a study by the Pell Institute, students from wealthy families are nine times more likely to attend and graduate from college than students who come from poverty. Those born in the middle to upper classes can afford this socially sanctioned time to navel gaze and philosophize about the meaning of life, to debate for hundreds of hours essential life decisions such as whether to become an urban intellectual or a vegan nomad peddling feather earrings.

If you do have the chance to go to college, this is where you might very slowly learn to take on essential, everyday tasks—such as changing your bedsheets and not eating more cheese pizza than what feels good. Life is challenging. Then, you start reading works by the likes of Michel Foucault, Frederick Nietzsche, and George Gurdjieff, and your mind opens to both the abstract reality of existence and the implicit injustices of society. This idle time and deep introspection is poison for conventional adulting; just look at Tony.

A few centuries ago, people in their twenties were considered middle-aged, and they were dying from smallpox or the Black Plague. Now, millennials are barely reaching stereotypical indicators of adulthood by age thirty. I've heard story after story like Tony's, from people who are highly intelligent, well-intentioned, and socially aware. The gist is always the same: *I don't know what I want to do with myself in the long term. Every time I try to pursue a stable identity, I feel like I'm surrendering my creativity and my ideals; I am reducing myself to a commodity for the machine. This isn't my idea of life lived well. This is what I said I would never do. I am miserable.*

The study "Emerging Adulthood as an Institutionalized Moratorium" by James Cote says that there are certain types of people who psychologists have found tend to struggle longer and harder in their twenties than others. These people embark on what is called an "extended adolescence." The common characteristics they often share are a resentment toward the concept of adulthood, a history of trauma, skepticism of authority, and a desire to change the world.

I stayed up all night reading this study; I couldn't sleep. There are have been many times throughout my research that I've had to digest some pretty unsavory information that has challenged my youthful convictions. I quickly realized that the type of person these PhDs were talking about was . . . me!

THE AMERICAN DREAM

The traditional indicators of adulthood, as outlined in psychology and sociology, are when you finish your education, solidify a stable career, buy a home, get married, and have children. All of this is otherwise also known as "the American Dream." This middle-class lifestyle America has provided for so many people—white people especially—is why a lot of us have been bred to think this is the best country in the world. The American Dream is at the heart of the myth of American exceptionalism. And millennials are challenging these two concepts.

To be an American comes with its own propaganda. American exceptionalism is the nationalist notion that America is the world leader of democracy and the ultimate purveyor of a free world, and thus we should follow its cultural mandates. It preaches that for anyone to have any value in a society, which is by far superior to all others, they must subscribe to the conservative fiscal and social values of its founders, even when these policies and philosophies have been contemporarily distorted.

American exceptionalism is, in reality, a fallacy. The US ranks thirty-eight in math and science (according to the Programme for International Student Assessment) and forty-third in press freedom/reporter rights (according to the Press Freedom Index), and it has one of the highest rates of violent crime compared to other developed nations. The American Journal of Medicine found Americans to be ten times more likely to be killed by a gun than people in developing countries. According to the United Health Foundation, the US ranks twenty-ninth in infant mortality and twenty-sixth in life expectancy. In 2016, a report by the Commonwealth Fund reported that 43 percent of low-income Americans went without healthcare—compared to 8 percent in Britain. These few rankings debunk the assumption that the system we have is the best in the world.

But that doesn't keep the US from being a superpower that enjoys exerting our dominance over other countries and telling them what to do, often under the pretense that we're doing them a favor because our model of society works so damn flawlessly.

Nations and cultures have fragile and inflated egos, just like people. We're really good at sweeping our own dark history under the rug.

Slavery. Segregation. Displacing indigenous peoples. Aggressive competition manufactured by economic scarcity. Incompetent politicians who don't do anything for the people they supposedly represent. Blood money—billions of tax dollars spent subsidizing war in the Middle East and dirty energy. A bloated defense system. We could go on and on.

The truth is it isn't just millennials who are "entitled"; America herself, the geopolitical imperialist, is entitled. We must recognize that the American Dream is one of entitlement and that not everyone is going to get an equal opportunity to realize it—not everyone may even desire it. But no matter how much we may rebel, millennials do feel a subliminal pressure to conform to this cultural norm.

American millennials want to be exceptional too—exceptional at challenging this. And if we get enough Instagram followers (really!), we just might be able to make a difference with our wide influence. We're not racing toward marriage, home ownership, or having two-and-a-half kids like previous generations. Many of us are dangerously close to becoming what some psychologists classify as "abnormal adults"—people in their thirties, forties, and onward who don't have homes or spouses or children or any kind of linear career track.

Scratch just an inch below the surface and it's easy to find that the values this country advertises itself as being founded upon are nothing but a false flag. We could also pick the millennial condition apart and find the same inconsistencies. We say we want to change the world, but all we engage in is click-bait activism. We say we're above this materialistic culture, but we're still sucking from the tit of it.

I believe hypocrisy is a huge part of the human condition —and that one reason we're here is to learn to mend the rifts.

Halfway into this project, I had to put it down for about two years just to work on clearing the haunting discrepancies with what I thought my message was and the person I actually am. We are all, individually and collectively, slowly working out all of our issues with power, money, and sex—and no one can avoid falling in and out of interpersonal balance. What we first need to do is recognize this.

WE ARE A PRODUCT OF THE ECONOMIC TIMES

Amid the realities of American egotism, mediocrity, and corruption, there are many reasons to be grateful that we live here instead of, say, South Sudan. The whole middle-class conformist package that elicits so much contempt in young, critically-thinking, noncompliant millennials would be paradise to a displaced refugee struggling for shelter, food, and water. There are immigrants who come to the United States and kiss the ground they land on, because it is a place where they have a chance to meet their basic needs, earn money, and make a life.

When compared to the struggle of others, it's easy to see why some people say millennials are coddled. We were overindulged as children, fragilized and overprotected by our parents, and it's one of the reasons we're perpetually underperforming. That's why when the going gets tough, we apparently get going.

Is our behavior attributed to some kind of intrinsic characteristic common to the whole generation? Or are we simply the products of our environment? The science discerning the ratio of nature versus nurture is still mixed. However, as B. F. Skinner's philosophy of behaviorism states, millennials—just like everyone else—are a product of our conditioning, of stimulus-and-response. Behaviorism says that human actions are largely, if not entirely, a reflection of our surroundings. If we want to change the behavior of people, we have to change the environment that created them first. And in order to change our environment, we have to enlighten ourselves first by changing the conditions of our inner world.

There are plenty of external variables that are causing us to stay childlike for longer than ever. And it's not necessarily because we have some millennial gene that makes us perennially socially immature.

The system is rigged, and this is the main variable impacting our success—or at least what is conventionally defined as it. From the person who is selected to run for office to the one who gets the tax breaks—our entire system is run according to rules that increasingly favor the 1 percent, the top income earners in the country. This system helps the rich to get richer, as social security nets dwindle away. All this is a natural byproduct of what happens when capitalism, a bastion of the American ideal, is unfairly regulated by corrupt government.

Trickle-down economics has proved to be another illogical fallacy. There was an idea in economics that people at the top, the highest performing individuals in society, are the ones who generate opportunities for others and create the middle class. This supposedly explains why our government offers tax breaks to corporations, high-income earners, and investors. According to this theory, the private sector would reinvest additional earnings this back into the economy, redistributing resources and reducing the need for government agencies.

But really, trickle-down economics is just a theory. The wealthy aren't creating new jobs; they mainly hoard their wealth. Think about it. What's better for the economy? For one rich person to buy an airplane? Or for one million people to be able to afford a vacation? Having a strong middle class is what stimulates the economy. Whenever the legitimacy of trickle-down economics has been tested in smaller environments—as it was in 2017 in Kansas, when Republican governor Sam Brownback slashed tax rates, eliminated state tax, and cut welfare programs—it has failed. Growth stops, debts accrue, and vital services are no longer provided. The people perish.

Life in America is not what it once was, for better and for worse. For the first time since World War II, the middle class is shrinking so rapidly that 44 percent of millennials think the American Dream is dying.

The middle class is the magical place where your bills can be paid, retirement is saved for, and a medical emergency won't leave you bankrupt. Once you make a certain amount of income and gain entrance into the "club," the risks of social maladies like malnutrition, disease, and being the victim of violent crime are reduced. For millennials to be a part of this coveted middle class, we need a government that will responsibly redistribute resources. Essentially, we need to be coming of age in a different social environment.

This earth is already magnificently abundant with human capital and natural resources; it's how we've divided up and allocated our resources that makes fiscal wealth only available to a small population. We haven't yet invented a way out of a system that has divided us into the haves and the have-nots.

Millennials are futurists. A lot of us see how the system "could" be. There are no guarantees, and our visionary inspirations could fail. However, we try anyway because many of us see that integrity and innovation just might be the only things that can bring balance back to this country. And it's going to take everyone to tip the scale.

I should also note that some of us do choose to go down the conventional path into lucrative, stable careers, such as commercial real estate or finance, because we want to avoid financial struggles or wish to live a certain lifestyle. As one millennial real estate broker anonymously told me, "I will not stop until my name is jizzed on the side of six Manhattan skyscrapers." It is going to take status, power, and wealth to make these shifts anyway (and a whole lot of entitlement).

BLAME CHARLES DARWIN

In his theory of evolution, Darwin coined the concept of "survival of the fittest." It says that everything that evolved in the animal kingdom and natural world is here today because it had the intelligence and strength to compete with and outdo whatever stressors or threats existed in its environment.

Social Darwinism emerged in the late nineteenth century and applied terms like "survival of the fittest" and "natural selection" to justify the actions of the people who were able to rise to the top of society like cream on buttermilk. Social Darwinism states that the people who "win" in this society and the people who "lose" do so because we exist in a meritocracy, where the smarter and more adaptable people are able to work their way to the top. This theory, however, fails to take into account the fact that the top 1 percent have redesigned the rules to ensure that they and their ilk remain in power, meritocracy be damned.

A well-functioning democratic society is akin to a living, self-correcting organism that's designed to provide the means for as many people to fulfill their basic needs as possible when every member of society contributes to the whole. The problem arises when this model is exploited, greed is rewarded, and certain individuals—the rich, white, male oligarchy—have the most say in creating and molding our environment simply because they are already at the top of the pyramid. They are the right skin color, and the right gender. They have the right connections. They inherit family wealth. And all too often, they rule with a false authority. Instead of using their power to create a society where everyone can prosper, they create a society where they prosper at the expense of everyone else.

There are more people on the planet than ever. The US started with 2.5 million citizens when we first became an independent nation in 1776; now our population has reached more than 300 million, and we're forced to compete for limited resources. Millennials are pitted against each other in a race to accumulate: numbers in our bank account, formal degrees, people to legally bind by our side, and children to carry on our family name. And by in large, we're just not that enthralled by the whole pursuit. These are evolutionary, biological imperatives and also the social markers that traditionally define us as normal, successful "adults" in a civilized society. In a capitalist system, these badges of adulthood were considered forms of property in the days of yore: my wife, my kids, my land, my slaves. Possession is nine-tenths of the law.

But can our quality of life and value to others be measured by our levels of consumption? While so much of the world still has no access to basic amenities, consumption is considered the indicator of success in the developed world. It has become one of our predominant cultural *memes*—a pervasive thought pattern that has infiltrated our social structure. And millennials are challenging it, because we know it is contributing to the compounding environmental catastrophes we're inheriting. Instead, we are questioning what we really need to be happy.

One person in the US consumes as much energy as 370 Ethiopians. We produce 70 percent of the world's hazardous waste. We consume 815 billion calories of food per day—and 200 billion of those calories aren't needed. The amount of wasteful consumption in the US is a major force that is destroying our natural world, and the resulting climate change will affect the lives of people in the third world who've done very little to create it.

And millennials aren't into it. Only about 25 percent of us are actively engaged consumers. We're keener on the concept of community. We've seen and experienced firsthand living in collectivist cultures in other parts of the world that work—where people don't have much; but they have each other, and that makes them happy.

When shit goes south, humanity is going to have to remember really quickly that we can't survive alone despite what our individualistic cultures have prescribed. It's going to take many hands and deep pockets to repair the destruction that's forecasted to go down—disease, drought, famine, war, and economic collapse.

THE SEARCH FOR A BETTER LIFE

"I was searching. I was searching for happiness, for fulfillment outside myself. Outside of the partying. The sex. These empty, empty things."

—James Hilton, twenty-four, ashram resident

Our "emerging adulthood" years are mostly spent soul-searching. Life becomes about how you are going to fill the empty void, the hole in the heart some of us have from living in a broken world—until many of us learn, after much searching, that we've been whole this whole time.

James Hilton was in so much suffering, trying to comply to the social norms of the world, that at one point he attempted to commit suicide. He was looking for connection, guidance and wisdom, and a sense of ease; he wanted to get rid of the constant fear inside him that society shoves down everyone's throats—the anxiety of having to be someone and do something. But he didn't want this. James says he just wanted to be around love, spreading its contagious vibrations and lighting other people's spiritual fires. So, he went searching . . .

James has found a bit of solace living a slow, domestic life at an ashram in Taos, New Mexico. The safe, tranquil space of the ashram helped him get out of survival mode so he could heal himself.

Scientists are now proving that the body has two modes: protection and growth. You can't reach a spiritual state of love and self-actualization when your body is trapped in a state of stress, which in turn creates disease. For most young people, this stress manifests as the dis-*ease* of the mind.

"I asked the universe: if I need to be here on Earth to do work, then show me what I'm here to do," James says.

Ultimately, he has found that his needs are better met in sequestered spiritual communities than in a mainstream urban environment. In the ashram, life is easy. He cooks vegetarian food. He cleans. He meditates. Here, he can sustain a state of equanimity. He's not part of the problems society is creating around him.

James sees that humanity is at a tipping point. "We're sucking the Earth dry," he says. "We take and take and take. She will get angry and she will destroy, but she can regenerate herself. The earthquakes and tsunamis are here, waking us up."

Mother Earth has every right to be pissed because of our carelessness, and she has every right to want to wipe humans from the planet after all the ways we've exploited her. I don't want this impending destruction to happen. I don't want us to lose what we've spent a lifetime working to gain. I don't want to see wars and famines and plagues; I don't want to see billions of people displaced.

I do know this, however, about people: we are stubborn creatures of comfort and habit. We are so often blind to ourselves and will keep doing the same thing over and over again, until we hit rock bottom and open our mind to the idea that there could be a different way—one where we don't have to suffer and cause suffering. The select few of us who can intuit where all this is heading have known for a while that it's high time for humanity to birth a new system, one that benefits and respects what is different, but also universal, in everyone. But in order for that to happen, the majority of us must decide on a plan of action.

Millennials (and everyone else who cares about our lives and those of our children) are being called to crusade for the alternative ideas (some described in this book) that have the potential to solve the problems we're inheriting. We're in that critical time in the cosmos, when it's time to intercept.

WHICH WOLF WILL YOU FEED?

Conflict and duality are at the heart of the human experience. There are powerful, polarizing forces that exist within each of us, and it's one of the biggest reasons why humanity is in the situation we're in.

You can call these forces whatever you want: angel vs. demon; id vs. superego; adult self vs. child self; higher self vs. lower self, etc. I like to describe this duality through the terms of the conscious and subconscious mind.

Our conscious mind, which includes the thoughts we're aware of and approve of, very much wants to be of service to the world, to forge a unique life path and create a sense of meaning and purpose—like millennials say we're about. Our unconscious/subconscious mind, however, has different priorities. It chases after sexual gratification, material wealth, and security, and it likes to honor convention.

Until we make what's lurking in our unconscious conscious, it tends to take over when we're not paying attention. The subconscious mind explains why society seems to stay the same at the core of its design, even if it undergoes superficial changes. Women, ethnic minority, and LGBTQ communities are still oppressed, and there's a stark division between the rich and the poor. The urgency is palpable, but alas society will stay the way it's always been if we let our subconscious run the show. We will follow the path of least resistance unless we intentionally resist it, because it's the way we've been programmed. We've got hundreds of years of evolutionary biology to disrupt. And it takes true maturity to confront how you individually contribute to what you collectively say you're against, and true courage to change your ways.

We all want to believe that we're altruistic. Millennials can say—in our youthful idealism—that we desire to save the planet, be ourselves, and live for each other; but deep inside each one of us are powerful urges that cause us to behave otherwise. As we get older, these beliefs start to take over. Don't fool yourself for one second by thinking you don't have it in you—not in this day and age where all of our issues around security, money, sex, and power are being surfaced.

The good news is that once you admit that you are full of the shit you detest, you can start to ascend. You can reprogram yourself to live extraordinarily. It all boils down to this question: Which wolf inside you will you feed?

Becoming a healthy adult who can make a positive impact requires us to face our inner demons. It's not about the job and the kids and the money as much as it's about *that*. And emerging adulthood is the ideal time to start integrating both the light and dark sides of our personalities if we want to mature and become the type of people the world needs.

"Will you persevere in spite of fear?" asks Dr. Seth Schwartz, who lectures on the psychology of emerging adulthood at The University of Miami.

"Sometimes forcing yourself to follow a dream is the only way to force yourself to face all your fears," Dr. Schwartz tells me. "You have to face them before you can get to where you really want to be going in life. Understanding yourself has nothing to do with age. It has to do with what you've experienced."

And millennials are gaining just that—life experience. Just like Dr. Arnett in chapter one, Dr. Schwartz says that he wasn't much more productive, in a conventional sense, than his students when he was their age. He, too, was busy looking for himself. This story is nothing new. Schwartz says that identity is a combination of individual, relational, and collective elements—and he was learning how to relate to the world so he could give something back to it.

"Our society doesn't reward self-actualization," he says (in fact, if you're successfully self-actualized like many great prophets and political liberators, you may be assassinated). "You have to work really hard to self-actualize in a society that actually represses it."

There is a point to all our navel-gazing. Maturity requires self-esteem, and self-esteem starts with self-discovery. If you want to get a grip on your subconscious mind, you've got to travel inward and trust what comes up in your emotional world—so it can be released and we can start to unlearn what this society has taught us to believe about who we are, what is possible, and the type of treatment we deserve. And this pursuit is time-consuming.

But it's worth it. Because if you don't have this self-worth and self-awareness, perhaps the worst thing a young person can do is make a legally binding decision with another person or create a baby because they buckled under the social pressure to grow up and "be someone"—decisions that are still a product of the subconscious mind. And there are big decisions we make as emerging adults that we can't undo, ones that will determine the outcome of our entire lives.

If you want to learn about what's hiding in your subconscious, here's a trick: whenever you get a result that's different from what you consciously intended, it's usually a sign of the toxic emotions and cultural programming within you. For example, if you say you want a simple life, but you constantly find yourself attracted to difficult people and overly ambitious goals, something unconscious is motivating your behavior. Investigate it.

Millennials have seen too many members of previous generations do what they thought they were supposed to before they knew who they were or what they were getting into. We've seen too many people who missed the opportunity to go after that one thing they really wanted. We've seen people give up right before their big break because fear and doubt took over.

I think it's time to celebrate that becoming an adult is a slower process. I believe it's a sign that the human race is becoming more conscious. We are becoming more conscientious with our decisions. We're taking so long to funnel into traditional paradigms because they are outdated. It's not that we don't want the dream job, the house, the kids, and the social recognition one day; we just want to arrive at it at the appropriate time, after we've done the necessary inner work and our lives reflect who we authentically are.

The rugged individualism of our culture is turning into a generational pursuit for *individuation*. Coined by Carl Jung, *individuation* refers to the process of integrating the components of the psyche to form a mature personality. To individuate, all the parts of yourself that you hate, repress, and deny have to be faced and properly channeled into a more effective expression. Peace is the journey, and life is the calling. And this book is about a generation choosing consciousness over conquest.

Becoming an adult is ultimately about individuating. Because once we commit to the process of taking responsibility for our own lives, we begin to realize that we are gods and goddesses in monkey suits. Spiritual adulthood is a state of mind.

Chapter 3

The Many Different Expressions of Success

"The biggest challenge our generation is facing is choosing to find one's talents and offer them to the world, rather than follow the step-by-step program we've been taught is the only way to make a life work in American society."

—Becca Roth, twenty,
student at California State University

GAYLORD "ROCKY" SMITH, TWENTY-FIVE, TAKES ANOTHER BONG rip in his apartment outside Encinitas, California. He hits it like a champ. He doesn't cough. It seems he's grown quite used to the feeling of marijuana smoke in his lungs.

"I've done nothing for six or seven years," Rocky confesses. He's wearing a sweatshirt. His brown, curly hair is shaved short. He looks like what kids these days are now calling "ethnically ambiguous"—a mixture of black, white, and Asian.

Speaking of ambiguity, I can't tell if Rocky is totally fucking with me in between his bong rips. He speaks in a matter-of-fact tone, but what he says is ridiculous. He lives in a messy two-bedroom apartment with his twenty-one-year-old girlfriend, Sarah, who canvases during the day for Greenpeace as people walk by and yell profanities at her. Sometimes, they throw things.

Rocky's apartment may be messy, but it doesn't smell. Clothes, food packaging, and other items are strewn around the floor. Sarah says she hasn't been home to her parents' house in over a month because they are drunk and chaotic, so she stays with Rocky instead.

"The original agreement was that my dad would pay for my rent if I went to college," Rocky says. "I kind of went to class. I got in the habit of playing video games and reading comic books. I pretty much spent all my money on pot and snacks. On my twenty-fourth birthday, my father told me, 'You probably need to start doing something.'"

Rocky's mother died of cancer when he was a kid, an event that he calls inconvenient. I'm starting to get it—Rocky uses sarcasm as a defense mechanism. Underneath his aloofness is someone with feeling, someone who's experienced loss and other tragedies. I'm surprised that Rocky has let me into his home to interview him. As I watch him take another rip, I think about the black hole of sorrow and inertia that's gripped me in the past. I imagine Rocky is struggling with his own internal black hole—just like James Hilton and Tony Dee in chapter two.

Rocky's father is an attorney, and Rocky now works in his office scanning documents, copying paperwork, and doing all the odds and ends that lawyers can't bill clients for. In return, he gets an all-expenses-paid apartment.

"It's a combination of love and fear," Rocky says when asked why his father has enabled his idleness and pot addiction for so long. "He fears for my safety and survival. It's not unlikely that he thinks it's a fifty-fifty chance that if he hadn't set me up with a job and place to live, I'd either sit and rot or get myself killed."

Someone had to do something to intercept before he turned into a puddle of mush in a hoodie. Rocky's father got him off the couch by dangling a bunch of money over his head. Necessity is the mother of invention. Maybe if our parents would just cut us off, millennials would be forced to do more with our lives.

It's no secret that millennials struggle with money, as do most people. Money is one of the most effective ways to control humans, more than power and sex (those things can be bought if you have enough money). We're either enslaved to our debts or privileged enough to proclaim that we hate or don't need money.

We fight with being bought, with selling out our dreams to work at some crappy job just to keeps the lights on. We struggle to declare our worth, to demand a living wage for our time. We strive to prioritize the parts of life that money can't buy. Millennials and everyone else are fighting for their lives in a system that puts profits over.

We need money to survive.

THE GREAT RECESSION EFFECT

Any study on our generation has to inquire about the psychological effects the Great Recession had on us. It split the millennial cadre in half: those who graduated after it and those who graduated before. Reporters Emily Esfahani Smith and Jennifer Aaker, in their *New York Times* article "Millennial Searchers," found that twenty-somethings who entered the real world postrecession are more focused on creating a positive social impact with their lives. Those who graduated before are more focused exclusively on personal happiness and hedonism.

Millennials grew up during a middle-class boom. Besides a brief dip in the late eighties, household incomes grew steadily throughout the last two decades of the twentieth century. We were brought up during a time when the concept of unlimited growth seemed feasible, but now we're recognizing that unlimited economic growth is what's destroying the environment. Everything has limits, and so does our economy.

However, back then, this financial boom created a stable foundation for many of us to see the world as a friendly place, one that was full of possibility and where we'd always have a safety net to fall back on. Millennials have the luxury to choose to follow our dreams. This is a far cry from the boomers who were brought up with parents who had made it through the Great Depression and who believed that the bottom could fall out at any moment.

Now, juxtapose our upbringing with coming of age during the recession. Millennials entered the working world at a time when inflation rates, high employment, and massive amounts of student debt have made it harder for us to achieve middle-class status than ever.

We question: when is the next bubble going to burst? It could be the tech bubble, the student loan bubble, another lending bubble, or the collapse of the dollar's value. The world is only getting more chaotic and volatile. We know this system is unsustainable. And yet the flaws of this financial system, which is too large and complex for the average person to wrap their head around, affects the entire world.

This is probably another reason why millennials enjoy reaping the fruits of experience rather than material possessions. We realize we don't really have control over what happens. And we saw what happened to our parents who spent decades working their way up a corporate hierarchy with respectable jobs, prioritizing material security, above all else. We watched them lose their retirement savings, their homes, their jobs. We saw them go from having the coveted middle-class lifestyle to falling hundreds of thousands of dollars in the hole, forced to live in whatever apartment they could afford, or out of their car, or in Motel 6, with their now-awful credit.

But this doesn't mean that we don't still desire to contribute to life—to make it more wonderful for the people around us, to be rewarded for those efforts, and to have security to fall back on. These are some of the most important human needs that exist. And the Great Recession made us prioritize the importance of doing good in the world, as well as doing well for ourselves in it. The traumatic loss that we witnessed made us search for meaning in our lives.

WHAT, THEN, IS SUCCESS?

Being either rich or poor comes with its own set of challenges. You can throw money at a lot of situational problems, and, sure, they might go away. Money buys you access to resources, which we need to thrive, but it can't buy you love. It can buy you a therapist to sort through your emotional garbage, but it can't buy you a satisfied mind.

The kids who had the fortune of growing up with everything—who lived in unfettered excess and were fed with a silver spoon—still have to deal with inner demons. They have to reconcile with their privilege in a world that deals it out unfairly. They have a greater responsibility to others and opportunity to give back and lead from a place of compassion, if they choose to assume it. They have to learn how to go out there and get for themselves what they spent their whole lives being handed on a platter. Growing up in the lap of luxury doesn't always teach a person resilience.

Even the Bible declares that it's difficult for a rich man to get into heaven—perhaps because rich people have been conditioned to center their lives around materialism, fleeting desires, and the false self above all else. There is a witchcraft to money, and even those who start off trying to use it for noble intentions are vulnerable to its sorcery.

Those who live in poverty have a different type of struggle. According to a study in the book *The Vanishing Middle Class* by MIT economist Peter Temin, it takes a person twenty years to climb out of the hole of poverty—and only if nothing goes wrong. And let's face it, shit goes wrong all the time.

People who are dealing with a lack of opportunities to make a living wage have constant economic stress. They're vulnerable to homelessness and sickness. If you're poor, you won't be able to access certain places and activities that would be beneficial to your difficult situation, for example, those promoting mental health. It isn't a desirable situation for anyone. However, perhaps the thinnest silver lining present in this situation is that it's a bit easier to find gratitude for what you do have. When you have very little, every little bit matters. You can find solace in an immaterial world. People matter.

I remember seeing people in India share their last bite of food and comparing it to the people I grew up with who were chronically dissatisfied because they didn't have the latest Louis Vuitton handbag—even though they already had three different styles sitting in their closet. Happy humans tend to be more humble.

In postrecession America, millennials have surrendered the notion that wealth and power are the only indicators of success. We've heard too many horror stories from people at top of the social pyramid who talk about the pains that accompany conventional types of triumph. Financial rewards become meaningless when health, happiness, and authentic connection are sacrificed for indulgence in the ego.

Western civilization's obsession with power, wealth, and status is a mind virus that Native Americans called *wetiko*, which they consider as the greatest threat to mankind. Wetiko takes over humans like a parasite to its host and convinces us that we, too, have to overpower and conquer others to achieve wealth and personal security. The indigenous peoples saw it in the European colonists as soon as they landed.

You could call it the cultural epidemic of narcissism that is spreading like a deadly plague. When we're under the spell of wetiko, we can't see that other lives are as important as our own. We can't see that there's enough for everyone—but only if we take just enough of what we need. Wetiko is what we need to confront as a society.

The propagation of the cult of self that our culture promotes is sexy and alluring. We're bred to believe that for *me* to win, *you* have to lose. But what we're fed is two truths and one lie. Yes, we need money, safety, and security. But no, they won't buy you peace, true belonging, or the kind of nourishing love that lasts—especially if obtained at the expense of others. What's promising is that people are waking up—even the ones with power—to the fact that you can't enjoy the riches of the world if they cost you your soul. So, they're spreading the wealth around.

Take Ariana Huffington, for example. The woman who ignited the trend of blogging when she started *The Huffington Post* woke up one day in 2014 face-down on her desk in a pool of blood after passing out in a narcoleptic-styled bout of nervous exhaustion. The whole experience caused her to change her entire outlook on work, her company culture, and the importance of wellness, so much so that she used her power and influence to start a social movement promoting balance and wholeness after stepping down as the editor-in-chief.

"It's not 'What do I want to do?'" Huffington says in her book *Thrive*. "It's 'What kind of life do I want to have?'"

It's said that there are eight types of capital: financial, material, spiritual, intellectual, social, experiential, cultural, and living capital. All are necessary for a life of balance, joy, and abundance. Humans need exercise, leisure time, and intellectual stimulation; we all have an innate need to be with nature; most of us feel a drive to volunteer and be a part of a community. Huffington calls wellness "the third metric"—a vital component to productivity and energetic vitality that has been absent from the capitalist conversation until now.

This is why so many millennials are adamant about designing our own lifestyles, going as far as to call ourselves "lifestyle entrepreneurs." Those of us who are happy and balanced are finding ways to monetize what we know. Because we know that most people could successfully work themselves into a state of clinical depression in three days if they went to a job they hated, fought traffic for hours, watched the news, ate processed food, sat on a couch, and scrolled through Facebook for an entire evening, comparing their lives to others. The dilemma is that this is the riptide of mainstream life.

If this society cares about making money, we should also give a shit about depression. According to the Analysis Group, for every dollar that's spent treating major depressive disorder, another $6.60 gets spent on reduced workplace productivity and other direct and indirect costs related to the illness. our myriad needs were met by our institutions and health was prioritized, we could have a highly generative society.

In the midst of all this, more and more Americans, including plenty of millennials, are challenging what defines a person's "success." The 2013 American Express LifeTwist Study revealed that 95 percent of Americans believed that being open to change is what makes a person successful. Prior to the Great Recession, most believed that success was defined by having a lot of money, but values changed when the economy crashed.

The question for humanity, at this point, is can we adapt? What values will we pursue with the freedom of choice we have?

As long as millennials refuse to be gluttons for punishment and destruction, we are making an impact. In fact, our bleeding hearts and misanthropy, which are so often criticized, are actually part of a humanist movement. We know that the solutions to our planet's problems probably won't be found by swiping a credit card. . However, we also have to be careful about shooting ourselves in the foot. We don't have to throw the baby out with the bathwater. We can contribute, in our own ways, to society, using a different mindset.

DO ALL ARROWS HAVE TO POINT STRAIGHT?

I've never been a straight arrow, and I don't know if the wonky, schitzy path I took through my twenties has ultimately helped or hurt me. I definitely gained some experiential capital: I learned how to live with the land (natural capital), and I made a bunch of amazing friends (social capital). However, I also acquired a long list of shitty ideas that didn't work. I've learned that you've got to meet others and the world halfway. You've got to learn how this whole thing works before you go disrupting it.

Not every young person tussles with tradition, like me, Rocky, Tony, or James. By no means is the progressive agenda that's delineated in this book uniform to the entire millennial experience. There are some of us who believe that our society works well. There are millennials who think that climate change isn't real, that America's gigantic defense system is necessary, and that our main problem is all the misandry man-hating that's going down in the streets. However, the rest of us—the dissenters, the skeptics, the informed dreamers—form the moral millennial majority.

A 2015 poll by Harvard's Institute of Politics found that millennials basically trust no one.

- 88 percent of us "sometimes" or "never" trust the mass media or press.
- 86 percent of us don't trust Wall Street.
- 82 percent of us don't trust Congress.
- 74 percent of us don't trust the Federal Government to do "the right thing."
- 50 percent of us don't trust the cops.

If we aren't following traditional paths, it's because we don't believe the rhetoric we're being told. It doesn't matter that millennials are zig-zagging toward adulthood, because the journey is the destination. Our job is to transform the system, not conform to it. There is no roadmap to making a world that no one's ever made before. We're figuring out our individual paths step by step. Turns out, this strategy isn't so unusual.

The 2013 American Express LifeTwist Study also found that:

- 13 percent of Americans had a clear path plotted and were determined to stick to it without wavering, i.e., they moved from start to finish in a straight line.
- 56 percent had goals but were open to life taking them on and off that path.
- 25 percent went wherever outside forces took them like a balloon in the wind.
- 11 percent sought out change for the entirety of their waking days—reincarnating their identities over and over again in reaction to external events.

It takes all kinds. You don't need a thirty-year plan. There are these things we have called instinct and intuition that guides us in our decision-making. If you're open to listening, you might find that you're being summoned by some kind of inner power or knowing, a balance between emotion and logic, desire and strategy. A spirit, perhaps, that will guide you toward making our institutions noble and compassionate again.

A SENSE OF SELFISHNESS

There's a reason why our culture looks the way it does. From the perspective of evolutionary biology, it makes perfect sense. Humans are hardwired to seek status, social recognition, and wealth. I don't know if there's ever been a society in recorded human history where these types of vanities weren't valued to some extent.

"What's in it for me?" That's the question that rules all human behavior. We have what is called a selfish gene. And because of it, it's safe to assume that everyone is doing what they believe is best for them at any given moment. Yes, humans are capable of compassion, empathy, and justice. However, time and time again we see how people turn this sense of compassion and drive for justice on and off as it best serves us. Most of the time, we're not even aware we're doing it.

It's important to realize that this is an evolutionary mechanism. We've talked at length about the more liberal "beta" millennials who seem too sensitive for the world; now let's explore the mindset of a millennial alpha—a traditionalist and a conservative. There's sincere logic to both sides of the coin presented here.

John Klein (name changed), twenty-six, became a registered banker at Wells Fargo after working a few less-than-lucrative jobs postcollege (see: cashier at Best Buy and insurance salesman in a pyramid scheme, where he ended up driving around making zilch dinero most days). He became a banker because he needed to support himself in an expensive city like Los Angeles.

"I realized I can't rely on anyone else," John says. "I have to take care of myself. No one else in this world is going to take care of me. It was only once I got this Wells Fargo job that I could start supporting myself. I'm now lucky to have enough to get things that I want and save a bit on the side. People value money because it makes the world go around."

He's absolutely right. As I've gotten older, I've also realized that I have to become more like John in some ways. This is exactly what happened to the baby boomers who were formerly hippie revolutionaries in the sixties. They started out as iconoclasts who were part of the liberal social upheaval by championing the civil rights movement, protesting the Vietnam War, and running around naked during the Summer of Love; but when their time in emerging adulthood was done, they returned to the establishment, who had control over the resources, to make a stable life.

John says he values personal freedom. His parents are wealthy, but they refused to enable him. As soon as he graduated college, he was on his own. Freedom for John means having access to financial and material capital. He wants to buy a car without having to ask his parents for money; he wants to be able to buy a plane ticket to Vietnam on a whim to scuba dive with his girlfriend. And, on his way to Vietnam, he wants to sit in first class, eat filet mignon and baby carrots, and recline in leather seats with enough legroom. Freedom to John is being able to hire a housekeeper to clean the layer of grout off his bathtub so he doesn't have to bend over and do it himself after a long day on the job. Freedom means having mobility. And since John likes being a consumer, his definition of freedom requires money.

"Listen, I still am not 100 percent sure of what I want to do with my life," he says as I sit with him outside the house he rents in the Hollywood Hills. "Working at Wells Fargo was a better way to make money than the minimum wage I was making everywhere else."

He knows he's sold himself to the Man. Yet, he also knows that there aren't too many professions where earning this kind of dough is guaranteed. The people who work with money in our society are usually ensured that they will make good amounts of it—because they create, regulate, and monitor it. They collect dividends and derivatives and score bonuses in the elaborately complex institution that is our financial system. That's why John became a banker. He doesn't care that the bankers chasing paychecks crashed the economy in 2008 by selling a bunch of subprime mortgages. He's not interested in challenging the ethics of his industry or calling out the corporate environment he works at for its unethical practices. He's living in survival mode and enjoying sensory perks along the way.

John says he works to live; he doesn't live to work. He accepts the necessity of hierarchy and capitalism.

There is, however, a catch to John's master plan for freedom. Until that fat payday arrives when he'll earn the lucrative salary that will place him at the top of the human food chain, he lives in figurative chains. He's a slave to the sixty-hour workweek that many millennials are doing everything to avoid. John spends two hours fighting traffic each weekday morning and evening on the Los Angeles freeway driving to Wells Fargo, where he sits in a cubicle from precisely 8 a.m. to 5 p.m. He helps students open checking accounts and old ladies reorder lost debit cards, and sometimes he gets stoned during his lunch break. He hasn't missed a day of work in two years. He believes in the morality of being hardworking.

This kind of work is not John's passion. He's studying to get his license to trade stocks and other commodities, and he hopes he'll eventually find pleasure at his finance job once he works his way up and starts taking on more interesting tasks. Every step he takes is a means to an end to one day have the conventional type of success he craves and to achieve his definition of freedom.

MONEY-LESS AND HAPPY

Now, let's examine a very different case study on the other extreme. Some millennials have beliefs that are opposed to John's. They believe that chasing money is an impediment to their freedom. They are the anti-institutionalists who deem that the pursuit for numbers cripples a person's ability to care for the other facets of life that create health and happiness and wholeness.

Working a job they despise for a company that propagates the cultural sickness of economic growth despite consequence; living in a cookie-cutter house made with unsustainably harvested materials and chemicals that they barely have time to spend in; investing in a market system that is destroying the environment and could crash at any time—these are not their ideas of security. They are their definition of insanity.

These types of millennials would rather work odd jobs in the informal economy (or even the black market), traveling wherever they can to volunteer at farms or schools across the world. These young people aren't conventionally ambitious; they aren't working on some magnum opus like *The Millennial's Guide to Changing the World* to make their parents proud or validate their existence. They don't think they carry the fate of the world on their shoulders.

If you think of society like a molecule, you have protons (the conservatives) and neutrons (the liberals) that are smashing into each other in the nucleus. And then you have the electrons (the counterculturalists, the mystics, the wanderers, the recluses) that orbit around in a cloud far away from the center of the activity.

These people are lighter. They choose not to participate in the war of dualism and distance themselves from the race for resources. They don't have a lot of money, but they've got free time. And they spend it worshipping the moment. They get to sit on the sidelines and philosophize, dropping in to experience the realm of the eternal. They focus on the esoteric and on leading a low-stress existence. They contribute as little as possible to corrupt institutions and try not to interact with the busy, modern world.

Some live in nature. Some live off food stamps. Some trim weed once a year and live off the earnings. They're always on the go. They find ways to hack the system. They aren't working toward financial security. They have no five-year plan, let alone a thirty-year one. They believe that god laughs when you make plans and that there is no way to make a difference in the system by working inside it, so they practice radical self-reliance instead. Many believe that the only way to be free of the shadows of society is to turn your back on it. And maybe this is spiritual bypassing; maybe this opposite extreme is just another form of complete selfishness—a way to evade taking responsibility for oneself that only really works when you're in your twenties.

Briz Smith, twenty-two, works as a housekeeper at the Earthships headquarters in New Mexico. Earthships are a revolutionary eco-friendly building construction method that creates homes that look like spaceships. Briz describes herself as apolitical. She's been traveling for three years, living on farms on many different continents, and she's not sure where she'll end up. She owns few possessions. When she hears the call, she takes her backpack and follows the wind. She's not punching herself in the face like I am, trying to figure out how to the change the world. She just trusts it.

"I threw myself out into the world, and I was caught so well," Briz says while we sit in an arid field of yellow grass. She has short, pixie-cut hair and a calm gaze in her eyes. Briz is totally tapped into the fifth dimension. "The people I met were so sweet and kind."

Briz says she never felt like she fit into society (though that doesn't mean she doesn't want to eventually fit in somewhere with someone). Briz is spending her twenties searching for what she loves in hopes that it will lead her to who she is.

"Love drives me the most in the moment—all kinds of love," Briz says.

Briz's goals are more qualitative and abstract than John's quantitative ambitions. John wants to make more money and further his career; Briz wants to care and give and receive and grow.

God bless the diverse spectrum of humanity. It takes all kinds of people to make this world go around. Every type of consciousness that exists on the planet is a valuable one, and if we can just learn to live and let be, perhaps we'd all have a safe place to be ourselves by now.

MATT ERLICH'S MIDDLE PATH

"You know what makes people happy?" Matt Erlich, twenty-five, says as he puts his spiral-bound notebook on the deck table. "Options."

Matt is currently a sales manager who indirectly manages 250 people daily at TEKsystems, an IT firm that *Fortune* named a top place to work at in 2013. Matt is one of those mid-decade millennials who is "#winning" inside the market system that is slowly and possibly becoming more humane. He works for a company that doesn't put profits over its people.

There are conscious capitalist initiatives that use business to create vibrant and enjoyable cultures, where positive social values are the cornerstone of the empire. These are the types of social enterprises that millennials want to work for. If the private sector listens to millennials, we can create a world filled with goods and services that we actually want to live in.

TEKsystems is what I call an emotionally intelligent company. The HR policy at Matt's company requires him to open up about his feelings on the regular. He gets to bring his whole self to work: his daddy issues, his tears if he's having a bad day. He gets to reveal the reality of his inner world without fear of getting punished for being what we all are—vulnerable. We're humans, not machines.

Corporations lose hundreds of millions of dollars training millennials who quit their jobs every year because they're not happy. Companies that need millennial employees to thrive are realizing that retention rates rise when they create a nurturing and creative internal culture of transparency, loyalty, emotional health, and psychological safety.

Millennials want self-actualization, and if we can self-actualize while making money, that's ideal. Matt has benefited from working at a company whose HR policies allow him to do personal work at work. They want to build him up, rather than suck him dry. His employers recognize that every single millennial employee they have is going through an emotional process due to on-the-job and personal stress. These employees need support through the ebbs and flows, and they have to want to choose to stay at that one company, even when there are thousands of other things they could be doing across the globe. They could be drinking ayahuasca in Peru, teaching English in China, or starting their own company in the comfort of their home. How do you get a millennial, who has a world of options, to hunker down and stay put? The answer is for companies to commit to our personal growth.

In his book *Flourish*, Dr. Martin Seligman explains well-being as a theory of uncoerced choice: "what free people will choose for their own sake." Seligman, who spearheaded the positive psychology movement at the University of Pennsylvania, would most likely agree with Matt's statement: having options is fundamental to both psychological and physical health.

There are other academics who would challenge this notion, such as neuro-economist Baba Shiv. They say that, yes, having the freedom to make decisions on our own terms is important, but options themselves don't make people happy. Because having too many can hijack a person's ability to function with a sense of direction.

Options are what millennials crave, but options are also what drive us crazy. It's the paradox of our modern privilege. We have choices, but we don't know what to do in spite of them. So, we find some kind of internal guidance system. Some people call it god. Some people call it their intuition or going with their gut. Some people consult spirit guides and angels and the deceased avatars or their ancestors. Whatever works for you, we need to find our flow in a world filled with cruelty and wickedness and engineer positive, meaningful experiences.

CREATING A CULTURE OF HAPPINESS

There's a spectrum of well-being—on one end is languishing and on the other is flourishing. According to the theory of flourishing (which has been around since the days of Aristotle), happiness happens when we feel "in the zone"—growing, trusting our resiliency, and being creatively productive, all with a sense of power and ease and feeling of goodness.

Dr. Corey Keyes, a pioneer in the flourishing movement in positive psychology, tells me that our society has made a lot of attempts to deal with symptoms of unhappiness, but we haven't done much to create a culture of true healing. Seeking virtuous activity is part of it, and so is having a sense of social well-being and environmental mastery. This is what millennials are seeking as we strike out to find ourselves.

"It's not about finding yourself," says Keyes. "It's about finding your well-being. This is your time to start." Keyes said in our interview that, according to his research, only 37 percent of emerging adults are flourishing and that the environment we're coming of age in is a huge contributing component.

So is mastering our own cognitive and emotional processes. With every thought we think and everything we do, we're shaping our brains. We can't change society overnight, but we can first learn to manage our inner landscape. The whole purpose of life is happiness, at least that's what Keyes thinks.

And that's what I believe success is, too.

Chapter 4

Reinventing the Quarter-Life Crisis

"It was medical school or sex, drugs, and rock 'n' roll. I chose the latter. Finding your purpose at first can involve a lot of experimenting."

—Mariah "Aum" Reed, twenty-nine, shaman

AT THE TIME OF MY QUARTER-LIFE CRISIS, I WAS TWENTY-FIVE and had just moved back in with my parents. This was when I first decided to write a portrait of our generation. I saved enough money to travel around the country to interview millennials (who are now featured in this book) by baking pies, selling diamonds on Saturdays, and dancing at bar mitzvahs. I spent all my free time reading books and trying to understand how our world works from an economic, political, sociological, psychological, and metaphysical standpoint. I was intensely anxious about striking out on my own and sharing my thoughts publicly. While everyone around me was getting serious about the more practical things, I was about to take the biggest leap of faith in my life, all in the hope that I could make a difference. If everything inside of me was telling me to do something, what would happen if I listened?

This book has been a product of my quarter-life crisis, of an aching desire to find my purpose. Back then, I thought I needed something bigger than myself to make my life worth living. I needed to believe that I had some say in my environment; I needed not to feel like a helpless victim to it. I needed to be anchored to a sense of direction. In my attempts to "save the world," I sabotaged myself left and right. I've burned bridges. I've been self-important and ugly. I've felt despair. I've tossed and turned over whether or not these are my wars to fight. I shot off about nine of my ten toes trying to make a difference, spending all the money I worked to earn. I've been laughed at, silenced, and backstabbed. And I wouldn't take back any of it.

My quarter life crisis was the defining point for me, as it is for many, when I had to ask myself some big questions and make a decision. Was I going to go for my dream that every pulsating cell in my body was crying out for me to pursue? Would I dare to do the things that everyone told me were impossible?

I've been running around for a decade telling everyone that the sky is about to fall, but no one seemed to want to hear it. Maybe there's nothing any of us can do to stop humanity from evolving to extinction; maybe it's god's business. As the world spins madly on, the people around me were "growing up"—they got jobs at big companies and took out Roth IRAs. Meanwhile, this grown-up Alison I was anticipating getting to know was still frozen inside of me, unable to thaw and get on with the program.

But at the end of the day, I chose to cherish life—mine and others'. I decided to believe in the purpose of this book. And maybe people will listen now. Maybe now is the time when we can make a difference.

This world is filled with tons of people who are trying to change it. "Changing the world" is not an original concept. I've realized that those of us who drive ourselves crazy trying to change the world are just adding to the madness if we're not changing ourselves at the same time. Taking on a pious, sacrificial role won't save you from yourself. In order to write a book that provides people with a sense of peace and empowerment, I had to first become that for myself.

At twenty-five, I was having what psychologists call an *identity crisis*. During our early to mid-twenties, young people start obsessing about this thing called *the self* and our need to have one. Quite frankly, I believe the people who flip their lids during this period are often just dealing with pains of coming into awareness. Once you become acutely aware of what it means to be a feeling, thinking, and energetic being, you're suddenly connected to the chaos and suffering around you—you start to feel what's real so deeply that you can become it. I've noticed that it's so often the people who've gone crazy who try to change the world, as if changing the world will make them become sane somehow. Now I know it doesn't work like that.

The quarter-life crisis is a relatively new sociological phenomenon that is often seen in millennials. I see it as an initiation, the time when we're truly meant to transition from girls into women and boys into men. It is caused by a myriad of forces, including:

- too many life path options
- economic hardship
- changes in brain chemistry
- wanderlust
- comparison and competition

Let's break these down one by one.

TOO MANY LIFE PATH OPTIONS

Before I begin, let me start with a disclaimer: I am privileged, which has opened me up to a world of options. Living in America—and the developed world in general—has its perks. I can choose to hide away on a tropical island paradise that my imperialist government took over by force without having to obtain a visa. I can pay for the plane ticket by putting it on a credit card that awards me with 80,000 free miles. When I lived in New York City, I could have any food I wanted delivered to my doorstep. Roast beef sandwiches on sourdough with a sweet onion jam at midnight? Done. Am I craving a booty call? I've got 350 matches on Tinder. And what if I wanted to change the world? There's a social cause for every day of every week and every month of every year that I can sign petitions for.

It's enough to make your head spin. If you're seeking insight into your identity, look no further than to what you feel attracted to in this world of options. It reveals a lot about your values and your self-image.

Markets are becoming more and more saturated, with plenty of stuff for us to buy and activities to do. Information technology and social media have connected the seven-plus billion people on the planet. We can find anything we want with a Google search. Society gives us so much variety, and the caveat is that a huge chunk of it isn't even healthy. The products we consume are made with slave labor, they poison our bodies, and once discarded they are left to stain the earth.

As millennials come of age, we are forced to find our way through all this and add our own unique signature to the clusterfuckery—just to make a dollar and a life for ourselves. And as we do, our options keep growing—for potential mates, places to eat pho, and possible career paths. As we step into our roles as creators, the World of Things keeps rapidly expanding along with the universe.

In this day and age, you can choose your haircut or preferred gender pronoun; you can be in a consensual clown orgy at Burning Man or live off the grid on an island. Social norms have become so liberalized that there is a multiplicity of paths to go down. Some people think this is good, while others believe it contributes to the identity crisis young people are experiencing in droves. You may not like tradition, but there is something about conforming to convention that makes this stress go away. The hundreds of mundane choices we make each day add up and create either health or disease in our lives.

It takes pressure to make a diamond. But very little in this world ever made me truly satisfied until I decided to follow the whisper within. I decided to write this book and embarked on what became a twisted, uncertain, and redemptive adventure. I believe there's no accountable way out of the life process, but there *is* a way out of the pain—it starts with being committed to the process of living, no matter what obstacles appear on your path. It starts with having a sense of direction and following your inner guidance, come what may. And often, satisfaction and confidence arise from that.

ECONOMIC HARDSHIP

If you are going through a quarter-life crisis, odds are that most of it will start and end with the need for money. For many of us, our crises mark the point when many people have to choose between the practical need for money or following their dreams.

It would be utterly irresponsible of me to deny the obvious—that if you chose to play along with the system, you *can* come out on top. You can get a good paying job after college, work your way up the company ladder, start saving two hundred dollars a month to appreciate in a 401K (the sooner you start, the better), cash out with a million at age seventy, and sell the home you bought with a bank mortgage for twice the price (market value depending)—and then you and your wife or husband of forty years can retire and move into a board and batten ranch house on a great lake somewhere.

This is convention. And there's something really sweet about it. Some millennials *do* aspire to this path; we're just not sure that we can do it without sacrificing our desire to make a difference along the way.

Keri Hunigan is twenty-six and still interning in the peace-building field. She has just earned a graduate degree in political science. She lives at home with her parents. Keri is currently experiencing a quarter-life crisis.

"I'm at the point in my life where I wonder if I did the right thing by getting a graduate education. I see people who didn't make the same choices as me who are happy and getting married and having babies. I wonder if I had gone straight to work what my life would be like."

Keri has loans to pay. She has applied to fifty jobs. Her main "problem" is that she wants to make a difference in a world, and she has only applied to jobs that are meaningful to her. Unfortunately, so far all are already taken by some other bushy-tailed, wide-eyed millennial. Keri is nervous and experiencing high levels of self-doubt. She wonders if there's going to be a light at the end of the tunnel, but she refuses to give up on her values and convictions and the positive impact she wants to make.

"It bothers me that there are so many people who don't care about making the world a better place," she says. "I'm not saying that everyone has to be an activist. Not everyone has to dedicate their lives to building peace the way I would like to. But I do think everyone needs some sort of cause. It does something for your soul. I think everyone needs more soul."

Keri is not alone in her gridlock. Many young people now spend the majority of their twenties competing to earn money in nonlucrative environments. We write articles "for exposure." We intern for years to build resumes. We get degree after degree, hoping it will help an employer see our value. We do work in exchange for a place to sleep. In this era, twenty-somethings are modern-day slaves. Many of us work without seeing a dime.

So, should we put on our own oxygen mask before helping others? That would be wise, but it might also make us part of the problem and not the solution. Keri is someone who has done everything according to "the plan," but she's now in an identity crisis because she can't move forward. She wonders, *Will I ever be able to move out of my mom and dad's? Will I have it all, as I was promised?*

Within three years of our interview, Keri's prayers are finally answered. She lands her dream job and finds a husband, though it happens in ways she could never have predicted.

Keri is just like Molly Finneran, age twenty-two. Molly is a pearl of a girl and a do-gooder. She works at Planned Parenthood. Luckily, Molly hasn't had her quarter-life crisis yet. I met her while couch-surfing at a group home. Her presence felt so safe and nourishing that we snuggled all night in her bed. Molly says she doesn't like the words *good* or *help*. When asked what she wants to do with her life, she says that she simply wants to connect.

"Human connections make me feel the most alive," she says. "I feel the most alive when I can genuinely share a personal part of myself with someone, and it never has to be the same part."

Millennials start off with a lot of good priorities. We want connection. We want to do good. We want to build peace, and we grow up thinking the world will reward it. When years pass and we have yet to see the fruits of our labor, we are faced with enormous stressors that shake our convictions in the dreams of our youth and our visions for a better world.

But here's the thing that few people will tell you: your dreams will change, and there's no need to hold onto something that no longer serves you. It doesn't mean you've failed; it just means you're evolving.

During a quarter-life crisis, your perceptions about how you want the world to work are met with a steady onslaught of contradictory evidence. You may have wholesome ideals, but this isn't a chivalrous culture; it's a kill-or-be-killed society. You're going to need to money to survive or you'll end up in a gutter. Your quarter-life crisis is a call to find balance; it's not about abandoning ship.

To find a way to merge purpose with profit, you're going to have to keep hitting the damn until it breaks, while changing your strategy along the way. You can find a way to monetize your dreams. You may need a side hustle for a bit. Manifesting requires a lot of perseverance. Things don't always come easily—maybe they're not supposed to. But I believe that they come when they're meant to. And we'll do a whole lot of growing up in the process.

CHANGES IN BRAIN CHEMISTRY

The quarter-life crisis is also biologically wired. The part of your brain that comprehends the need for future planning and stops you from doing impulsive things in public—like throwing your glass at a bartender when he messes up your drink order—is called the prefrontal cortex. Neuroscientists are proving that the prefrontal cortex doesn't fully develop until age twenty-five, and for people with cognitive challenges like ADHD, it sometimes takes even longer.

There comes a time in every young person's life when they realize they must stop fucking around. That epiphany is likely the prefrontal cortex talking. Some psychologists believe that age twenty-five is when adolescence officially ends; others believe it happens at age thirty (and to think you can be officially tried as an adult in court at the age of eighteen). Until then, our emotional regulation, self-image, impulse control, the ability to learn from our mistakes, and judgment are still slowly forming.

Actions have consequences! It's the darndest thing. The quarter-life crisis comes in the form of a wake-up call to this reality—and it's ultimately a benevolent one. Because if more people were willing to finely tune their awareness of the cause and effect of their actions, we just might be able to collectively work our way out of this ditch. It may come as quite the shock to some millennials when our parents are no longer willing to buffer the blows of our mistakes, but it is necessary for us to start making long-term, sustainable decisions for ourselves. We don't live in a safe bubble.

Another thing that happens during the development of our prefrontal cortex is we start to fathom our own mortality. Before we turn twenty-five, it's easy to live life in the fast lane like we'll stay forever young—because we don't know anything else. It's easy to make decisions as if we'll never grow old, but eventually the time comes to quit the binge drinking and getting arrested. The party is over, and we need to get serious. Your body won't be able to assimilate liquor without a gnarly hangover for much longer, and all the good jobs—the one with the benefits—administer background checks.

Ladies and gentleman, you've got to learn to mind your wake. You've got to understand that while real-world responsibilities may seem regular and lame, most people are just trying to do their own thing or live their lives in peace. When this prefrontal cortex thing switches on, conforming to social norms starts to become more appealing. It's a survival tactic, really—when we blend in, we deal with less conflict.

If you've had an abusive or neglectful childhood, the painful memories we previously buried in order to live with our tormentors are also going to start popping up during this time in our early twenties. The onset of many types of mental illness typically surface in the early and mid-twenties, and it's a huge contributing factor to the quarter-life crisis. Call it your Saturn returns, call it whatever disorder you like, but many people during this time are forced to confront the fact that the behaviors they learned to adopt to survive childhood aren't going to help them get to where they want to go in their adult lives.

I eventually reached a point when running around emotionally disheveled and crying about my victimhood stopped being a cute look for me—it also just gave people the green light to take advantage of me. I was wired in a certain way, and I had to do some rewiring in order to become a functioning member of society.

WANDERLUST

Katy Blanton, twenty-four, is on the hunt to discover viable alternatives to convention. She's championed a lifestyle of living in and out the bag. As soon as she saves up a thousand dollars, she hops on a plane to places like Costa Rica to reside at an anarchist farm, where she eats rations of avocados, cuts lettuce for the community, and lives off-the-grid to escape the contemporary world of madness and try to free her soul.

Do millennials want to be able to afford a temporary vacation, or do we want to permanently live one? This is the question older generations seem to ask whenever the topic comes up of where we'll be galivanting off to next. Millennials have traveled 23 percent more than previous generations. We are spending our emerging adulthood chasing after a sense of place. When we don't know who we are or where we belong and when we're fighting to make sense of a painful past, sometimes the only thing we can do is pack up and go—far into the unknown to unpack ourselves.

My personal advice is to have a quarter-life crisis now so you avoid a midlife crisis later. You're freer in emerging adulthood than you'll ever be. You have no roots and no obligations to anyone else. If wanderlust takes over, you can roll with it. You're young and resilient. You can start over anywhere you please, again and again. It's easy for you to assimilate into new environments. There is a whole international culture of backpackers and hostels and communes for you to explore.

When Katy suffered her quarter-life crisis, she dropped out of college during her final semester. Life was throwing emotional grenades at her, and she didn't see the point of suffering through the onslaught to finish her degree in the humanities in a place where she felt like she was spiraling out of control. It was a decision that didn't make much sense to the people around her, but she stuck with it nonetheless.

"Dealing with the psychological issues I was going through and having to navigate the material world wasn't easy," she says. "I was always given money for everything, and when I dropped out of college, my dad said he wasn't going to support me anymore."

When no psychologist or pill can fix your problems, sometimes you've just got to hit the road. There are tons of places in the world where you can go to heal. Just try to not be ignorant or disrespectful to the native people who live there, especially in places that have been colonized by westernized powers and packaged into destinations for predominantly white people to run away to, retreat, and relax, while they leave spoils in their wake.

"I've done a lot of personal work and meditated on the life I want to pursue and live every day, one that fosters self-education and growth and mindfulness and exploration and nature," Katy says. "I know I want sustainability, community, healthy and awesome food, and intimacy, love, and genuine connection. Things that I find hard to find in most of . . . society. I don't want to curse myself, but in the normal nine-to-five pursuit of life, those are hard to accomplish. They are put on the back burner."

Millennials want to pursue our passions *now*—not when we retire. *Now* is our time to heal, and humans can heal just about anything in the right environment with the right tools and the right kind of people. Perhaps this is why many millennials are delaying our adult responsibilities—we need to heal ourselves first, and we go on the road to do it.

COMPARISON AND COMPETITION

There are 7.6 billion different realities coexisting on this planet at the same time. If you start comparing yourself to all the different people you could be, you're going to start sinking into a black hole of quicksand. You will erase yourself into an existential crisis.

When we leave home at age eighteen, most of us scatter ourselves across the country. We go to different colleges and get jobs in different cities. We chase romance. We zig-zag around—though most of us manage to move forward—dovetailing into the next phases of our development at varying paces. As hard as this emerging adulthood thing can be, real adulthood is supposedly even harder. So don't rush the process, and enjoy exactly where you're at right now, while you're at it.

During the phase of emerging adulthood, the people we've known forever start to differentiate themselves. They develop diverging values, goals, and lifestyle preferences. Take Yelena Nam for instance, the girl I used to hang out with all the time in high school. Over the years, the differences between us amplified, and she is now a corporate attorney. When I found out, I judged her at first. I was quite the anti-capitalist at the time; in fact, I was quite anti-everything. Meanwhile, Yelena looked at me like I was crazy for living in a van, spending all my time and money writing a book that might suck and that wouldn't provide me with any security. Luckily, we are still friends. Kindness is what counts at the end of the day.

Yelena is a conventional person, and she has her reasons. Her parents, both doctors, immigrated to the US with Yelena and her sister after the fall of the Soviet Union to start over. Yelena is grateful for the educational and professional opportunities that living in America has afforded her. To her, it is the promised land, at least relatively speaking.

When I interviewed Yelena for this project, I realized that her story and values make sense. In the process of learning the life histories of hundreds of my peers, I've learned that everyone chooses the appropriate and reasonable life path given what they've been through. What gets to us is when we start trying to compare apples to oranges.

Not everyone is meant to be like Yelena. The artists, mystics, dancers, poets, activists, and entrepreneurs will embark on a less prudent path. If you resist pursuing what you're truly passionate about, you might spend the rest of your life wondering what else you could have been doing.

Embarking on the path less traveled comes with its own costs; your quarter-life crisis might emerge from dancing on life's edges with nothing solid to lean on. Meanwhile, those who choose the nine-to-five may experience a crisis from the monotony of landing a secure job, complete with the cubicle and cork board. These millennials have an avenue to develop security, but they might find their work spiritually empty.

A quarter-life crisis can happen to anyone living on every point of the spectrum—those ground to dust by the daily routine or those exhausted by our own ephemeral instability. Whichever type of crisis you have, uncertainty is the only thing that's certain. The anxiety of not knowing what will happen—if you will create the life you truly desire or if you will become just like your parents—drones on and on in your head until you're one tea-kettle whistle away from hyperventilating. And—because of this little thing called Facebook, we see never-ending pictures of all the different life paths available playing out all day, every day. When we're feeling insecure about who we are and uncertain about the outcome of our own decisions, comparing ourselves to others is often all we do. As we scroll through our feed, it's easy to think that surely this or that person who looks so perfect has it all figured out. We assume that they don't have the same kind of doubts and fears that we do. But believe me—they do.

Some respond to their quarter-life crises by trying to drop an anchor. I almost impulsively married an emotionally unstable accountant, thinking his corporate health insurance would solve all my problems. It would have been a huge mistake. There are no shortcuts to becoming and standing strong on your own two feet. The only way to keep the mind from churning is to feel what's in the heart that's hurting. Once we can do that, we will evolve. What once terrified us won't seem so scary. We will become more confident painting on larger and larger canvases and being seen and heard for who we are.

The only way out of a quarter-life crisis is to allow yourself to get through it—to breathe in, sit with the issues that arise, and navigate the outer storms by following your inner compass. We've got to believe that we have the power to change the world before it changes us.

MILLENNIAL AVATARS, DESTINED TO MAYBE, POSSIBLY SAVE THE WORLD

There is an indigenous American prophecy that says that when the forests die, when animals are born mutated, when people are at war but can't remember why, and when an evil spirit has taken over the soul of mankind and corrupted them into living lives of greed and ego, a generation will arise from the control of the colonial empire to make the Earth beautiful again—and they will do it by following the Great Spirit within. If this prophecy is correct, that generation is probably, maybe, possibly . . . the millennials!

(Or it might be Generation Z.)

We're seeing these forecasts transpire before our own eyes. Experts say we're losing about 80,000 acres of tropical rainforest daily. Fish, birds, and other animals are being born mutated in the aftermath of Fukushima. We're at war in the Middle East for reasons cloaked as "terrorism" that no American can truly explain. We've turned our backs on our neighbors, our communities, and our family members in their times of vulnerability. We justify our actions through the paradigm of consumerism and venerate excessive consumption as the ultimate indicator of triumph.

And in the midst of this, you have the millennials, who are struggling to find our place in a chaotic world. Our elders can't seem to see the forest for the trees anymore, but we are still sensitive and we can. Turning the tide in the grand scheme of human evolution may be up to us and our intergenerational allies. We're walking a razor's edge of tropical storms, wildfires, and threats of nuclear war. We cannot sell out our spiritually attuned sensibilities as they are important tools for the task at hand; we have to find a way to evolve the system so diversity on Earth can thrive again.

The Iroquois Great Law of Peace talks about a principle known as "the seventh generation rule." It said that every decision made in governmental, corporate, and personal realms should consider the impact it would have seven generations down the line. In 1870, modern imperialism began with the Industrial Revolution. Colonist countries declared themselves the rightful rulers of other territories and created satellite markets around the world to stimulate their economies from a depression. They used war to gather resources from foreign lands, imported cheap labor, enslaved and displaced indigenous peoples, and embarked on a mission to "civilize" the world with Western medicine, Christianity, Social Darwinism, law, and technology.

Here's the math: if a generation cycles every twenty or so years, that would make millennials the seventh generation to come of age since modern imperialism. We are now feeling the devastating effects of this worldwide colonial empire and the Industrial Revolution. The expansionists of Western civilization did not exercise the kind of consciousness the indigenous people embraced. They did not consider the cumulative effects their actions would have on their children's children. We're living in a time period called the "Kali Yurga" in Sanskrit, the age of vice and destruction, where people worship false idols and lack morality. In this time period, I can't help but wonder if perhaps the millennials have been chosen, not forsaken. Maybe we are meant to save the day in the last inning like the "Lost Generation" during the Great Depression.

Millennials may not be the generation to turn the tide and usher in an enlightened epoch. The truth is it may take generations after us to bring the dawn. But that doesn't mean we should throw in the towel or that our lives are insignificant. It's still up to us to do our part, to at least try to walk as best we can in a state of integrity, for the sake of the children to come after us.

The quarter-life crisis represents a turning point when the autonomy of adolescence shifts. We age out of our self-seeking independence and are called to step into our interdependence. We have to find an answer to the question: What will our role be in all of this?

Chapter 5

To School or Not to School

EVERYTHING IS A BUSINESS IN THIS COUNTRY, INCLUDING education. For boomers and Gen Xers, going to college used to be a ticket to the middle class. But now that information is everywhere, tuition is inflated, "good" jobs often require more education than a bachelor's degree, and starting your own business requires no degree at all. The revolution will include access to accurate and empowering information, and the role of formal education is being questioned more and more by millennials. What was once considered a prerequisite to life in this society is now being examined by millennials for the return on its investment.

Because you know what? Steve Jobs didn't go to college, and look at what he accomplished.

WHAT YOU NEED TO KNOW FOR LIFE?

"It's easy to get stuck working at restaurants. Go to college, yes, but don't be attached to finishing. If anything,

go to get out of your hometown. If you have strong inclinations to create a business or pursue a creative passion, I say screw college and double down on that. If you don't know what to do, go to college to meet people. It's a money sink. My college was paid for by my parents, but my school was cheap. By itself, it didn't do anything for me, and I don't know if it ever could."
—Edwin John Leskin, twenty-seven, social media strategist, serial entrepreneur, and college dropout

There are plenty of things I didn't learn in college that I desperately needed to. I didn't know how to handle rejection with resilience. I wasn't trained in how to de-escalate conflict, be assertive, and speak out for my needs in my relationships or recognize unhealthy dynamics. I wasn't taught about professionalism or how to negotiate a salary or manage my finances. I didn't understand the realities of the industry I studied and what it would take to get my foot in the door to actually start a career as a journalist. I didn't learn how to manage anxiety, avoid depression, or regulate my emotions. I didn't know how to market myself.

I did, however, binge drink to the point of vomiting. I rolled out of bed and went to class in my pajamas. I spent my parents' money on nachos, swallowed a bunch of Adderall, and crammed information into my brain before my exams. I can't remember one fact I learned at all, though I did pretty well.

A lot of people share my experience when it comes to college. They remember all the fun times they had behaving badly, but they don't remember the facts and figures they stored in their short-term memory and regurgitated the next day for a test.

Luckily, I did have a few professors who really made a difference in my life because they worked in the industry in which they taught and were passionate about it. They believed they had a responsibility to support the rising generation in finding their purpose, and they served as living examples of what's possible to accomplish in the real world. A teacher can be a mentor, a person who cares about our future and who will call out our talents but also hold a mirror up to our weaknesses. They can help us see the essential details of life that are easily overlooked and the mistakes learned the hard way that will limit our effectiveness in the world. A good teacher can give us a reason to believe in ourselves when we aren't able to see our value yet.

I entered the workforce shocked and debilitated by how little I knew about getting by in the professional world. It was remarkable that I could be high-performing academically in school and an emotionally stunted, delusional dunce at work. I'm not alone. A large portion of millennials who graduate from college have never worked a real job in their life beyond a summer internship. Navigating life after college requires understanding the practical concerns and codes of conduct of the professional world a lot more than what passing a trigonometry test can teach you.

I view college as a halfway house of sorts that buys the economy some time until you emerge into the world needing a job. (So much so that when there are no good jobs available, millennials go back to school.)

Doing well in academia requires jumping through a series of hoops that someone else designs. We complete courses, pass tests, and turn in assignments. In college, most people learn to live independently for the first time in their lives.

College will teach you a bit of critical thinking, but it won't prepare you to build a healthy life. It will help you socially by introducing you to friend networks. For those of us who come from sheltered backgrounds, college exposes you to the diversity of political, cultural, and religious stances that exist in this country. Sure, we'll read some Chaucer, we'll study calculus. Some of us will figure out what we want to do with our lives while at college. And it's a resume builder. But it is that experience worth up to $65,000 a year?

Edwin John Leskin says the connections he made at school are what ultimately led him to a fruitful career. He dropped out of college during his final semester when someone gave him seed funding to start his own company. A chain of events transpired that would have never happened had he not gone to school; however, it wasn't the diploma that he ultimately needed to pursue his goals. Edwin says that most of his friends aren't even working jobs in the fields in which they studied at college. So, what is its true value?

Some say that the value of college is based on your belief that it does, which it helps you sleep at night as you struggle to pay off your loans. The quality of your college experience also varies depending on what caliber of school you attend.

Society starts pitting us against each other from as young as middle school in a competition of who's going to get into the Ivy Leagues. Education is so often less about fostering a lifelong passion for learning and more about creating more capitalist-driven competition. Higher education produces people who are good at taking orders but who aren't the kind of innovative leaders who will challenge the mold.

Don't get me wrong. School is necessary for some of us, especially those who wish to work in technical fields. I don't want my airplane pilots flying without a license or my brain surgeons cutting me open without credentials. The question is: Does everyone need to have letters behind their name to succeed professionally in this country? Maybe we don't need a degree to make a difference.

THERE ARE OPTIONS

Most kids are going to want to go to college. Not because they believe a degree can earn them more money, but likely because it's what all their friends are doing. Nearly 90 percent of millennials who graduate from high school will go on to college within eight years of graduating. In a way, college is a rite of passage.

I would argue that the most important thing a millennial can acquire during their emerging adulthood is an education. You must learn a trade to start participating productively in society, and going to school is a way to do it. However, there are alternative options to go about it that might make the juice more worth the squeeze.

There are jobs you can perform with a high school education alone that can end up earning you up to thirty-five dollars an hour. What's important is how well you learn on the job. Take notes. Make your boss's life easier instead of harder. Do the heavy lifting that no one else wants to do. Remember your mistakes so you don't repeat them and cost your company money. I learned most of what I know today by fumbling around at my jobs and creating a long list of no-nos. It's said that behind every successful person is a lot of mistakes. Plus, you don't need to get shot to know that it will hurt; your bosses and coworkers have already laid down the groundwork. Learning from people who have made mistakes before you is a good strategy and something we rarely learn at traditional schools.

You can also start your own business and be incredibly successful without a college degree. It's not just Steve Jobs—Richard Branson of Virgin Group, Larry Ellison of Oracle Corporation, and David Geffen of DreamWorks are just a few other wildly successful CEOs who never completed their degree. You can be a self-made, self-taught person in the US without investing in higher education. You just have to convince others to invest in your idea. And you have to invest in yourself.

School is expensive. Some millennials believe they actually wasted time in college when they could have been building a professional foundation to start making money doing what they love. Instead of directing their resources to starting a business with the one-hundred-thousand dollars they spent on school, they graduate with so much debt that they have to work for someone else. Why leave school with debt when you can spend those years earning actual money and building a resume?

If you are going to go to school, one way to save money on tuition is to start at a community college where tuition is far less. Professors at community colleges are often high-performing industry leaders who decide to teach a class or two on the side to give back to the community. They are the kinds of teachers who do—and nothing is more valuable than that. After you've gone to community college for a few years and maintained a certain GPA, you can easily transfer to a college or university with a better reputation. It can even be one that you wouldn't have gotten into right after high school. Your diploma will bear the name of that school when you graduate, and you will save massive amounts of money. The average yearly price of community college is about $3,500.

If you already know what you want to do, you can go straight to vocational school to learn a very specific trade. You don't have to waste your time with prerequisites and other unnecessary courses that teach you theory but not an actual, marketable skill, and you'll leave school with a service you can offer society.

If you're not sure what you want to do and you value gathering knowledge for knowledge's sake, then a liberal arts education at college can help you become a well-rounded person. This is all well and good. However, college is much more effective if you know what you'd like to devote your life to so you can spend your time and money delving into that, especially if you have limited resources. There are professions that require a certain type of college degree to perform, such as nursing, and others where a college degree is necessary for you to go on to graduate school, if you plan on being a doctor.

Graduate school is another beast entirely. That's when it's really important to make sure that you're studying what you truly want to do. Many millennials go to law school, thinking it's a path to good income, before they realize that they will forever hate their lives if they become a lawyer.

Then there are for-profit colleges, which are easy to get into and especially notorious for being predatory, providing little return on what it costs to attend them. A degree from a for-profit school is often perceived to have the same value as a community college, though they are far more expensive, and many of the people who take out loans to attend them end up defaulting.

Right now, people in the US have more student loans than credit card debt. That's why if you don't know what you're getting into, college can be a traumatizing experience. But it's good to know that you have options and you can take your time figuring it out. It's one reason the gap year movement is so trendy now, where high school graduates are taking time off from school to travel, work, or engage in other activities before choosing what they want to study and where.

TALES FROM THE COLLEGE CRYPT

Kara Gilligan, thirty-three, calls her college experience a horror show. Today she's a divine feminine life coach and thought leader (which basically means she posts a lot of long, smart, and vulnerable messages on Facebook to her audience of followers).

Cheers to you, Kara. Her career path was directly inspired by her time studying English at Dartmouth College, but not because of the academics. Kara witnessed firsthand the dark side of the Ivy League while dating a brother at Bones Gate, a cultlike fraternity, where she was made privy to violent and secretive hazing practices.

Fraternities and sororities, or Greek life, are a big part of college culture. At some colleges, your social network is entirely reliant on them. Certain frats and sororities are associated with different class statuses. It's all another way to categorize and rank people, keeping certain circles together and others outside.

Kara refers to what she saw in Bones Gate as black magic, ritualistic initiations embedding heartless belief systems into the psyches of young men. The mob mentality and brainwashing incorporated into the culture of Greek life became frightening. Kara says Bones Gate had a rage cage where she would watch the brothers fight each other with weapons. They would pour chemical lye on their arms to see who was tougher. They were forced to do heavy amounts of drinking and drugs. If someone was reaching their limit and couldn't partake any longer, he was called "a pussy." The mascot of this elite frat was a ghost in the shape of a dick and balls; they called it the Thick Dick.

"The Thick Dick was everywhere—scenes of the Thick Dick in hell were painted all over the walls. I was walking around with dicks and balls all around me, watching these brothers sadistically torture each other, smoke bongs, worship Christian Bale in American Psycho, and talk about how they were going to fuck up the world once they got to Wall Street. Let me tell you, that shit changes your perspective on reality."

Kara left Dartmouth highly traumatized. But she found a way to alchemize her negative experience into the service she now gives back to society. Bones Gate revealed to her how Greek culture trains male leaders to associate violence with power and desensitize themselves from their bodies as they bond with each other through shameful and humiliating acts committed in secret. Kara also realized that these are the men who, after college, are funneled into high-power positions at corporations and financial firms. These practices and mindset are part of what's seeding the current dysfunctional culture of patriarchy, which is robbing entire communities of their rights around the world.

After college, Kara went on a painstaking and time-consuming journey to make sense of what she witnessed. Bones Gate ultimately made her realize that it's imperative that we bring empathy, compassion, self-care, and intuition into the business sector. That's why she started her business, Waking Beauty, where she coaches men and women on how to create what she calls "sacred wealth" by monetizing their mission and message in the world in a way that promotes humanity and personal balance.

HOW TO TEACH HAPPINESS

In this era of STEM (science, technology, engineering, and mathematics), the humanities are viewed as less and less valuable. Lessons on what it means to be human and how to cultivate qualitative aspects of life—the moral, emotional, and artistic components of human nature—are being neglected. That's what the humanities—history, religion, comparative literature, sociology, etc.—teach. However, if you get a degree in the humanities, you won't leave college with any kind of trade-specific skillset to support yourself financially. It's a situation that hundreds of thousands of millennials have found themselves in.

In the book *Excellent Sheep: The Miseducation of the American Elite and the Way to a Meaningful Life,* William Deresiewicz critiques the Ivy League from the perspective of an insider who's worked within the system for decades. Deresiewicz, an ex-Yale professor, says that he consistently saw a legion of highly disciplined, high-performing students in his classroom who couldn't think creatively or find answers to life's deep questions. He found his students philosophically devoid of insight. They may have been considered the upper echelon of talent preparing to enter the workforce, he says, but as far as he could see, they would not be the young people who were going to change the world.

Making our society more efficient, complex, and technologically advanced won't necessarily make life happier for people. It could be argued that perhaps none of the innovations, diversions, or the time that's been "bought" through the process of society's industrialized advancements (besides things like medicine) have truly improved the quality of life of humanity, because there hasn't been heart fueling it. You could argue that it's up to our educators and educational institutions to cultivate that in students.

In a dominator culture, some people will always have more resources than others, and some are considered higher performing in relation to the type of intelligence that culture deems profitable. All of this is now being measured quantitatively through test scores and bottom lines. "No child left behind" may be the motto of our school system, but children are left behind all of the time. If you don't finish school, you have no place in this society. No one will look at your resume if you don't have a high school education. And now, millennials are competing with a substantial amount of degree inflation.

Our education system reinforces all the values of a capitalist, industrialized model of society. It teaches us how to fit in; it teaches us what we need to know to pass the test in a factory-farm-like style of education. In this "conveyor belt of education," people can go from high school to college to graduate school to getting a salaried job at a corporation to being able to save a down payment and get a mortgage approved to buy a house and a Roth IRA and to save enough for retirement. The conveyor belt proves that the system works—if you fit the mold and this is the life you want. But the one thing it doesn't teach us is how to transform the system so it can work for everybody.

EMBRACING ALTERNATIVES

Social theorists of contemporary education refer to the subconscious or unconscious lessons that a student learns during their education as a *hidden curriculum*. In a hidden curriculum, public and private education serve the interests of a dominant group in society by educating people differently based on race, geographic location, and class. Because of social service programs like Teach for America, scholarship programs, affirmative action, Head Start, Pell Grants, and more, these hidden curriculums are becoming exposed, and people are attempting to dismantle them to extend educational access to marginalized populations.

The inequities of our education system are not necessarily conspiratorial. It's just that it's designed to benefit those who created it, like everything else in our society. Millions of people are working in earnest each day as teachers and faculty members to make one of the most important institutions in our society function. Being a teacher can be a thankless and tiresome job, and we should be grateful for everyone who enters the field to serve the community. But it is also a job that is highly bureaucratic and regulated because it is overseen by the state and our government. It takes a lot to be a teacher and not have the inspiration of innovation be beaten out of you by these entities.

The Department of Education plays a huge role in the creation of curriculums—and so do principals, teachers, and the school board. In private schools, the school administration has the majority of the influence. Basically, a bunch of adults from previous generations are deciding what belongs in the contents of our mind—people who have already been indoctrinated into the mainstream way of life and whom the system currently serves more. Those who control the media—and education is a form of media—control our psychology. Unlearning what we've learned in schools is part of the process of awakening to the deeper truths about this society.

81

So, what's the alternative? Should students be in charge of our lesson plans and determine the information we are forced to ingest? Or is that request just more entitlement on our part?

There have been movements away from a standardized style of education. You can get homeschooled. You can send your kids to a Waldorf School, where they can spend their days in nature holistically cultivating their mind, body, and spirit. You can go to colleges like Oberlin that are so liberal I hear you get bonus points for walking out of class in protest. Top tier schools even offer free courses online on platforms like Coursera.org. Yes, you can go to college online now—for free. With the Internet, no matter where you are, you can learn if you have a thirst for knowledge and a computer. You can go to the library to read. Some of the most free-thinking, well-read people are self-taught, creating their own curriculums in the university of life.

College culture varies radically according to each institution. These days, there is more and more room to create your own major and make every class you take something that is important and interesting to you. Students are also given many opportunities at school to have a say in the environment where we work, eat, learn, and live. Education—it's all about how you go about it.

A CHANCE TO BE YOU

Johanna Williams, twenty-four, has a bachelor's degree in cinema and media studies from Carleton College. Now she works as the community relations coordinator at Challenge Aspen, a nonprofit for disabled athletes. Johanna is a paraplegic herself who is bound to a wheelchair. She was one of three people with a physical disability at her liberal arts school, and none of the campus housing or classrooms at Carlton were wheelchair accessible. So, she had to petition for her college to accommodate her special needs.

Johanna says her biggest fear is not accomplishing anything with her life. She may be disabled, but she's certainly done more than a lot of the people I interviewed in her short life. It's all about having an internal locus of control. If you're an optimist and a go-getter, you'll be an optimist and a go-getter even in a wheelchair.

"Just because I don't do things as perfectly physically doesn't mean that what I do is less important. My best is enough, and it's better than not going for something at all," she says.

For her senior thesis, Johanna created a documentary about disability and sexuality. The film covered everything from a quadriplegic who felt orgasms in his thumb to what it's like to grind on the dance floor with someone in a wheelchair. College provided her with the right environment to do some me-search, a nurturing setting where she could explore the world and her capabilities while her material needs were met.

Anslee Connell, twenty-eight, is a jack-ess of all trades, a very millennial occupation indeed. She's a Zumba teacher and a talented seamstress who makes stylish, form-flattering dresses for plus-size women; she also works odd jobs and sings in a band.

"I hated high school," Anslee says. The classes were easy for her, but she says she was an outcast. "I felt very, um, out of place and misunderstood. I had a whole lot of body image issues. I was also a creative in the middle of a school filled with noncreatives and people who had no ambition to realize their potential. I felt very alone. I had this constant feeling of wanting something better and wondering how to achieve that. I felt so different and apart from everyone else. It was really hard to go to the same environment every day, never being fully known or seen."

Anslee was diagnosed with polycystic ovarian syndrome and insulin resistance when she was thirteen years old. The conditions come with a host of side effects, such as excessive weight gain, mood imbalance, and unwanted facial hair. She says she felt like a freak, not because of her personality but because of her body.

Things became better for Anslee once she was able to leave her hometown of Statesboro, Georgia, to attend Berry College to study photography and visual communication. Anslee says one of her top needs in life is acceptance. College became a place where she finally found herself accepted and liked. She made good connections within a few months.

"I found that sense of belonging."

Anslee and Johanna's stories bring up the topic of ableism, which could be an entire chapter itself. Not everyone is going to be able to perform at the same capacity, but it doesn't mean they don't have gifts to contribute. College, ideally, should help foster this kind of empowerment. For some people, it does.

But is higher education for all people all of the time? Is it always worth the price tag? Not always. Don't get duped into thinking that a college degree can solve all your problems or guarantee you your dream job. Design your own path to education, to learning a trade, or to creating something that will contribute to others. We are living in a time when it's safe to deconstruct linear pathways if it will bring your best self forward to take real action in the world.

Chapter 6

Entering a World of Working

I'VE BEEN "LET GO" AT A FEW JOBS AND WALKED AWAY FROM even more—because of my millennial hang-ups. I'm sensitive. I mouth off at times. The minute you think I'm disposable, I think *you're* disposable. Older generations have no idea what to do with us in the workplace. They say we're disloyal, we collapse under the slightest pressure, we're disrespectful, and we don't know how to pay our dues.

This is all true. But here's the thing about our peer group. Most of us crave meaningful work far more than money. We want to know that our professional work is making a positive impact on the world. We want to feel safe, free, and inspired at our jobs. Some of us will quit every single position we have until we find an employer who is willing to invest in us in a meaningful way. The days of working at one corporation for decades to rack up a retirement fund and benefits are just about over, and companies are losing millions of dollars each year training millennials who leave their positions—usually within a year of being hired.

Millennials are always looking for the next best thing. We fear missing out. If a company wants a millennial's loyalty, it has to strive to operate holistically. It should position itself as one of the better companies a person can work for. It needs to value ethics, environmental sustainability, employee accountability, personal growth opportunities, and a fun company culture. Millennials are multipassionate, multidimensional people— we will likely experience multiple professional identities in one lifetime.

WE ARE HERE TO MANIFEST IN OUR WORK

Humans have an incredible capacity to create, and we are always creating—whether consciously or not. I've noticed in my interviews that my peers who fail to live productive lives usually entertain some belief in their own victimhood—they blame the system or an outside force, be it a person or a supernatural being, for keeping them from living lives of prosperity and purpose. To remain in a victimized mindset keeps us powerless.

All this talk about how the system is broken is logical, but if we continue to make this our excuse for underperforming, we'll never be able to make a better world. It's easy to project all our psychological struggles and hang-ups onto the power structures that organize us, but unfortunately, change cannot happen through this mentality. It keeps the status quo in place and gives our present leaders continued power to decide the social architecture. What we believe, we eventually become. So, let's believe in our empowerment.

If we are to organize a social revolution, it has to emerge out of the current framework (unless mother nature demolishes it in a maelstrom of fire and brimstone so we can start over completely). And a primary way we can achieve it is through the working world. Even if nothing changes in our toxic society, we can still consciously create healthy lives by filling them with positive people, places, and things. At the end of the day, the only thing stopping you from creating the life you want is an excuse.

Millennials may not have much confidence once we enter the working world, but we are full of potential and energy—the vital energy of youth. We're a slab of marble ready to get chiseled into masterpiece statue.

But it will take discipline to prevent your negative, self-defeating thoughts from controlling your actions or yielding power over what you'll eventually become. Believe that you are an epic creator and claim your role as the captain of your destiny instead.

Turning our visions into reality is a creative process. If you have a thought you can't shake, it may be a sign that you're supposed to follow it. If millennials aren't provided the opportunity to follow our inspiration or life calling at a company we work at, many of us will quit our jobs to create businesses of our own.

I've personally found that while it's empowering to get excited about changing the world, it helps not to get too wrapped up in fixing, rescuing, or saving the entire fate of the human race. It's not that we collectively can't; but rather, it's dangerous to place the entire weight of the world on a single person's shoulders—the pressure just might kill you.

Remember: the ends never justify the means. It's easy to start out with high-minded intentions, only to end up using the same Machiavellian traits of the people who are destroying the world to accomplish your goals. Instead, recognize that we're all here to do our own special part. You cannot make saving humanity about your ego.

Repeat after me three times: *martyrdom is not a valid career choice!*

The future is not in *your* hands; it's in *ours*. Many hands make light work. And the world of professional work is one of the areas in which we can tangibly contribute back to society together—sometimes in big ways.

We will likely face difficult moments on this path, no matter what we choose to do. I just try to remind myself that the work I have chosen—even if it's for a grander purpose—is not supposed to be endlessly painful. If my life purpose hurts that much, then I'm playing the main role of the wrong show. It's time to reroute.

PICKING A POSITION

We've talked at length about how the financial futures of millennials are impacted by structural disadvantages that range from inflation and debt to the transition from salaried to contracted labor. According to the National Center for Education Statistics, it took boomers 300 hours of minimum-wage work to pay off a year of public tuition; it took millennials 4,459 hours. One in five millennials are still living in poverty, says the US Census, and the majority of the rest of us are one accident away from bankruptcy at any time. And still, millennials don't seem to stick around at our jobs.

Most people believe you either work to live or live to work, but we are challenging this notion—beyond wanting opportunities to grow at our jobs and actualize some grand vision for ourselves, we also crave work-life balance. We want to succeed at work, but we're also not willing to sacrifice our well-being for it. Our surroundings play a huge role in our health and happiness, and a toxic work environment filled with bullies and sycophants can strip us of our life force. For many of us, all it takes is one bad apple to spoil the show in a workplace, and we're out.

It's natural to want to pursue a calling—a vocation that suits one's strengths. If you're able to wake up feeling excited for your day and who you'll spend it with, you're winning. However, in this society, choosing a career is a loaded decision, because not all career paths are created equal. Choosing a career also means choosing your social status. It determines if the opportunistic people of the world will suck up to you or step on you.

The truth is that not everyone will get to be a famous celebrity, athlete, CEO, or hedge fund manager. We can't all become life coaches who sit poolside, taking pictures of ourselves in swimsuits and telling everyone on Facebook how they, too, can live the life of their dreams if they buy this e-course for $1,599. This society needs dentists and nurses and teachers and mechanics and accountants and city planners and politicians and sanitation workers. All of these industries are part of the revolution of the system. It's going to take all of us working within them to crusade new standards of compensation, workplace conditions, product resourcing, corporate responsibility, and more.

I like to believe that if the majority of people are on board with the global goals of eliminating poverty, making medical care accessible to all, creating gender and racial equality, and building sustainable infrastructures and peaceful and just institutions, we'd happily do all the work that needs to get done to accomplish these goals—whether that involves mopping the floor or balancing a checkbook. Millennials need to realize that they are not going to like every aspect of their job all of the time—and that's not an excuse to jump ship. There are pros and cons to every industry, and it always helps to see the bigger picture. If there's a social purpose behind a company or organization that we can rally around, millennials are more likely to make the many necessary sacrifices that come with creating a livelihood while staying loyal and committed to an employer.

There will be tedious moments. You will likely have to do tasks you despise. You will have to answer and be obedient to people who will disrespect you. But this is all done to achieve common goals.

HOW TO MAKE US STAY

As I have mentioned, millennials are professional reincarnators and shape-shifters. Our multiple passions help us to thrive when we're able to wear many different hats inside an organization that utilizes our various strengths and skill sets. We may have a hard time deciding what we want to do, though the one thing we know for certain is that we're probably not going to stick to the same job for our entire lives. But to get started, we need to eat a slice of humble pie.

When we start out at the entry level, we have little experience, big dreams, a lot of enthusiasm, and not too much knowledge about how to be professional in the world. We may not always like where we start out, but opportunities for advancement can make us stick around. For millennials, this advancement doesn't always mean pay raises. According to Gallup, pay raises are attractive only up to a salary of $75,000 a year.

A workplace will keep our attention if it can help us improve our mental health; allow us to be healthy in mind, body, and spirit; show us how to manage our finances; give us the time and tools to have fulfilling relationships inside and outside of the office; and mentor us toward making an impact in the world. But first, to achieve all of this, the paradigm of the majority of our working industries has to do a one-eighty-degree turn. Companies have to start gearing their efforts toward pleasing employees first, rather than making short-term profits.

The field of conscious capitalism is finding out that when companies take care of the needs of their people, the money can follow. Even the largest, most notoriously corrupt companies are starting to clean up their acts—because the people are demanding it. Conscious capitalist companies exist now, and they are starting to face the impact they have on the larger community. They are choosing to uplift the world rather than endlessly extract from it. Today, people are starting to explore a different way to do business, and it's coming from "the millennial mindset." Companies that are looking to bolster their workforce with new, fresh-faced members of the incoming generation and are adapting their company cultures to what we value. (Some of us want sleeping pods and free yoga classes at work—and are lucky enough to get it.)

Millennials are the least engaged generation at work in history, which has a number of consequences. It keeps us underproductive. We get into more accidents. Some of us hate our jobs so much we'll purposefully sabotage the business. Companies are making less money—thousands of dollars per employee per year—due to the negligence of millennial workers. And all of this could be changed if we have a reason to believe that our work has an impact on the world and that our input can help shape a company. If a company wishes to stop millennials from leaving their jobs, they have to give us a seat at the round table and let us innovate companies from within. They can give us opportunities to engage in what's known as *intrapreneurship*.

And believe it or not, we want feedback. This world runs on people doing the things we say we're going to do, and millennials want accountability. It inspires us to act with integrity. It helps us realize just how much everything we do matters and that we don't exist in a vacuum. We have to be taught to mature beyond our own depressive self-absorption.

However, until every corporation on the planet cares about their people as much their profits, the fact of the matter is we're going to have to work some shitty jobs to survive. There is no safety net for many of us, and some millennials *are* in fact content to work as cashiers and bus drivers. Because there is something honorable about being able to support yourself, no matter what you do.

MAKING ENDS MEET

The average college student graduates with $25,000 worth of student debt. The average monthly payment for a ten-year student loan at 6.8 percent interest ends up being $280 dollars a month. Add to this the average monthly rental payment of $992. Tack onto this amount car insurance, health insurance, groceries, and utilities, and you have a generation that's working poor. Millennials will have to work about ten times as long as previous generations to afford home ownership, and some of us may never get to retire.

Our incomes also vary according to our identities. According to a study by the Institute for Women's Policy Research, in 2013, millennial women earned a median of $30,000 a year. Millennial men made $35,000. The wage gap between the genders is unfortunately still present. Between African Americans and white Americans, it's even worse. The Economic Policy Institute found that black women have to work seven months into 2017 in order to reach the same salary as white men made in 2016. By 2020, the average white household is predicted to have 86 times more wealth than black households. The numbers are staggering.

What we need right now are government-subsidized job programs that encourage companies to hire new employees and shrink the wage gap between men and women and minorities. We need our start-ups funded. We need affordable housing options. We need to raise the minimum wage. It's going to take larger, financially stable companies to crusade for these reforms on our behalf—if the baby boomers are willing to join our fight so we can campaign for the good of the whole. The millennial struggle is the fight to make ends meet without sacrificing our impact on the world.

In the meantime, I see it over and over again: young people who are somehow able to skimp by on side hustles, sometimes earning us next to nothing, just so we can pursue our dreams.

We can do this because we're still young—some of us busk for change, some take on work trades, others look for freelance gigs. Somehow, we swing it. We've got the Internet, which means everyone can create an income, whether it's selling soy candles on Etsy or bidding on copywriting gigs or driving people around for Uber. We can teach ourselves how to build websites by watching YouTube videos; we can distribute handmade products around the world. These side hustles are not the same as having a fat salary and benefits, but we've learned that having multiple income streams is the only way to protect us from falling into zero income if we're thrown under the bus by a downsizing company. Side hustles also help us bootstrap our startups and allow us to grow and shift as new opportunities and ideas enter our spheres. If our lives are not owned by anyone, we can avoid corporate slavery.

There are multiple ways to hack the economy, and one of them is paying special attention to location.

Take Destiny Howard, twenty-three, for instance, who lives in Norman, Oklahoma. She makes about $11,000 per year babysitting and was able to save up enough money in a few years to buy a new car while she lived at her mother's house. She now supports herself on the same $11,000, which is below the federal poverty line. Her rent is about three hundred dollars a month (ideally, rent should only make up a third of your income). She can live off her pay quite comfortably, but that's because she lives in Norman.

Now, let's look at Samantha McCurdy, twenty-six, who graduated from Maryland Institute College of the Arts with a degree in painting. She was one of the few millennials I met who knew as soon as she left school what she wanted to do—be an artist, even though it is considered an impractical path. Nothing and no one was going to stop her. She was smart enough to pick her location wisely, moving to Dallas, Texas, with its up-and-coming fine art scene and a cost of living more than 30 percent less than a place like New York City.

"There are people here with money who are uninspired," says Samantha. "These people are looking at me to be cage-less. They are begging to throw money at me for my work. There's a serious art market here."

Samantha currently has a side hustle as a fashion stylist for an affluent boutique, where she can earn a consistent income. There are months when she'll sell ten paintings and months when she'll sell none. Half of her income goes to rent. She also has student loans that she's paying off. She chose to live in a giant industrial artist loft space with two bedrooms and a roommate, splitting the rental cost of $2,500 per month. She hosts gatherings and art exhibits at her home cum studio, which she named THAT THAT.

"My greatest dream is to make art and sustain myself monetarily. Art to me is not a choice. It's something I have to do. I have to create and build and think and invent. I describe it as 'art guilt.' I start to get real moody and bitchy and lash out because I haven't been in the studio.

"I have to fulfill this desire to create constantly. When I think of myself as an old woman, I think of myself as a gray silver fox, with white hair, hand tattoos, and a lot of rings, teaching a ceramic class somewhere. I just want to make art. Whether it's through art alone or through a side hustle, to make art is the dream."

WORKING TO LIVE

Haydon Camp (a.k.a. Haydon Hoodoo), twenty-five, received a psychology degree from the University of New Orleans. He calls it a bullshit degree, one that's almost impossible to monetize without further education. Right after graduation, he moved to Austin, Texas, to find a job.

"I looked for psychology jobs and tried to work with children," Haydon says. "I started going through the training to work with kids with behavioral problems, and I got stuck with the worst one. I had to change his diaper. I had no idea what I was doing."

Sometimes, the kid would hit Haydon.

"I couldn't help him. He needed his mom. I didn't want to affect him negatively. It's funny now, but at the time it was awful. I started having panic attacks and quit."

Haydon applied for a job at the University of Texas but was underqualified. He gave up on psychology positions and started canvassing for the Democratic party, reminding people of two upcoming propositions and to vote in the next election, but it didn't make him any money. So when he found a Craigslist ad for an online marketing position with local businesses, he took it. He cold calls people for $150 a week, on top of the $1,600 a month he already makes with his music gigs. It's enough to get by.

Haydon knows it's a shitty job. He's passionate about many things, and online marketing is not one of them. Haydon is an emotional soul who loves playing music—he is generous with his affections and attention, writes love songs, and is kind to animals. All of this makes Haydon beautiful. He knows he's not his job, but he's grateful to have one, and he's grateful to be able to have enough money for lunch.

The odd jobs we take on can get pretty hilarious. I've worked over seventeen jobs, or rather "gigs," to supplement my income writing over the years. The list includes a frozen organic food distributor, newspaper delivery girl, line cook, martial arts instructor, barista, and more. What a long strange trip it's been for me in the working world thus far.

I've realized in my own personal journey of being self-employed and working for others that what I learned in school didn't do diddly squat to prevent me from making a total ass out of myself once I was in the workplace. I've learned that the codes of professional conduct are far more important than subject theory. I've learned that if you know how to be professional, you can excel.

Here are some examples of what not to do:

- Don't write emails to your boss that go on and on about your feelings.
- Don't ask to change your schedule repeatedly.
- Don't go home early while other people are still working.
- Don't displace all of your repressed resentments toward authority onto your supervisor.
- Don't make excuses about why you didn't get the job done.
- Don't make out with your coworkers.
- Don't talk about how hungover you are.
- Don't take constructive criticism personally.
- Don't show up late.
- Don't text on your phone during a meeting.
- Don't talk about politics and religion or stir up philosophical debates while on the clock.

It's actually pretty simple. When you're between a rock and a hard place, just do what you need to do to get the job done. Don't make work about your personality or your personal issues. Millennials may want to be our authentic selves at work and to be nurtured in the workplace, and it might be suitable in certain work environments, but that's not the state of the working world at large. The work environment we are entering into is largely conservative and competitive. When I was working in kitchens, I remember asking everyone if they wanted to do group yoga, and they laughed in my face. When I broke down crying during a work evaluation, it got even worse. Somehow, we've got to strike a balance between growing thicker skin and refusing to accept abuse as a management tactic.

MILLENNIAL WHISPERING

Gabrielle Jackson Bosché, twenty-nine, is the founder of The Millennial Solution, a consulting agency that helps corporations understand and retain their top millennial talent. Gabrielle says she's in the mediation and reconciliation business—she's doing her best to help four different generations work together, The baby boomers, gen X, millennials, and gen Z.

She focuses on the divide between the baby boomers and millennials the most because they are the two largest generations. Millennials job-hop so much that some companies are afraid they won't have enough people to step up and take on their positions once the old guard retires. Just look at the statistics: 65 percent of millennials are currently looking for a new job while they're working at the job they're at, 67 percent of millennials plan on starting their own company one day, and 50 percent of millennials are freelancing. Gabrielle's company is filling such a necessary role that it's taking off rapidly. She had forty-eight bookings in 2016. The story of how she started The Millennial Solution is a common one: she says that the millennials who turn out to be entrepreneurs tend to do so accidentally—especially during the recession years. Why wait for opportunity to be handed to you when you can create it for yourself? All you have to do is type a few key phrases into a search engine to learn how to form an LLC—and boom! You're a business owner.

"When you see someone doing something that you know you can do better, and it makes you mad, that's your calling," Gabrielle says. "People were providing a lot of context and answers to explain millennials. I'd been researching and writing about them for a decade. My first book about millennials was called *Not Another Teen Rally*. It's not in print anymore, thank God. I studied politics and theology during undergrad, and my senior thesis was about millennials and politics. I've always been passionate about explaining who we are. I never thought I would start a company until someone suggested that I should."

She's learned that a lot of magic can happen when companies orientate their cultures to meet the lifestyle demands of millennials. But millennials also have to realize that the people who sign our paychecks gave their lives to get the positions where they currently stand, and they're reluctant to go against what seemingly "worked" for them in the past.

The good news is that eventually—and not too long, actually—the power is going to transition and change hands. And millennials will have more agency to do away with all that's outdated—systems, unnecessary rules, modes of operation. By 2020, we'll make up 50 percent of the workforce. We've inherited an economic infrastructure with endless dysfunctions, but we can use the power of our number to create a world where we can have the lives we want.

LIVING IN A CIRCLE OF SOVEREIGNTY

We live in a pyramid, where the small amount of people at the top have material excess while the majority live in scarcity. The people at the bottom are stuck in a perpetual place of poverty, building an empire that someone else rules.

In a healthy, balanced capitalist democracy, social division should look more like a New York City pastrami sandwich. The upper and lower classes are the thin slices of rye bread, while the middle class makes up the majority of the sandwich. Think of a nine-inch stack of meat. Capitalism in its ideal essence is supposed to operate as a meritocracy where people are rewarded for being smart and working hard, where they own their own labor.

This is what draws millennials to entrepreneurship, where we can take power over the future of our livelihood. It's a risky, even terrifying, decision to venture out on your own, but once you cross a certain threshold, most people don't regret it.

AJ Leon, thirty-one, says he started his own business Misfit, Inc., with his wife Melissa because at his core he sees himself as someone who doesn't fit in. AJ left a successful banking career to pursue his dream—the idea of living an inauthentic life was scarier to him than not being able to pay rent. Melissa supported his decision because, in her words, she preferred to live with the real AJ than an impersonation of him. Today, their company employs a handful of other creative, sensible people.

Misfit, Inc., is a publishing house as well as a foundation that initiates mission work abroad. It also creates digital art and cultural projects. Today, AJ gets to travel around the world doing what he loves. But when he first started Misfit, Inc., he used to trade website design for bagels.

"The dictionary defines a misfit as a bonafide individual, a person who constantly stands in defiance of the colleagues and friends who want us to live the lives they'd prefer us to," AJ says.

Alas, a prophet is never recognized in their hometown. When AJ struck out on his own, he faced a number of challenges. The first of which was that no one in his previous circles was able to understand his decision.

"For people who need the validation of family and friends, know that when you go out on your own, affirmation is probably not going to be there."

AJ issues this warning to his fellow millennials who want to follow their visions to be entrepreneurs. "When you start to make choices that are wildly different than those around you, you're not going to get support. People struggle to understand what it means to carve your own path, to create your own adventures, to be more project oriented. Don't listen to anyone."

He says there's never been a moment, even at times when he was left with no plan B, that he looked back—even when he and Melissa slept in train stations and cars. AJ gets to run a business that's completely aligned with his values. He gets to make a difference. He'd rather have that than security and compliance.

LIVING FOR WORK

Necessity breeds invention, and some of us, more so than others, feel the urgency of these times. We are the game changers, and we are working to change the system from the inside-out. There are so many people trying, and giving, all of their energy to the very last drop to be a part of the organized resistance through creating products and services and pushing for policies that can really solve the problems we face as a civilization.

I invite you to question as you go about your professional pursuits: What does the world really need? If we want sustainable and regenerative human systems, we've got to dream bigger. We need to use the power of business to influence politics and culture and make the absurd conventions that confine us obsolete.

Miki Agrawal, serial social entrepreneur; founder of Wild, Thinx, Tushy, and Icon; and the author of *Do Cool Shit*, is an example of one such disrupter. She is a millennial cusper who has achieved so much commercial success before even turning thirty that she makes me wish I hadn't spent all that time living in a car and eating lentils to escape the evil of society when I could have been hustling to change it.

Miki started her social entrepreneurial career with her gluten-free pizza company, Wild. Tushy, her other venture, is an affordable bidet attachment that eliminates the use of toilet paper, and Icon is a panty liner for women who suffer from incontinence. Her claim to fame is Thinx, period-proof panties that eliminate the need for tampons or pads. Thinx operates with a give-back model—just one example of an initiative that falls under the umbrella of corporate advocacy. For every pair of panties bought, a sanitary napkin is given to a girl in Africa, where, in some places, periods keep women from going to school every month. Thinx is a product that also has a message, one that sheds light on the absurdity of a social taboo—the cultural shame imposed on women for having bodies that bleed for the procreation of humanity. Thinx's marketing was considered so scandalous for promoting a natural bodily process that the company's billboards were almost banned from the New York City subway.

Miki knows that producing one product can have a myriad of effects on the larger social ecosystem, and she designs her initiatives accordingly. She knows that she has a platform to inspire others to create companies with brands that solve problems and promote generosity. Social entrepreneurship is good for business.

"People will care more about your product if there's a give-back mission attached," Miki says. "There is more potential to create revenue than if you're making a product to just make a product. The numbers prove that social enterprise is more valuable than just enterprise. In a nosey and challenging market, social enterprises differentiate themselves."

THE SOCIOPATHIC CORPORATION

We live in an egocentric society that models the arrogance of the separate, self-image of man. From Koch Industries to Trump Towers, business in this society has previously been about making an empire for your ego. No matter what sector you find yourself in—academia, nonprofit, or corporate—it seems that self-importance and competition among individuals can dominate all interactions unless we work to create workplace cultures that embody something else. It's publish or *perish*. Be the *best* do-gooder. Make the *most* quarterly profit. It's all about output, output, output. But this breeds the same culture of useless busyness for the sake business and interpersonal hostility that divides instead of connects us. We lose sight of what's important when we believe our assess are constantly on the line.

A lot of our problems can be solved if we redefine what it means to provide humanity with basic public services that are mandatory for our survival. Today, in the United States, institutions like prisons and hospitals are registered as for-profit private enterprises. This means corporations are making money off crime and disease—issues that an ideal society would want to minimize. Why aren't these nonprofit entities instead?

Corporations have become sociopathic entities on the planet, unaccountable for the havoc they wreak on the environment and the people they employ across the globe—but there's a reason for it. Traditional corporations are legally bound to produce the most profit possible to redistribute to shareholders. When a corporation seeks to grow at all costs, it is doing what corporations are designed to do. But if we don't disrupt this business as usual, these entities will control the fate of the human race—by producing disposable, poorly made crap that eventually ends up in a landfill; through buying out our representatives, creating massive wealth inequality; through outsourcing jobs to the third world where there are fewer labor laws; through refusing to switch to renewable energy. Think how weird it will look when the Earth is studded with deserted strip malls, and the next intelligent species to evolve enters the ruins and thinks to themselves—is this what humans used to do in their free time? They worked jobs they hated for companies that destroyed their civilization just to able to shop at Old Navy?

But how do you battle with a sociopath? When you fight with a crazy person, you become crazy by proxy. Until there are alternatives to traditional corporations, people will accept this as the norm, and the corporate state will continue to suck everything into its profiteering exploits. My friend Lloyd once told me that the only person who can take down a sociopath is a truly brilliant individual who can prove what else is possible—and people have to choose to follow the brilliant person instead of the disturbed one.

Luckily, not every business has to be a traditional corporation. A truly brilliant alternative to the traditional corporate model are social enterprises. Millennials are doing good when we choose to invest in, work for, and purchase products from these types of companies because we're taking away power from the corporate entities that abuse it. There are a number of different organization styles that people can file to create what is known as a conscious company—a collective of people who act intentionally to uplift everyone involved in the means of production, from the neighborhoods where stores are located to the people on the supply chain to the employees to the customers. Impact is measured as well as profit, and there is an emphasis on benefiting stakeholders instead of shareholders.

In the area of conscious enterprise, burgeoning types of organizational structures include B corps, social purpose corporations, low-profit limited liability company, cooperatives, hybrid organizations, and deliberately developmental organizations. These alternative structures are able to take into account the effect they have on everything they touch as they generate revenue. It's less about shareholders—the people who buy stocks in a company—and more about stakeholders—everyone who is impacted by the creation of an organization. Corporations and brands that are built from this vibration of self-awareness and intention are pioneering corporate responsibility and innovation. They are experimenting with what can happen when we make goods and services out of love for people and the earth.

Classifying organizations in an appropriate manner is a key way to restore balance in the system. Every type of business model has its pros and its cons. Nonprofits are hard to financially sustain, social enterprises are still figuring out how to measure impact, and for-profits can only make decisions to maximize capital. That's why hybrid organizations that include aspects of both nonprofits and for-profits are gaining popularity. A mission is becoming just as important as the money.

It's time to question if strictly for-profit models are even ethical, if it's right to profit when so many other stakeholders are suffering as a result of the negative externalities of a business. Imagine living in a world where all businesses merge social programs with their enterprise activities, where the quality of life of every person is considered in the cause and effect of a company's actions. It is possible, but it's going to take pioneers.

For all life to thrive on this planet, millennials have to evolve what's already been done by our predecessors. And it's up to our predecessors to use the power they've accumulated to allow this social transformation to take place. Everyone, regardless of their generation, will be birthing this do-no-harm paradigm shift in business.

"It's our duty to make improvements in this world," says Miki. To make these improvements, it takes boldness.

"Your gut is everything. If your gut is saying it's right and the practical world says it's not, you can't ignore it. Go with your gut."

A lot of millennials question what they can accomplish and the purpose of one life. I think part of our existential anxiety stems from impatience, because what needs to happen won't happen overnight. Many millennials expect to be rock stars as soon as we enter the working world, and that's why Miki's number-one career advice for our generation is as follows:

"Don't expect to be CEO at age twenty-three. It's annoying. Be humble and rise up the ranks the way you should. Prove to me that you deserve that position."

The change we seek and need is happening. And soon it will reach a critical mass as we, one by one, choose to dedicate our lives to conscious innovation.

Chapter 7

The Ritalin Kids (Try to) Grow Up

QUESTION: Am I mad, or is the world mad?
ANSWER #1: You are mad—and so is the world.
ANSWER #2: You are also beautiful, healthy, vibrant, and plentiful—and so is our planet.

Where will you focus your thoughts?

IN HIS BOOK *PSYCHOPATH FREE*, JACKSON MACKENZIE CALLS PSY-chopathy the most important issue of our times. The world is full of predators, prey, and power plays, and mental health is at the heart of many issues in society today.

According to the National Institute of Mental Health, about 9.1 percent of the US population has a personality disorder. According to the same study, only 39 percent of people diagnosed with a personality disorder are in treatment. Add to this the prevalence of attachment disorders—that an estimated 50 percent of people didn't learn how to securely emotionally bond with their parents during their childhood—and you've got a population of people who are going to create a lot of drama in our attempts to relate to one another. A lot of the time, it is unintentional.

Everyone is impacted by the mental and emotional flaws of humanity. We're still, after thousands of years, trying to figure out what to do about the phenomenon of human pain—how to stop it from spreading and how to make it go away. People have been so hurt in their past that a defensive mechanism kicks in to prevent them from feeling more pain, and in the process of protecting themselves, they hurt others. Pan outward, and we start to see that our current culture of colonialism, industrialization, and white male supremacy is propagated by this type of psychopathology.

I'd say that the biggest problem millennials face is that we're suffering from mental illness in droves. Unfortunately, we need to be exceptionally healthy if we're going to embark on a mission to unite humanity. We have to commit to facing reality at all costs.

Millennials are known as the "Ritalin Kids." We are the first generation to grow up in the pharmaceutical boom. Some of us have been on meds since childhood, and we have become completely dependent on them. Amid this crisis, we've been called "adult children" and are still struggling to grow up.

The signature sensitivity of the millennial generation is both our gift and curse. It allows us to empathize with others and tune ourselves to our environment, but the flip side of this is that we're fragile and afraid of going out into the big, scary world and making a difference. Our active imaginations may grant us the ability to dream of a different society, yet we still have to navigate in this one.

This requires a degree of mental health and emotional stability. Many millennials find it difficult to tolerate uncomfortable feelings. We make the problems of others our own, rather than tending to our own business, until the burden of daily life is too much to bear. Most of us don't know how to communicate our feelings; and the most unfortunate aspect of this is even if we did, there is a deficit of people who seem to care.

This world is full of darkness and light; death and life. What will you grow in the garden of your mind—weeds or flowers? We all have personal wounds and collective complexes, but with fastidious pruning, our individual psyches can be a source of sanity within the insanity of the outer world. I'm living proof.

You are a system of neural networks—and so is society. No millennial is an island. We have to interact with the world of things to survive, and we have to interact with people, each of whom has their own separate neural networks and habitual ways of interpreting the very same world. Every mind is unique, and it's up to you to become the captain of your own. Changing society starts with altering your mind patterns first; it starts with shifting how you interpret yourself in the world.

As conscious beings, we are forced to live with the awareness that, one day, we will die, including everything we love. Somehow, we've got to come to terms with the feelings that accompany this knowledge—the hopelessness, the futility, the fear, and the grief—with the belief that we can heal while we're still alive. The point of human existence is to overcome suffering.

The paradox is that to do this, you can't ignore the hurt. Suffering must be allowed to rise and be felt until there is a shift. You can't make the sun stop from setting with positive thinking alone, but you can train your mind to focus on growth. We grow and we let go—and that is how we find our freedom from the conditions we were born into and the painful situations we've been through.

Human sensitivity, our capacity to be empathetic and aware of the impact we have on others, can become our greatest asset. Sensitivity and intuition will help us to steer clear from danger. Our sensitivity lets us know how to take care of ourselves and what boundaries to maintain with others.

When we're open and sensitive, we can start to engage in the energetic process of remembering our true nature, pretrauma. The poison becomes the cure, when we learn from the past and how to forgive. New experiences and beliefs will emerge when we stop projecting all of our self-worth issues and baggage onto others. We can be born again.

We are victims no longer. No one needs rescuing—because no can do this emotional work for someone else. There's no need for revenge or for anyone else to suffer just because we have. We can make peace with the lessons that have taught us how to heal.

THE ANSWER IS ALWAYS *BOTH*

We are growing up at a time when there are more mental health resources available than ever, more pills to treat the symptoms of being human, and more research conducted about the nature of human suffering and how we can overcome it. Psychology is often considered a soft science because little of its practice can be tangibly measured in the same way a chemist observes the effects of mixing an acid with a base. Psychology deals with people and their behaviors and their neuroses, which can be subjective and open to interpretation. You can be diagnosed with a different mental illness with every doctor you see—and none of these labels will restore a person to sanity.

Some time ago, the field of psychiatry asked the question, "What's wrong with you?" Today, more and more therapists ask instead, "What happened to you?" The latest findings on the etiology of mental disorders revolve around trauma. You could say trauma is at the root of almost all of our social problems. And reducing a human's pain to the three hundred diagnoses in the *Diagnostic and Statistical Manual of Mental* The terms *dependent personality disorder* or *body dysmorphia* can't even begin to address the true cause of what's disrupting you from embodying your essence.

It's hard to tell if young people are more screwed up than we've ever been or if we're more willing to go and get help. (Maybe previous generations only knew silence to preserve the social order.) A 2012 study by the National Survey of Counseling Center Directors reported a 28 percent increase in mental health visits since 2000. What's for certain is that the youth of today are burnt out by the demands of modern living—western civilization's "first world problems," if you will—before we've even begun our adult lives. We are suffering from extreme low self-esteem.

Openly expressing our aches and pains can be a bane for our abusers, and it is also a sign that the movement of humanism is spreading. Today, we're at less risk of being fired from work or sent to a psychiatric ward for expressing normal responses to distressing situations. Now, researchers are truly invested in the idea of happiness and how to attain it—and how to capitalize on it, too.

We are realizing that sharing what's going on in our inner world is a good thing. It may be the only way to exist in this life and keep your peace intact. Many of us are taught by older generations to reject feelings that are painful, but any mentally healthy person will tell you that pain is the greatest gift life can give you. If you listen to your pain, you can correct your course. If you're cut off from your feelings, you're cut off from your instinct and joy and from interpreting your body's survival signals.

I believe we can choose to live in either a universe of chaos or order. In a universe of chaos, everything happens *to* you. Life conspires against you. The pain never ends, and there's no rhyme or reason to the situations we find ourselves in. There's nothing we can do about any of it. But if we choose to live in a universe of order, then everything happens *for* us, no matter how excruciating and complicated it may seem at the time. We are here to overcome our weaknesses. There are lessons to learn and compulsive patterns to be broken, and the end goal is our empowerment. The world is responding you, and you play a big role in creating your own reality.

To be healthy, we've got to transcend the duality of right and wrong or good and evil—and make space for the many different facets of ourselves. We've got to get comfortable with paradox and the unknown in order to stand tall on our own two feet as a well-adjusted adult. We've got to be able to trust all our felt sensations and express them in a way that fosters good relationships with others.

IT'S NEVER TOO LATE FOR A HAPPY CHILDHOOD

So much of our sanity and disposition as adults are dependent on our childhood experiences, even ones most people think they can't recall. I don't believe we ever forget what happens in our childhood; we simply block it out. If you look carefully, every time we're emotionally triggered by something, it directs our attention back to a wound buried deep inside of us that is probably the cause. No matter how much you try to forget, the body remembers. If we don't address the pain, it will continue to create the biggest blocks in life that prevent us from feeling healthy, happy, and free.

This theory in psychology, which argues that early childhood trauma stops our emotional development, explains why there are so many emotional toddlers running around as grown-ups. Some of us never get over what happened when we were at our most vulnerable. Our ability to healthfully relate to others starts being formed during infancy, when we need to be cared for by people we can trust. If we don't receive the things we need from our parents—affection, attunement, protection, and safety—we may develop issues later in life.

It's said that our entire subconscious mind and personality is programmed into our being from the time we are born up to age seven. So, if we experience trauma at an age before we have the capacity to process it, a part of us may get stuck at that emotional age. A part of us goes into hiding. And subsequently, we will try to avoid whatever we've come to associate with that particular event like it is the black plague—either that or we'll be attracted to it, like a moth to a flame. We've got to face it, if we are to move on.

The big issue with trauma is how deeply it impairs your daily functioning and your ability to handle stress. People vacillate from a spectrum of disassociation to emotional activation when they are exposed to something that reminds them of the original event. And there is nothing abnormal about this. The body and the brain of someone who has experienced repetitive deliberate harm or undergone a life-threatening event are simply responding to an abnormal situation in a completely normal way. These defense mechanisms would serve us well if we were still primates living in the wild, but instead we live in a highly complex, stressed-out society that doesn't give us the time or the social graces to float outside of our body or overreact to everyday stimuli. This society runs trauma survivors over, when we need to cross the street to the other side.

What's interesting is that in order to heal from trauma, which is at the root of most mental diseases, you simply have to have a safe space and support in order to feel. Research shows that trauma is stored in the limbic system, the part of our brain responsible for emotions and the unconscious and our fight or flight mode. This part of the brain does not process language and is not responsible for higher reasoning. In other words, healing from trauma is rarely a mental activity; it's more of a heart thing. It's a painful process of remembering and reclaiming all the difficult feelings that we have not allowed ourselves to feel in the process of living. It's about learning to meet ourselves there, in the pain, until we start to identify it as something else. It's about taking care of ourselves when we are most vulnerable.

We've got feel the frozen emotions left by the original event. We've got to unpack all of the associations our traumas have taught us to make about what is bad and what is good; what is safe and what is dangerous. By dealing with these triggers in a different way, we have the power to create a new, trauma-free future.

We're all seeking closure. And I believe that everything we do on this life journey is merely an attempt to finish an uncompleted story, where love is the universal ending.

THE COMPULSION TO REPEAT

> "The patient cannot remember the whole of what is repressed in him, and what he cannot remember may be precisely the essential part of it . . . he is obliged to repeat the repressed material as a contemporary experience instead of remembering it as something in the past."
> —Sigmund Freud, *Beyond the Pleasure Principle*

Some people have a chronic compulsion to recreate the same traumas in their lives over and over again. According to numerous studies, people who were sexually victimized during childhood or adolescence were 2 13.7 times more likely to be sexually victimized again in adulthood. This phenomenon is known as *revictimization*, which, despite its definition, is never the victim's fault. According to a study published in *Psychiatric Clinics of North America*, there are a few theories as to what causes revictimization. People might engage in self-destructive behaviors that put them in high-risk circumstances; they might be drawn to social attachments that are reminiscent of an old relationship with an abuser and confuse abuse with love; they might engage in self-blame and doubt and have trouble communicating, which can perpetuate violence. However, when we change the one common denominator in all these experiences, we can reclaim our power.

I have experienced my own fair share of traumas, and I spent most of my twenties unconsciously recreating them. In the process, I hurt others, but mainly, I hurt myself. Healing has been an exhausting, but rewarding, process of putting my mind back together again after being completely fractured by loss and violence. I could never have done it alone; I needed people to support me and access to resources. And part of the healing process is also in remembering.

It's important to note that your healing is not a courtroom of facts and figures. Recollections of how situations went down will always vary according to the different perspectives of those involved, and every time we revisit a story, its contents can change. But content isn't always what is most important; it's more about venturing into our psyche and retrieving forgotten feelings, images, and impressions of environments and people so we can learn how our past experiences have shaped our current reactions to the outer world. Once we are aware of this, we can respond from a place of consciousness. This explains why the denial of a disturbing memory is more damaging than facing a past that could have killed you, but didn't. The bitter truths can liberate us; it's the sweet lies and self-deception that keeps us in the haze of craze.

In the process of writing this book and interviewing many people, it's become undeniable to me that although everyone experiences challenges and hardship, life unfairly shits on some much harder than others. I've come to the conclusion that humans are not wired to experience violence without damaging results. But I've also come to the conclusion that humans have an extraordinary capacity to move beyond even the most tragic circumstances, and we can be remarkably resilient.

Dorthea Hudson, twenty-seven, is a millennial with a background of extreme childhood abuse. Dorthea also has synesthesia, and she has been diagnosed with bipolar II, ADHD, and PTSD. She had her first mental breakdown at age sixteen due to a psychiatric med she was taking.

There's an index called Adverse Childhood Experiences (ACE) that measures the amount of physical and psychological stressors of abuse and neglect that a person has had to endure before turning eighteen. The amount of ACEs a person has directly correlates to their physical and mental health—their likelihood to contract certain diseases, get pregnant prematurely, become an addict, fall into crime, develop depression, or commit suicide. Childhood is a huge indicator of your future success or failure—but it can be hacked.

Dorthea starts off her story. "The summer before I went to my junior year high school, my dad beat the shit out of me. I got sent to a hospital, and they transferred me to the psych ward when they found out I was reacting badly to meds. I was raped by a staff member there. Then they kicked me out when my insurance ran out."

That was just the beginning for Dorthea.

"My mom was medicating me with pills that made me crazy, and I started to realize that it was all this emotional manipulation and meds that were making me coo-coo. Once I was off them, I started having all these memories of my sister catching my dad molesting my brother. I realized that my parents were pedophiles. I've never had so much terror in my heart."

Dorthea made a plan to sneak out of her mother's house. She ran away with her sister and went to a beach in Delaware. Dorthea noticed that when she was off her meds, she was stable. Her parents put out a missing person's report, but since she was already seventeen, the cops didn't care. Away from the people and the places that brought her misery, Dorthea says she had a great summer.

"Throughout my whole adolescence, I'd been crusading for people to believe me that my parents were pedophiles," she says. "If I talked about it, no one would believe me. I told my sister about my memory, and she said she had the same one. We tried to take it to court but the case fizzled out. The government, in my experience, has not cared. I had a therapist once tell me that courts don't believe children in child abuse cases."

It's one of the saddest experiences a person can have the day they realize their parents don't love them the way they need them to because of their own anguish and character failings. It's a harder pill to swallow when you know that your day of justice is never coming. In the midst of so much turmoil, Dorthea had to wake up to the realization that love is not supposed to be painful, despite the mixed messages she received when she was young. So, she went seeking for truly loving people and healthy situations.

On the day of her college graduation, Dorthea made the decision to never talk to her parents again. She's now living in Portland, Oregon, where she has a full-time job. She says she's happy most of the time, but she always has to be on her guard to ensure that her surroundings are safe and that the people she attracts into her life are a source of true support. Serenity comes and goes, but as she learns to accept it as her norm, it is steadily building. Most recently, Dorthea is studying to take the GMAT. Her dream is to go into marketing for green energy, and she wants to get her MBA at her reach school, Stanford. Her practice test scores are high enough that she has a chance to be accepted.

CELEBRATING MENTAL VARIANCE

People are very unique. Everyone interprets this life differently; it's part of what makes us humans so fascinating. Our culture would benefit from celebrating mental variance, instead of seeing difference as something that makes us ill.

Dorthea has learned to turn her synesthesia into a tool, a gift she can offer the world because she sees it in a different way. When Dorthea is in love, she sees the color gold. She calls it faint but vivid. She uses colors to fuel different life activities—and, of course, gold is her favorite.

Dorthea used to suffer from psychogenic nonepileptic seizures almost every day. For a while, she stopped being able to go to work. Then, one day, she realized that her seizures and her synesthesia were linked—whenever she resisted the way her mind sees the world, she would trigger the seizures. Dorthea began using her synesthesia, especially the color gold, to ease her nervous system. Today, she's back and ready to make a difference. Dorthea is living proof that personal transformations can occur when we learn to lovingly embrace our inner world.

"I want to do something good. I want to do something that's . . . not bad. Saving the environment is the most important issue of our times. It affects liberals and conservatives alike. Climate change is going to kill all of us. There's no point crusading for civil rights if we're dead."

The problems of the world are scary, and what Dorthea has endured is exceptionally frightening. However, she's realized that being proactive helps her move beyond her past. When she's not paralyzed by fear or focused on her victimhood, she can finally do something about what she wants to change in the world—so that perhaps one less person will have to suffer the way she has.

Everyone is in recovery from the traumas of this world. We've all got a little dysfunction within us, and some have more than others. It doesn't mean we're crazy; it just means we're human. But will we choose the courageous path of "working" on ourselves?

Dorthea is learning to listen to her body—to be risk-averse, to stay away from triggers. She does the responsible thing: she takes her meds, the kind that truly help. She stays away from drugs. She chooses to believe in the future of society and wants to function in it.

"I am reconstructing every part of myself," she says. "If my self-esteem is low, then I accept abuse. When I'm confident, I don't."

Those of us who are broken by life can learn how to put ourselves back together. Through our actions and thoughts, we get to shape the quality of the person that we become. Emphasize good qualities of your nature until you begin to identify with your strengths more. Speak to yourself with a voice of self-compassion, and you'll be less engulfed by the dramas of the world. You'll start to attract the people who reflect the self-love that's budding inside of you. Moreover, you'll be able to accept loving treatment. Your trauma is not who you are. Surviving through the unbearable and resurrecting yourself to revel in life again carves an emotional depth into your being that cannot be created any other way.

Dorthea is becoming more and more attracted to healthy people, which is another huge part of the healing process. Every relationship is part of the journey to piece ourselves back together. While it is within our power to heal ourselves, we can't heal alone. We need allies. Millennials are lucky to live in a time when the human potential movement, modern developments in psychology, and the arts of spiritual healing are everywhere.

The process of facing our collective problems is enough to send us barreling down a dark hallway, but I have come to find that when I'm proactive and open to a miracle, I always discover a light at the end of the tunnel. Beautiful things can come out of tragedy, though I believe they also happen in spite of it.

There is a long-held notion that a correlation exists between genius and insanity. Dorthea and I both think that it's bogus. People who go through deep traumas and go on to create works of art have simply overcome the hell they were in. Trauma does not create genius, but *when* it is released, the genius within all of us just becomes brighter.

THE RX GEN

It takes a lot of time to karmically purge the sins of our ancestors. Who has time for it when class warfare is being waged and money must be made? And so for that, big business invented pharmaceuticals and pills that come in all different shapes and shades and sizes.

This pill stops racing thoughts! This pill gives you energy! Got restless legs? Try Mirapex!

I can remember the day in high school when I found out about the magical pill Adderall. It helped all my friends get their homework done really, really fast. It was supposed to be a miracle panacea to an affliction known as ADHD, where people get bored and zone out and have trouble focusing on doing things they don't want to do but have to if they want a future in this society (which is a description that could apply to most of us). I gobbled that shit up to get through school.

What can millennials who are crippled by our own emotional pain do but take drugs to keep up with the hustle, which itself relies on our desensitization? It seems like the easy cure, but these drugs, which are so freely administered by healthcare professionals, create chemical dependencies. They have side effects that doctors often use other drugs to treat, and we become trapped in a cycle of self-medicating that keeps us from understanding who we really are without it all.

Humans used to ingest botanicals to create a heightened state of inner balance, but today, they take synthetics. Pharmaceutical drug development has steadily increased since the mid-1800s, and millennials grew up in the middle of a pharmaceutical boom. We were stuffed with meds before the medical community even knew about the side effects. Meds may make us behave as desired so we fit into the program, but they also make some people vulnerable to developing other forms of mental illness later on. Depression at age twelve turns into bipolar disorder at age twenty-two; meanwhile, you're swallowing a different pill each week just to deal.

Many of us were also given drugs before we were of a legal age to decide if we wanted to take them or not. The younger a person is when they begin taking meds, the less of a voice they will have in their own treatment decisions down the road. Ideally, a child psychologist would encourage parents to repair the dysfunctions in the family system that are creating the emotional and behavioral problems in their children in the first place, but that would require the entire family participating in a process of reconciliation and healing. Few therapists have the gall to call out an abusive parent when they're the ones writing them the checks. There's also the consideration that the household situation, however damaging or challenging, might still be better than foster care.

The question to ask, though, is why so many pills are pushed onto us, and why so few holistic or natural alternatives are taught or prescribed that can treat the source of our issues instead of the symptoms. Why are we not taught other ways to understand our bodies and minds so we can live in optimum emotional, physical, and spiritual health?

Not all mental illnesses can be treated without meds, but some can. I've seen millennials, who were first given drugs as teens to treat issues they could have managed in a different way, going through hell trying to get off medication. And I've seen people who do need their meds going through hell trying to find the right combination and dosage to suit their unique constitution. Basically, I've seen a bunch of people struggling to get out of hell and into heaven.

Amid these problems, there's always time for a good conspiracy, and Big Pharma leaves a lot of room for it. I've often asked myself if all this suffering we're experiencing at the hands of this system is deliberate. Is Big Pharma in the pockets of the Illuminati, trying to numb out the population so we don't overthrow it?

Clinical trials testing for side effects of psych meds are often conducted by the pharmaceutical companies themselves. According to ProPublica, doctors are paid off to meet with these companies, sometimes earning upwards of thirty-eight million dollars a year for pushing their products. The US accounts for a third of the global pharmaceutical market. The pharmaceutical industry is a certainly a profiteering beast. There's cash in illness—lots of it. If companies can convince us that there's something wrong with us simply because we feel things that are uncomfortable and respond naturally to less-than-ideal circumstances, they'll make billions.

If taking a pill can make your problems go away, that's great! What's scary is when taking these pills prevents us from addressing the things in our environment that make us sick in the first place—the root of the problem.

Kaitlin Bell Barnett describes her plight with pharmaceutical meds in her autobiography *Dosed*. "I spent years being depressed as a young teenager, and it took a lot of my life away from me," she tells me. "I've been on anti-depressants for fourteen years. I've tried to go off them."

Kaitlin was seventeen when she first went on Prozak. It worked, until one day, as a fresh college graduate, she started experiencing debilitating anxiety. Nothing was wrong with her in the conventional sense; she had a nice job, a nice apartment, and new friends and colleagues. But she couldn't sleep. She would wake up with her heart pounding.

Kaitlin says she started taking Klonopin, but the medications no longer provided the quick fix she needed. She started developing chronic migraines and unusual health problems that may or may not have been caused by her medications. In response, she started taking other medications, and soon the number of medications created a situational depression that was independent of the depression that had caused her to take medication in the first place. Things got complicated.

Kaitlin spent a long time hiding her problems from others because mental illness is considered taboo. She says she would weep all day long and then have to get ready for a work interview. She started to freelance because it allowed her to take care of herself whenever she needed to. I've found that this is one of the main reasons most millennials seek out self-employment—for self-care.

Kaitlin subsequently realized that lifestyle decisions made a huge impact on her mental health. She prioritized exercise, working on projects that gave her a sense of purpose, sleeping, eating well, and having a network of friends to talk to whenever she felt down. Having a good therapist also helped. Unsurprisingly, it turns out that humans need a lot of support and emotional resources to thrive. Kaitlin stays on top of it.

THE NEED FOR CONNECTION IN LIFE

"I see mental health as a state where we are aware enough of our shadows that we are not suffering from them," says Josef Rhodes, thirty-four, who works as a holistic healer. "We are not recreating our inner trauma in the world. Self-work is how we address this."

Josef is calling himself a "death coach" at this time. He thinks that death of the ego is a good thing and believes that an element of healing is learning how to let the part of our character that identifies with suffering kick the proverbial can so it can be replenished with unconditional love and faith in the ultimate reality of immortal life.

"We are, as a collective, well aware that we are way past the tipping point," Josef says. "We can still use our time on Earth to understand the Truth. I don't think we're here to save the planet. We're here to learn how to master the realm."

So maybe I should call this book *The Millennial's Guide to Letting it All Go in a State of Transcendental Oneness* instead . . . or how about *The Millennial's Guide to Realizing that Nothing Really Matters?*

I wonder how those would sell.

Mastering the realm comes with surrendering to the process of dying. If we walk with death as an ally, we will come to know immortal life. That's a nice, philosophical platitude for you.

On some level, I subscribe to it. We're just here dying little ego deaths again and again, recreating our identity until the body bites the dust. But I also believe we're here on this Earth to fucking be alive while we're living. I'm only here learning how to die so I can learn how to live. We're meant to enjoy the ride and revel in the pleasures of life. Personally, I believe that life is a virtue and that there's a reason the human body is built to want to survive. To me, mental illness is what causes us to behave in ways that violate that pursuit. If that's the case, then it's perfectly healthy to want to save and protect this planet.

Humans cannot escape trauma. Being born is traumatic. Ending a relationship is traumatic. Discrimination is traumatic. All of these common human experiences are painful, and you can bet that whatever you've experienced, someone else has as well. But none of these events can create mental illness alone.

There are people who go through horrendous tragedies and who don't develop longstanding psychological complications. According to David J. Morris's *The Evil Hours: A Biography of Post-Traumatic Stress Disorder*, one of the determining factors that contributes to who will develop posttraumatic stress disorder (PTSD) and who can experience a traumatic event without developing mental illness has to do with community. PTSD can turn into complex PTSD if survivors of a traumatic event endure social rejection in the aftermath, which is why it's so important to crusade for a trauma-informed society. If a survivor can come to a supportive social situation and receive acceptance, care, compassion, and a safe space to talk about whatever's happened, they are more likely to work through the event without developing a longstanding neurosis, shame, or fear of themselves and the ostracization of others.

Most of us aren't taught the proper ways to respond to someone else's tragedy, such as simply offering an unjudgmental emotional presence to a person as they move through the process of grieving. To give empathic emotional presence others, we have to be able to give it to ourselves first. Everyone has to be doing the work that it takes to become fully human if we want to move through our traumas with grace—both in our solitude and together.

Now, more than ever, it's important to remember that as climate change escalates and as our politics becomes more volatile, the amount of trauma we will have to endure will likely increase. Things may get worse before we collectively wake up and commit to doing better. Community has to emerge in the midst of all this, but it can only happen as we stretch our imaginations to learn about and embrace the sometimes horrific realities of our neighbors. Because the weight of this world is far less heavy when it's spread out among many shoulders.

Chapter 8

Cutting the Apron Strings

W HO CAN WE BLAME FOR THE ABSURDITY WE'VE INHER-
ited—tyrannical economic systems, the moral bankruptcy of the culture, the annihilation of the natural world, and
the international sabotage of progress?

The answer: our parents.

Yes, the burden of blame and cause and effect may fall on
our predecessors, but guilt, shame, and finger-pointing won't
help. What's been done has been done. You can't force others to
change. All this may not be the fault of millennials, but it's now
our responsibility.

It's been a long road for me to come to realize that I don't
need anyone else's permission to drastically change myself and
my experience of life. I don't need an apology to let go and
show up for people in the present moment. Receiving amends
and expressions of sympathy will certainly help build trust, but
it's ultimately not necessary. I alone can live out the amends by
choosing to live my life in a different way that stops the cycle of
suffering.

I am the sum of my ancestors. Every significant moment in life they faced, I will as well. But I have the potential to rewrite my DNA.

MILLENNIAL DEPENDENCY

First, let's recognize the accolades of the baby boomers. Our predecessors did some good. They created the civil rights movement. Diseases were eradicated. Experimental music and alternative lifestyles were accepted. Gender equality was crusaded. The Internet was invented. Their legacy hasn't been all bad. However, the wheels of the machine of their industrialized, capitalist society were put into motion, and it's now heading humanity toward self-destruction. And it's the baby boomers who are currently running the show.

We need to agree on something, moving forward: we can no longer continue to do things the way our parents did. If millennials chose to follow in their footsteps—in our public, private, and professional lives —we are bound to get the same results.

We get to choose our friends and beloveds, our careers and our geographic locations; but we don't get to pick our biological families. Families teach us the lesson of unconditional love. Because of their unique influence, we get to be exactly who we are. Self-love and acceptance start with gratitude, for all the relationships that got you here.

By the age of eighteen, we're legally adults. We can choose to run away from our family ties for good, though most of us would never dream of doing so unless under dire circumstances. Family is our shelter from the world, and many millennials stay dependent on their parents for far longer than previous generations. We stay hooked into their bank accounts, and some of us continue to live with them at home.

The relationship between parent and child is one of the most significant dynamics every human will ever have to unravel.

Being a parent is one of the hardest jobs on the planet. Kids are like little balls of clay, molded by their parents' every action. As we age, the clay starts to harden, and we either remain as fixed products of their decisions or turn ourselves into someone else while we're still malleable.

Whether we're affected by their absence or through their direct influence, our relationships with our parents form the foundation of our self-esteem and our capacity to trust in others. We plug ourselves into their nervous systems, we take on their emotions. We can't always process all the unconscious family dynamics or protect ourselves from what happens in our households as children, though these forces go on to program our personality complexes. We carry these imprints into all of our social interactions. Some are positive; others are negative. But, with steadfast discipline and self-inquiry, they can be rewritten.

PREDESTINATION BY BIRTH?

For some of us, our parents are a rock, the one loving constant in life's tumultuous ocean. For others, our parents are the ones who have betrayed us the most. Examples range on a spectrum from one extreme to another. This chapter is by no means an attempt to create a one-size-fits-all fix to the complexities of a child–parent relationship.

Some of us don't have parents. Some will choose to disconnect ourselves from our parents—temporarily or permanently—for our own mental health. Some will spend massive amounts of energy and the cost of a college tuition in therapy healing family ties to create a healthy adult child-parent relationship. And there are some who will choose to live our lives alongside our parents, never veering too far from their sides because we are nurtured by their presence.

But even if you had top-notch caretakers who devoted their lives to your development, there is still an undoing that needs to happen for any young person to fully come into themselves. To grow into adults, to become individuated, we have to cut the apron strings, as the old saying goes, even if we've had "good enough" parents. We have to break free from our dependency on them and gain a bit of emotional distance so our lives don't continue to revolve around who they are and who they aren't, and what they expect from us and what they don't. Every single family system is slightly dysfunctional, some more severely than others. We are all flawed creatures, and there's no way your parents haven't wounded you in some way or another.

The sociologist Karl Alexander conducted a study entitled "The Long Shadow" that tracked 790 kids from Baltimore, Maryland, for twenty-five years to examine how the family we're born into impacts a person's life decisions as they reach adulthood. He started studying these kids when they were in first grade, and what he found, almost unanimously, was that the number of resources and influential connections a family has largely determines what socio-economic group a person will belong to later in adulthood. Participants almost always made choices that recreated the situations they were raised in.

It went far beyond money. Dysfunctional family patterns were passed down in the ways participants interacted with work and education, the type of person they picked to partner with, and the ways they treated or mistreated their own children. For example, if you had a verbally abusive father, you'd be likely to be quick to lash out at others.

We pick people and situations that recreate the dynamics we've always known because there is comfort, as well as pain, in the familiar. I attach to you because you remind me of my wounds, and then I interpret your behavior through my wounds while you do the same. In the end, all parties get triggered and engage in a power play that is eerily similar to the ones we've always known.

We can easily say, "I never want to end up like my parents. I'd never do the things they did to someone else." Yet, some of us still have a way of recreating the same situations over and over again, perhaps because the desire to turn our greatest source of turmoil into love is so powerful. We become what we detest until we're conscious of it. Humans are creatures of habit, and our bodies record everything we do. Our subconscious is engineered before we even hit puberty. The more trauma and deprivation that a person experiences in childhood, the more likely they are to become a delinquent or an addict, develop debilitating health conditions or a mental illness, or experience domestic violence.

Being exposed to verbal abuse, sexual exploitation, and starvation, or having an alcoholic parent, for example, are all considered adverse experiences on the ACE index—but we have a choice. We can spend the rest of our lives suffering as a result, or we can devote energy to our own liberation. Once you've gotten past your own garbage, all that's left is service, and many people who experience adversity growing up will feel driven to pay it forward by guiding others out of their own suffering.

CHOOSING YOUR DESTINY

No matter what obstacles we face, our thoughts can spiral in two directions—upward toward freedom, opportunity, empowerment, safety, and emotional warmth and expansion; or downward, descending into a black hole of fear, helplessness, danger, and immobilization. With the first option, you're a creator. It's like that good ole' Serenity Prayer states: "Give me the serenity to accept the things I cannot change, the courage to change the things I can, and the wisdom to know the difference."

With the second option, you're a victim. Even the most obsessive seekers, self-help junkies, and rebels are vulnerable to repeating what we swore we never would, letting the downward spiral of thoughts determine our circumstances.

It can happen so quickly—it has for me. When I look back at my decisions, the crossroads I've encountered, and my situations in life, I realize that I'm living the same exact life as my mother. I had convinced myself that we were nothing alike, but I've discovered that we are. I'm susceptible to the same patterns. And when I listen to stories about my grandparents, I realize I'm destined to repeat the same situations as an entire generation of women who came before my parents. I've come to viscerally experience as true the theory that ancestral trauma is stored in our DNA. And now I'm here, trying to rewrite my story by first becoming aware of the stories of those who came before me. Like I've said: awakening is a painful process of remembering.

"So you mean I'm making the same mistakes that my mother made, that my grandmother made, that my great-grandmother made?" says Alila Sophia, thirty-three. Alila runs her own business called Sacred Cycle, which sells feminine empowerment products like menstruation cups and jade eggs, and leads her own retreats. At the time our interview, she is six months pregnant. The child was unplanned.

She is building a good life with the father, whom she has known for a few years but with whom she was only intimate with a few weeks before her pregnancy. While she is doubtful of many things, she is devoted to raising this child as best as she can. She wonders if she and the father have what it takes to make it as a couple in the long term. She says he's stoked to be a dad, but will she end up as a single mother?

Alila was raised by a single mother. After all that yoga, meditation, workshops, and many months spent at the ashram, she stands here doing what she always intended to never do—repeat that pattern.

"Who knows?" Alila exclaims in a cry of determination. "Maybe I'm healing my lineage by having this baby!"

She brings up an important point. There's no need to beat yourself up. Self-compassion is key to unwinding the tangled webs that have been weaved, and every moment is an opportunity to deepen your understanding of what love is and what love is not. If you're on that journey, you're already doing the work— even if you've set yourself up in a similar template. The people who overcome these generational patterns are the ones who have learned to sit in the fires of transformation and who turn their fate into destiny. They always choose growth.

What is going to steer your ship? Is it your insanity? Your resentments? Your traumatic memories? The actions of your parents? Is it the expectations of this society or my fears of growing old? Or will it be your free will?

SO, FORGIVE

> "Every single human being, when the entire situation is taken into account, has always at every moment of the past, has done the very best that she or he could do, and deserves neither blame nor reproach from anyone. This is particularly true of you."
> —Harvey Jackins, founder of Re-evaluation Counseling

The world may seem like it's crashing and burning. Your childhood may make you feel like a houseplant that's been trampled on and left out to dry for days without water. I may look out at my life and this society and think that the future of humanity is dismal. There is evidence to support all of these conclusions, surely; however, there is also evidence to the contrary. When I stretch the limits of my consciousness to look at others through the lens of compassion, I see that everyone, despite the unintended consequences of their actions, has always been doing their best. When I resource the deep reservoirs of energy and spirit within me, I know that I have everything I need to survive; I don't need to rely on others to be whole.

The truth is that my parents don't make my decisions anymore. My parents can't process my emotions for me or say anything that will rewire the self-sabotaging patterns in my psyche that were cocreated by their actions. I have to do that. It's up to me to figure out how to become the person I want to be and live the life I want.

Forgiveness doesn't mean you're excusing the things people have done. It simply means you're ready to stop making the situation about you. It means having the courage to move on from your pain; it means mining the tragedy for the gifts that you can turn into gold, and holding onto those, with no regrets.

Healing in many ways is the act of being seen, felt, and heard, but the sorry truth is not all parents are able to understand our perspectives, no matter how many times we try to explain ourselves. Some are too committed to their role of authority to meet you as an equal. Some can't face their own pains, so how could they ever face yours? The good news is that all we need to do is hear and feel and see *ourselves* in order to let go of the shame of what's been done, and what we've done as a result. Once we can do that, this whole adulting thing won't be so challenging anymore.

And no matter what your family looks like—single mom, single dad, or a blended Brady bunch gang—your family is yours. There is an emotional glue binding them to you. It goes beyond duty and obligation. We were put on earth to learn how to unconditionally love, and if we feel entitled enough to walk away from everyone who has ever let us down, there's no way we can ever learn this lesson.

If they did nothing else right, our parents still gave us the gift of life. No matter how many misdeeds they've done or how estranged you may have become, the essence of their being is the same as yours. And all of the pain and struggle that has been part of your journey has also provided you with lessons that led to your spiritual growth. At a certain point, we have to accept our families for who they are—not because the things that happened are okay, but because if we don't, we'll stay dysfunctional.

Gratitude—real, authentic, and raw thankfulness—is often the lasting sentiment accompanied with the final stage of forgiveness. Few people are truly able to reach this space. You've got to go through a lot of emotions to get there. It may seem easier to stay stuck in resentment than to plow forward, but think of the challenge of going through life carrying such a heavy weight on your shoulders. It doesn't have to be there forever.

In her book *Leaving My Father's House,* the Jungian analyst and mythopoetic author Marion Woodman calls this stage in the process of individuation "the painful recognition that we are all orphans and the liberating recognition that the whole world is our orphanage." It is then, and only then, that we can stop churning over the curses inherited from our family and start investing in who we want to be in our other relationships in the larger community. We can be our own people and claim our identity as children of the universe.

DO YOU SEE THEM TRYING (REALLY HARD)?

According to a survey by the Federal Reserve Bank, 48 percent of twenty-five-year-olds in the US are still living with their parents. Millennials have stayed financially dependent on our parents for longer than any other generation, yet another thing that makes us unique. It's part of the reason why breaking free to become people outside of their influence has been an ordeal for many of us.

During the financially difficult years, our parents often support our pursuits by giving us food and a safe space to sleep until we can get off the ground. This dynamic can be described as enabling, and it also reflects a cultural shift in the context of Western society. It's typical in other cultures for young adults to live with their parents until they start families of their own. Why not in America? Also, being financially supported by our parents in some cases can help us to help others.

Shira Zeman, twenty-eight, is an immigration lawyer working in Washington, DC, who recently started her own low-bono firm. Every night, she sleeps in her childhood bedroom. Shira's story reflects one of the reasons why we're called the Boomerang Generation.

"I was paying an arm and a leg for an apartment in Foggy Bottom," Shira says. "I was still sleeping at my mom's house all of the time. I don't think I would be able to start my own firm if my parents weren't so supportive. I wouldn't be able to afford it."

Shira makes about forty thousand dollars a year providing legal services to some of the most vulnerable members of our society. People assume that she makes a lot of money as a lawyer, but she mainly does social work. She says her clients make her realize how lucky she is to have the rights she has as an American. Though this country is deeply flawed, and even though our rights are still getting stripped from us, we are so much safer than many others in the world.

"My clients kiss the ground when they get to this country," she says. "They love this country more than I do."

And perhaps one day, even those of us who have struggled with our parents will know what it feels like to kiss and love them for all they've done for us and put up with from us. Perhaps we will come to realize that even if they failed to meet our needs as children, they were, and still are, trying their best. Perhaps, we will only realize this when *we* become parents.

Just like Shira, there's no way I could have completed this book and project without the help of my own parents. They don't always understand my reasons, but they've supported me as I've pursued my dreams and helped in the creation of this one.

HELICOPTER PARENTS

Millennials are known for our helicopter parents—hovering and controlling, attached to how well we perform as if it's a reflection of their own worth. The parents of millennials call university admissions offices to gloat about their children's achievements. They buy second houses near our college dorms. They put us on leashes when we were young. This is helicopter parenting at its finest, and the long-term consequence of this enmeshment is that it robs us of our ability to be independent.

In many ways, millennials are a strange blend of being over- and underparented. A parent's job is to protect us (up to a certain point) and nurture us, but we can't live in a bubble forever. We can't escape life's experiences of sadness, loss, rejection, and failure. We're going to bottom out at times and learn lessons the hard way, and no amount of parenting can keep it from happening. What a parent should ideally do is support us as we learn and recover from difficult situations. They should be there as we give life our best try, and even when we fail.

Helicopter parents don't trust that we can overcome our challenges and fight our own battles. They groom us to stay dependent on them (some unintentionally, some not). They are as much attached to their roles as parents as millennials are attached to our fading youth, which feeds the vicious cycle. What they are subconsciously doing is teaching us that we can't do anything on our own. We can't grow up into adulthood.

Helicopter parenting produces fragile young people who can't take responsibility for themselves. We collapse under confrontation. We don't own up to our mistakes. We aren't quite sure what we think or feel well enough to ask for what we need.

And we don't know how to express our thoughts and emotions effectively because we've always had someone telling us what to do and who to be and how to feel. It breeds narcissism, really. Helicopter parenting is one reason why many millennials grapple with such uncertainty over who we are and what we want to do. It's why we have inflated egos without proof in the pudding. We started our lives with an identity that was imposed on us, and when we finally reach an age when we have the freedom to carve out our own path, we go into crisis mode.

Then, there's the ego inflation. Millennials were often told that we were special and that we could do anything we wanted (you can see how that turned out!), and so often this statement was less about us and more about them.

Laura Lohnes, twenty-seven, is a researcher at a medical university. She says, "My mom told me all the time how great and smart I was. I grew up with this idea of myself that didn't match with the way the adult working world viewed me. All of a sudden, I entered the workforce and was the weakest link, goodbye!"

On one side of the parenting coin, we have aggrandizement, control, and domination. On the other side, we have absence. To keep a middle-class household during the time millennials were raised typically required two incomes; it still does. This means many millennials were raised part of the time by other people or were left to fend for themselves during the day. Add feminism to the mix and the ambition many women understandably had to prove themselves in a man's working world with only twelve weeks of unpaid maternity leave, and you've got the beginning of the shattering of traditional parenting roles. By the time dinner was on the table, parents were exhausted. The only interaction we had with them was usually about them getting us to perform or behave in a certain way. No wonder millennials have trouble with commitment. It's hard to deeply bond with someone who isn't around or who sees you only as something to satisfy their ego. It's one of the cruelest things a parent can do: rob a child of the right to have their own authentic sense of self.

FINDING THE IDEAL MOTHER AND FATHER WITHIN

Our parents aren't always meant to be our guides. Some of us have what's known as "good enough" parents—parents who knew how to love you the way you needed so you could emerge more or less as a healthy, balanced, and emotionally regulated person capable of lasting, loving bonds with others. But even so, no one has two ideal, ascended parental figures to show them what it means to perfectly embody the principles of being human. It's our job to create those figures within ourselves.

We can't look to others to fulfill the parental role, the way children look up to their parents when young.

So, we have to find the mother and father within. We have to locate our inner compass and trust it. We have to learn to love our wretched, poorly parented inner child the way it always needed, so it can grow up. We have to call these parts of ourselves out for what they are, forge a balanced relationship with them, and put our adult selves in the driver's seat.

And sometimes, we just have to leave home in order to do this. We have to press pause on our roles as children to become someone else. Parents, if I have one piece of advice for you, it's to let us do this. Let us go out on our own, and don't take it personally or feel like we've failed or forsaken you.

Brandon Martin, twenty-seven, dropped out of college, where he had a basketball scholarship, as a way to find himself. The decision deeply upset his mother, whom he says he owes a lot of his best qualities to.

Brandon says that family drama compelled him to leave home. He was going through changes as a teen, and those changes hurt his mother. She wanted him to have a good education; she'd worked her whole life for that. "I watched my mom struggle her ass off for us to be a middle-class family," he says. "I was one of four black kids at my elementary school."

But Brandon had his own goals, none of which were basketball. Brandon wanted to pursue the business of art, and he was willing to make the necessary sacrifices. For Brandon, the road-less-traveled wasn't easy. He even spent some time being homeless.

"For a while, it was really cool to be a thug. I was heavily affected by what plagues my race. These were messages sent to me my whole life. Slave syndrome affected my psyche—always feeling on the defense, not trusting the establishment to any extent."

Brandon recognizes now that his rejection of the system and of his mom's desires for him were also influenced by collective unconscious forces. He thinks the biggest issue facing our generation is an issue of identity.

"I don't think we really have a sense of identity as ourselves or even as a whole," he says. "We kind of pick whatever identity is presented to us, and we get really lost in that. Identity is the only way to be connected to what matters. It's our only moral compass, I think."

Brandon eventually returned home. Now, he is pursuing his vision with more knowledge about who the highest self of Brandon Martin might be—making music that offers a message of love, awareness, and empowerment to society. It's a calling he could never have followed if he structured his life around making his mother comfortable because of the sacrifices she made to lift her family out of poverty.

Brandon says that none of it has been taken for granted. It's just that he knew that his path was never going to be the same as her path. His mother, Sharon, was actually visiting him at the time of our interview. Her name is tattooed on his arm underneath the image of a sunflower.

Chapter 9

The Corporate Socialist Oligarchy

I USED TO THINK WE DIDN'T NEED A GOVERNMENT, WHICH OF course was young and foolish. Why? Because, anarchy. Over the years, I've simmered down a bit, and now I see that we need governance. But it can't look anything like the current governance we've got in America.

How would an ideal government operate? How big does it need to be? What should it oversee? What kind of laws would it impose on the people? If the United States is really a democracy, shouldn't the average person have a say in how they are ruled? It's been said that the US is a representative democracy, and it sure resembles one in theory and even in appearance. But perhaps that's the biggest myth we need to bust right here before we begin to discuss our options.

I've sat in on Senate hearings. I've watched white old men debate for hours about the consequences of passing legislation. From the outside, it looks like a bunch of well-educated people earnestly contemplating what the consequences of passing certain laws would do for the economy and civilian life. And often these are at odds—what benefits the economy usually damages our culture, and vice versa.

We are in the midst of a political milieu of little progress and much backward momentum. Our rights—like the right to a free Internet, the right to privacy, process, the right to healthcare, the right to a living wage, etc.—are being steadily stripped away from us no matter who seems to be in office. Democracy is meant to be slow and steady, but is this a democracy? All the checks and balances that were put in place can't prevent a dictator from rising into power if one party controls Congress. Millennials know that the two-party system itself is flawed.

And yet, we're told it's our fault. We're told that *we* voted these dimwits in. But did we? When you take into account gerrymandering, the two-party system, the electoral college, and the corporate financing required to fund the insane amount of money necessary for a campaign, the idea that a majority of the popular vote dictates who gets placed in positions of such power—and that people can rise to power based on merit alone—is quickly discredited.

Millennials have become beyond disillusioned with politics. We know that the time to act was yesterday, and yet we also know that there are things we simply can't do as everyday citizens. Though our leaders have to make the deals so the system serves the people, they refuse to do the right thing out of sheer greed. The system of our representative democracy is absolutely broken.

According to a Harvard 2015 IOP poll, only 20 percent of young adults considered themselves politically active. We are also, despite our high levels of higher education, politically illiterate. Most of us don't know how the system works; we only know the obvious—that it doesn't work for us.

Over the years, I've had to realize that I've no choice but to be political. And I've had to learn that my level of political agency is directly proportionate to my belief of how much agency I have. If the question is "how can we go about stopping the madness," then the answer is that everyone has to start participating in political acts.

If so, how can we do it? Do we take to the streets, yelling and screaming in protest against the actions of our leaders? Do we bitch on Facebook and write angry tweets? Do we sign petitions online? Do we call our representatives? Does any of this accomplish anything?

A CRISIS OF GOVERNANCE

The biggest problem with our planet is not that there are too many humans on it. Solutions are available that could enable everyone to equally access education, food, and affordable housing. The problem is that the task of implementing these solutions rests in the hands of the government. Unfortunately, people with missing empathy chips and extreme views are serving in very powerful positions. And we checked a box on a ballot to put them there—technically.

Politics is a path to power—and absolute power corrupts absolutely. Abraham Lincoln once said, "Nearly all men can withstand adversity, but if you want to test a man's character, give him power." It seems that the people we so often see becoming politicians may start out seeing it as a path of service, but because of greed and the desire to be winners above all else, they eventually lose their noble intentions. They rise to power through a family name, elite connections, false promises, and deceitful posturing. There's nothing fair about it.

A person can have the swankiest political platform and marketing, and they could have done some good things for the community throughout their career, but can they say no to a behind-closed-doors dealing that robs the average person of their daily bread so the rich can get wealthier? In an ideal world, politicians are civil servants working for the people, but the reality is that many use the system to bolster the interests and prejudices of the ruling elite, creating monopolies out of industries that harm our environmental and social ecosystems. It's a seductive proposition with payoffs that few can refuse when the cards are in their hands.

This is one reason why 50 percent of millennials have declared themselves as Independent. Despite their opposing philosophies, neither the Republicans nor Democrats in America's two-party system has done enough to repair this sinking ship. Beyond a few outliers, no one—on team blue or red—is taxing the rich and big businesses. No one is passing aggressive legislation to reduce carbon dioxide emissions, invest in renewable energy, and stop subsidizing fossil fuels. No one is denuclearizing and reinvesting military funding into schools and roads and other social programs to provide opportunities for undocumented immigrants, minorities, or indigenous peoples. This country was founded on "no taxation without representation." And here we are, watching our tax dollars spent. And if we don't pay up, we go to jail.

Speaking of jail, you can also go to prison for protesting all of this. Emily Reynolds, twenty-four, lived in Zuccotti Park in New York City during the 2011 Occupy Wall Street movement. She was arrested by the police for drawing on the sidewalk with colored chalk. Emily says she and the other girl she was arrested with were the only white women in the holding cell. She later completed her senior thesis about her experience at the University of Vermont.

It's said that our freedom isn't free, like it's a debt to be paid. But why do we have to give up freedom in order to have it? We have to risk imprisonment to simply show these distant talking heads that we've had it, and it's why so many people stay out of poli-tricks.

Millennials have to want power, too, to take back control from our government. We have to run for office and lead with integrity, or else every small step for progress that has been hard fought for by civilians, special interest groups, and the representatives who do care about the average person will be lost again as new leaders move in and out of Congress and the Supreme Court.

What's good about our Independent stance is it shows that millennials are ready for something different. We aren't quite sure what it is or where it's coming from. The Bernie Sanders campaign, which was funded entirely through grassroots campaign contributions, was seen by many of us as a glimmer of hope in half a decade of American politics. He lost to Hillary, after what was rumored to be a hostile takeover of the Democratic National Convention. We had a hero to believe in, but what we saw—once again—was that there will always be a way, just like in the turning point election of Bush and Gore, for the powers that be to intercept the electoral process so the status quo prevails when what we need is a revolution.

Can change happen peacefully within the system if we are engaged? Or is the crisis of governance so far gone that it's time for an overthrow, a coup d'état? If it ever comes to this, we need to have something in the works to replace and improve on the system in the aftermath, and I'm not sure we're there yet. All we know is that things can't stay the way they are.

A war between good and evil is being waged, and it has nothing to do with political affiliation per se. Instead, it has to do with the people and power structures in place that keep real issues from being swiftly addressed. It has to do with the gross neglect of the needs of the people by the powerful few who are in politics for their own gain.

UNDERSTANDING ECONOMICS

In an ideal world, it's the role of the government to keep our economy thriving. Government officials do this by taxing the assets of the rich and redistributing wealth to create jobs and social security programs that allow people to participate in society on a more level playing field. But, it's not happening.

The government also has to provide hundreds of services to civilians, from public transportation to sanitation, within a budget—another task they're failing at. Right now, millennials are poised to inherit the national debt racked up by previous generations, which is at the highest levels since the 1950s. Debt is part of how our system runs. The question is how much debt is too much (how about twenty trillion dollars)?

If you want to know how the system works, follow the money. Right now, our banking system is overseen by a centralized authority called the Federal Reserve, or the Fed, one of the most powerful organizations on earth. And there's nothing federal about it—it is a private organization. Whenever the US government needs to spend money, it creates treasury bonds that it gives to the Federal Reserve. Interest is charged on these bonds, and national debt that taxpayers have to pay off compounds. It may make you paranoid to know that the day-to-day ins and outs of our economy are being determined by a giant, mysterious institution that makes all the money, but that's the way things are.

The Fed has played a role in every recession through altering interest rates. It also contributes to the aggregation of all the big, national banks because it's run by the top bankers of these organizations that often favors the agendas of big banks over smaller credit unions. The big banks have been called "too big to fail"—they get bailed out of bankruptcy (as they were in 2008) because if one of them goes under, it could crash the entire economy. According to ZeroHedge.com, the five largest US banks held 17 percent of all US banking industry assets in 1970, compared to today, where the five largest US banks hold 52 percent.

That's big money. And people with this kind of money are the ones who pay for political campaigns and directly influence the decisions politicians make.

GIVE ME BACK MY RESOURCES

If the government won't redistribute resources, all is not lost. There are other ways to go about this—by creating an alternative economy. We don't have to rely on US dollars and the people who control them. It's said that nineteen out of every twenty dollars of new wealth created in the US goes back to the top 1 percent. That's how the deck is currently stacked.

If US dollars were circulating freely and everyone had equal access to them—and no one feared that there wouldn't be enough work in the future to support them and their family through to retirement—than relying on a giant central bank wouldn't be a problem. But this isn't how our society is functioning. In response, movements are happening in small pockets across the planet, where people are creating other systems to make this one obsolete. If the government is going to prevent progress and remain gridlocked, let's create our own money. Let's create resource-based economies that harness the abundance of what's around us so we can uplift communities out of poverty, stimulate productivity, and give people the means to govern themselves.

There's Bitcoin, a form of cryptocurrency that people are investing in and using to trade goods and services. Bitcoin is just one form of the now hundreds of digital currencies like Ethereum, Neo, Civic, and Dash that are being invented constantly. At the time of writing, Bitcoin has become an investment that is outperforming all stock portfolios.

Universal Basic Income is another answer to economic inequality, though it would most likely require the government to mandate. UBI is a form of social security that ensures that every person across the planet is given the same amount of money needed to survive each year. Instead of having different types of welfare programs where the government decides who gets what and how much of it they can afford, a universal basic income would be given directly to the people, who can choose to make whatever they want on top of that through their own enterprising. This would also eliminate the need for many types of non-profits and other NGOs. We would be on our way to eliminating poverty. What social experiments with UBI show is that when the basic needs of people are met, high levels of innovation can occur. It's good for society when everyone has what they need to live a dignified life.

WE HAVE THESE THINGS CALLED RIGHTS

Moses gave us the ten commandments because humans need guidelines for living with each other in a good way. Outside of religion, societies need laws to help us navigate this complex web of people, industry, and government without harming anyone else. These laws are supposed to uphold these things we call rights. We all have a right to live, a right to vote, a right to an education, a right to health care, a right to property. Rights also include civil freedoms—the freedom of speech, the freedom to peaceful protest, the freedom of religion, the freedom of the press. And we protect and promote our freedoms and rights through policies and legislation. That's why it's so important to understand how laws get passed.

Legislation gets passed through Congress when a representative from either the House of Representatives or the Senate sponsors and introduces a bill (the House of Representatives and the Senate make up Congress). The bill is assigned to a committee for study. It is debated and marked up, and once it's released, it is slated to be voted on. If the 218 out of 435 politicians in the

House of Representatives vote in favor of the bill, it moves onto the Senate. From there, if 51 out of 100 Senators vote in favor of the bill, it gets passed. The President has ten days to approve it and give it the final stamp.

That's how political change happens in this country, within this constitutional framework. Time evolves society, and legislation is passed, ideally, to keep all the moving parts that make up our society in balance as our environment shifts so we can grow with the times. However, what we often see is that the laws remain outdated and are held onto by old, stodgy stooges and the institutions who reap financial benefits from it at the expense of others. Passing legislation is a long process because it's built to be that way—with the appropriate checks and balances.

American politics is a giant social experiment, deemed as one of the greatest in the world, and the Constitution is considered one of the most genius organizing documents in history. However, not everyone who built our society has had a say in it—millennials certainly didn't get to choose the bill of rights. The society we currently live in is the product of the minds of a few white men who lived centuries ago—think Adam Smith's *The Wealth of Nations*, Thomas Hobbes's *The Leviathan*, and John Locke's *Second Treatise of Government*. These classic philosophical texts inspired our institutional political framework, originally crafted in an attempt to make America a free land.

There are people who will defend these doctrines to the death, but I question if they are still legitimate. Back when America was first founded, each delegate was responsible for only a certain number of constituents. The population of the US has multiplied by about a hundred times since then, but the number of people in Congress has stayed the same. That's a reason why we feel so divorced from what happens in the Federal Government.

"The People" may technically be able to pass a bill through Congress if we can get the attention of our representatives, but it's something that's still out of reach for most millennials. We need to pass new laws that solve our problems swiftly, and do away with the old just as fast. And a lot can get done if we focus on pushing a game-changing bill through Congress, such as an anti-corruption act, a single move that would help self-correct all that's broken in the system.

In 2011, senators Bernie Sanders and Mark Begich proposed a Constitutional amendment called the "Saving American Democracy Amendment." In it, for-profit corporations would no longer have the rights of a person, corporate spending in elections would be prohibited, and the government would be able to regulate those corporations and hold them accountable for their impact on the populace and the environment. This was a direct response to the Citizen's United Ruling in 2010, which many people think of as the beginning of the end of whatever democracy we had in this country. Government is here to regulate business; business isn't here to regulate government. For this to happen, they need to sleep in separate beds.

The amendment, of course, failed to pass.

"No matter who you vote for, they fuck you anyway," says Kyle Anderson, age twenty-six, an arborist who lives in Austin, Texas. "None of it matters. Staring off a mountain top and reflecting on yourself and what you can do in your sphere of influence—that does. Your immediate circle is all that matters—who can you positively influence for better or for worse."

Kyle went hiking across the Appalachian trail to get away from all the chaos and returned in a glowing, peaceful state. Kyle keeps out of politics because he doesn't like to surround himself with dramas that get on his nerves. He says he doesn't need a politician to give him the right to do whatever he wants; he just does it. "All I need is the woods," he declares.

His stance is certainly understandable. But is it sustainable on a wider, long-term scale? If everyone dropped out of the political process because they didn't believe in the system, the people with power and ulterior motives would continue to have their way with it. We've got some major battles ahead of us if we're going to usher in a paradigm shift that will allow our government to work for us again. At the same time, we also need to be fighting to extend rights now—not just to other humans but also to wildlife and nature.

The people in power can punish us for not following their laws. But who gets to punish *them*? Justice is a funny word, and there is not much of it in this country. In America, you have the freedom to call yourself an anarchist, a communist, a socialist, and more without being charged with treason. But you've still got to live in the system of representative democracy—whether or not you believe in it.

PLAYING THE GAME

Ben Droz, twenty-six, industrial hemp lobbyist, paces barefoot around the astroturf rug in the living room of his Columbia Heights townhouse apartment. He's wearing gray skinny jeans and a T-shirt that says HEMP. His shirt is made of it. Ben Droz loves hemp. I saw him on the streets of Washington, DC, one night when he handed me a bag full of hemp granola bars, an eight-ounce bottle of Dr. Bronner's liquid hemp soap, proindustrial hemp pamphlets, and some other paraphernalia. Ben spends most of his days giving out those granola bars to Congresspeople on Capitol Hill.

I can't help but grin around Ben, because he is what I would classify as a total ham. When he's not working for the small lobbyist organization called Vote Hemp that works on legalizing hemp so it can be grown domestically and used to create all sorts or renewable resources and medicinal products, he moonlights as a nightlife photographer with his photography company, which he called Say Cheese.

The Farm Bill had just passed in the Senate on the day I was with Ben—it is now legal to produce hemp for research purposes. It's a small step forward. Ben is on the phone with his boss talking about a press release they are about to send alerting the media about the passing of this legislation.

Lobbyists are the people who bring a concern to politicians' desks to persuade them to write new legislation and vote in a certain way. These lobbyist organizations , like the one Ben works for, can be run by a group of citizens creating a one-issue campaign, by labor unions, or by industry groups that are funded by corporations with the goal of passing laws that will help them make more money, often by deregulating their industry in a certain way. Pretty much every issue that's on a politician's radar is because a lobbyist brought it to a government official's attention through an interest group. But here's another reason why everything gets skewed: it takes money to lobby. You need resources to organize and present your needs to politicians. The better your lobby group is funded, the more power you have to influence your representatives.

For Ben Droz to lobby about hemp, he has to know everything about it. We're talking about hemp, not weed. You cannot smoke Ben's hemp shirt or his hemp briefcase. The reason why hemp is illegal is because of the drug hysteria that emerged in the 1930s. Ben says it's all nonsense. "The trace amounts of THC in hemp is akin to the amount of opiates in a poppy seed bagel." Hemp is not a psychoactive substance; it actually has a myriad of uses—from textiles, food, and all-natural cosmetic products to fuel, plastic alternatives, and building materials. Industrial hemp has a low THC content due to its high levels of CBD, a chemical that acts as an antagonist to the THC in the weed that gets you high. In fact, CBD has numerous healing properties for the human body. CBD is a good thing, which is why we need hemp lobbyists.

If you type "hemp lobbyist" as a video search on Google, Ben is one of the first people to come up. He used to dream of being a reality TV show star. He still does, in fact. He consciously uses his brilliant personality to walk behind the velvet rope, meeting politicians and getting attention from people in power so he can tell them about his cause. Ben Droz has deliberately made a character out of himself so he can make his cause a memorable one.

"I don't know about millennials, but I know about me, and I think the apocalypse could be sooner than they think," Ben says. He opens his Twitter page and tweets at the Center for American Progress about climate change. "Our generation needs to do something about this."

"We need biodegradable plastics," he continues. "Hemp can do this. My idea with hemp is for all the great products we have today to become environmentally friendly. The reason I'm into hemp is because it's an industry that can at least help things get better."

The business cards of every congressperson from every district are spread out on Ben's fold-out TV dinner table. He goes into his room to put on a suit. "When I moved to Washington, DC, four and a half years ago, I realized that when I wore a suit and a tie, I could do anything. And that's the truth."

As I sit in Ben's room, I've learned something about how we can make a difference. We've got to focus on the facts and solutions and learn how to play the game.

THE ROAD TO HELL WAS PAVED WITH GOOD INTENTIONS

Why can't we live in a self-correcting social system like Iceland? In the Nordic countries, the government provides everyone with health care and an education, where they can study for as long as they want to. While taxes are high (about half of the income), no one is ever hung out to dry. No one chronically worries for their safety or how they're going to make it in the world. There, tax dollars are spent wisely.

"The government takes care of us in every way," says Janne Henson, twenty-one, who is traveling in the US but lives in Denmark. "School teacher, doctor, dentist—whenever you need help, they're there. I cannot think of any way in which you are on your own in my country. In general, we have a very good system."

The situation in America is entirely different. Here, our government takes far more from us than it gives—and then we're asked to donate more money, on top of it all, to fund political action campaigns to stop these same politicians who are taking away our rights and spending our money on war. We do get some things in return for what we give through our taxes—programs like social security, food stamps, disability, and Medicaid. We get public education up until high school, a legal system, regulatory agencies like the Food and Drug Administration (FDA), a militia, police, sanitation, and more. But do these services help us or just support the agenda of the people who rule them?

Young people have always been known to be mistrustful of the government, rules, and the law. Millennials see the ways the system fails to live up to its potential and the ways it actively oppresses its own people. Is it a conspiracy? It's hard to say, though the answer is, probably. What's clear is that our government is based off a seminal founding document that has taken some major turns for the worst over the past few decades. It can, in theory, be improved on to solve the problems we're inheriting, but given the current state, it would take a miracle. It would require all of us being political and making large sacrifices for a bigger picture in major ways that may not have an immediate payoff.

Parker East, twenty-nine, is an author who, at the time of this interview, was about to bike across the country to build a cob oven. Parker says he's been living off his Jeopardy winnings from an appearance in January 2013, when he won around seven thousand dollars.

In 2008, he was on the verge of dropping out of society to live on a bicycle and pick food off trees, when he was convinced to work for five months on the first Obama campaign.

"I wanted to create change in the world. Once I had the first taste of volunteering for the campaign, I became very heavy."

Parker says he didn't make it all the way to election day. Though he was getting paid for his time for a while, he ended up working for free for a month and a half. "I had to ask relatives for money."

He left the experience feeling very naive—that despite his high hopes, politics would always be politics from top to bottom, bottom to the top, and all the way through. Parker believes that anything that can truly fix the system will have to come from the outside.

This brings us back to the reform vs. transform debate. Can we effect the change we need from the inside? Or do we need to create a new system entirely—and is this even possible with the power that be lording over us? Parker thinks the political framework behind the governing systems in the US is so corrupt and ineffective that it will engulf every scrap of a person's revolutionary ardor if they try to play ball within it—until all that's left is cynicism. His experience campaigning eventually pushed him to choose to live outside the "forced anxiety" permeating the collective psyche.

Parker did motivate himself to volunteer on election day, even though he had not stayed on for the entire campaign. And then, Obama issued a one-hundred-million-dollar expansion on Guantanamo Bay.

"How did I get fooled? I listened to that will.i.am song 'Yes We Can' over and over again. I was in, hook, line, and sinker."

Parker, who is somewhat of a whiz kid, still keeps up to date with current events. He still votes, usually for the democratic candidate, because he's most concerned for the well-being of those living in poverty. Yet, he goes back and forth, he says, because if the system is so broken, shouldn't he just vote for the people who will break it entirely?

"Let's just put it this way: I vote for the same reason I turn off the lights when I leave a room. If you're in a car, and you don't like where it's headed, you don't take your hands off the wheel."

There are plenty of backhanded dealings happening on Capitol Hill that the majority of the population will never know about, despite the efforts of sites like WikiLeaks. No matter how much C-SPAN we watch, it's impossible to keep up with every facet of politics or with what these politicians are up to all of the time. No one has the energy to be an unpaid professional politico watchdog.

The system is healing from years of gender inequality, classism, slavery, homophobia, and racism. These "isms" are so ingrained into how our government runs and who gets a say that it requires constant resistance to keep it from slipping back into its old ways. But, amidst having to navigate in one the most hopeless systems, one thing is certain: there are millions of government employees working day in and day out to run our country. It's not just our elected officials; the government is also made of regular everyday people who make up the nuts and bolts of how our society functions. And they aren't evil for doing it. Most probably started their public service careers with the desire, like so many millennials, to serve this country.

At the heart of politics is what social scientists call *wicked problems*. "There are two central characteristics of wicked problems," says Helen Kramer, twenty, a math major at Oberlin University with a concentration in peace and conflict studies. "The first is that there are no definite endpoints." For example, we want more equality, more well-being. Well, we can always have more and more of that. This is what Helen means. A wicked problem has no endpoint because the goal is abstract.

"The second characteristic of a wicked problem is that it's always part of a system that is constantly interacting with other parts, and once you start to implement a solution, the nature of the problem changes." In the realm of politics, we need to find a way to integrate all the various parts of a system into a tangible solution.

THE STAIRWAY BACK TO HEAVEN

Some millennials are focusing on participating in local government rather than what's happening on the federal level because it is a way to talk more directly to representatives and focus on the issues that hit home the most. An answer to the wicked problems of politics is to think smaller and pour our energy into bio-regionalism—doing what we can to affect positive change in our local communties.

Technology also provides a medium for citizens to propose their own amendments to congressional representatives rather than having to do it through a lobby. Perhaps in the future, we will be able to vote for politicians from our phones. We could take away campaign financing altogether and have a single website where every politician can showcase a multimedia platform of their campaign, their voting record, their past employers, and acts of service to the community. This way, those millions of dollars that are spent putting signs on lawns during a campaign could be spent somewhere else, such as feeding hungry children or bailing the people who can't afford it out of jail. Every candidate would have an equal shot at a job based on qualifications only, not their deep pockets.

If citizens were able to vote on specific issues directly through our technologies, then we wouldn't even need those talking heads to debate about what is best for us. Whatever is implemented will truly come from the people, instead of corporate lobbyists. The majority could rule this country and control the policies that affect our future. It could be a real and direct democracy.

If we don't like something, we have the power to change it. If nothing else, we can vote the most corrupt politicians out of office. In 2014, 90 percent of representatives were reelected into office, the same year Congress had an 11 percent approval rating. We actually let those people keep their jobs.

The future of our planet depends on our ability to make the priorities of future generations, minorities, the environment, and the impoverished the same priorities of our representatives. And we have to understand how the government works in order to engage with it. We have to work within a corrupt system to preserve our rights.

There is no way around it.

Chapter 10

Retreating to the Counterculture

"You know the phrase YOLO? I used to think it was a good thing. You only live once, so you should take chances. But it's almost more like, 'You only live once, so you should give up on everything and live for now as if there's not something better to work for.'"

—Lee Stewart, twenty-six, climate activist

WHERE WILL MILLENNIALS BE IN OUR MIDDLE AGES? WILL we still be living at our parents' or renting apartments at steadily inflating prices as our wages continue to decrease or stay stagnant, while we post sexy selfies of ourselves on Instagram?

Or will we be fighting for what's good in this chaotic world to stay alive, dreaming up solutions to the seemingly unsolvable problem of how to exist harmoniously in an incredibly intricate universe?

You may want to save the bees, save the trees, save Sudan . . . there's a lot that needs saving out there. You have to be a little crazy to think you can change the world. Yet, if there is any social group that can catalyze a cultural movement, it's the youth. We have the holy rage. We have the energy. We have a vision of unity. And we will rebel against you.

THE MANUFACTURERS OF *COOL*

Being cool matters to millennials. We're on a search for this thing called *identity*, and we can try on a lot of outfits until we find one that fits. Many of us are looking for the coolest one.

The notion of cool, however, like everything else, is a cultural construct, like everything else. And popular culture is a highly profitable enterprise concocted by mainstream media conglomerates and advertising companies. Are millennials creating our own identities, or are they being created for us? If individuation is what you're after, then you've got to release yourself from the master plan of who social engineers are breeding us to be.

Our consumer culture does not create happy young people, argues Robert McChesney, author of *Rich Media, Poor Democracy*. McChesney writes that there's a correlation between political apathy and levels of consumerism across the globe—the more obsessed we are with stuff, the less concerned we are with our impact on the world. Stuff becomes a distraction, and getting stuff becomes an end goal. Maybe this is why so many millennials aren't consumer-driven; we're more keen on finding our happiness.

Millennials are seeking wisdom and guidance in a culture that lacks a meaningful context to help us understand our place in the world as young humans. Millennials as a whole aren't into shopping and spending money in the same way previous generations were. According to the 2016 Gallup study "Brands Aren't Winning Millennial Consumers," only 25 percent of us keep up with brands and actively engage in the process of buy. We're not waiting for the next pair of Air Jordans or the latest version of the iPhone.

However, whether or not we're buying into what the advertising industry tells us to, we are all still absorbing the media and using what we see to interpret who we are and the world at large. The media is imprinting us with images of popular, socially celebrated identities, who often take on the rich, white notions of success that fuel the capitalist organism.

We're not born with a set self. We change over and over again throughout our lives. But until that change is organically birthed by the authentic energy within us, it often takes on the form of us trying to shape our image into someone else whom we think others might find valuable. And the media is feeding us lies about what is valuable and what is not.

Destroying public property? Cool.

Volunteering at a homeless shelter? Not cool.

Buying everything you want and worrying about the bill later? Cool.

Passing legislation through government? Not cool.

For teenage girls and young women to be cool, we need to be oversexed and promiscuous, while at the same time not being too "easy." For teenage boys and young men, coolness is about being as belligerently deviant as possible and aggressively demanding what they want. It is rare for the mainstream media to advertise young people as simply bright, conscientious, and creatively empowered inheritors of the Earth, as we have the potential to be.

Who's creating these identities, which in turn create America? The major media syndicates are now consolidated, funding the content that so often appeals to our baseline drives for sex, money, and power. If it bleeds, it leads. Violence sells. These media overlords know everything about us. Our Facebook data is being filtered. Our personal information is given to transnational corporate companies so they can market more crap in our direction—the guns and gold and the girls; the cars and the clothes. They're all trying to tell us what reality is and we've got to learn to filter these inputs. So often, these manufactured stereotypes teach us to have a negative self-image.

We're an insecure species, and we need validation, constantly. And now social media has created what people in Silicon Valley call "the attention economy." But what are we getting attention for? With few decent role models and many toxic ones, it can be a challenge for many of us to think about the kind of person we'd like to become. And so for some of us, the only way out is to challenge everything.

CREATING SUBCULTURES OF DEFIANCE

In the 1960s, a moral awakening erupted within the younger generation who were responding to the Vietnam war and the civil rights movement. People began to question all the conservative values they'd been taught. They began thinking critically about the notion of color. They started to care about the wars the US military was waging overseas, which was no longer a distant suffering happening far away in a third world when Americans were being drafted. They were bold enough to see the inequalities created by slavery, sexism, and the class structure for what they were. A spirit of love took over. The counterculture movement began. People experimented with altered states of consciousness and mystical intelligence, often through psychedelic substances.

Today, all the issues that surfaced in the 1960s are still present, with waves of crises exploding in other arenas. We're still revolting against war, sexism, and racism. Women, ethnic minorities, immigrants, and LGBTQ community members are still underrepresented in leadership roles.

By the time I was twenty-one, I wanted so far out of the mainstream lifestyle and value system I'd been force fed. I began to look for viable alternatives. My first social experiment was playing with the hippies, whom I found hanging out at a music festival one day. I thought, *This is the answer! Why didn't anyone tell me that I could be eccentric, make art, wear costumes, play music, and live in a tent forever? Why can't we all just share everything?*

There's a lot to learn from these transformational subcultures. Though they're largely whitewashed, there is merit to the arts of yoga, meditation, sound healing, dance, shamanism, and more that are being taught at these gatherings. However, my aspirations to live at music festivals and sell Bloody Marys, grilled cheese, and 5-HTP supplements to these free-spirited party animals were quickly dashed once I realized I would make a lousy hippie. I'm too productive to laze around all day. The peace, love (and disassociation) that those subcultures preached was surely aspirational, but at a certain point it stopped feeling authentic for me.

I needed people with whom I could express my darkness and existential turmoil. I needed a place to be a miserable, angsty millennial while also nurturing my blossoming inner light-being. The need to belong to a pack or a tribe where you can be yourself is a very human yearning. So, next, I tried hanging out in the anarchist/punk scene—a counterculture movement that was birthed in the 1980s. Punks are the hippies who got angry.

Jason Clark, thirty-two, is a professional chef who is also enrolled in nursing school. Jason is a former punk rock kid. He says he grew up in a dangerous, dysfunctional home, and so he naturally gravitated toward a community that violently stood against everything he thought was wicked and wrong about the world. Jason used to have black flames tattooed all the way up his arms and over fifteen piercings on his face. These tattoos and piercings identified him as part of a cohort; they also scared other people away so he wouldn't have to deal with his own fears of connection. Reassimilating himself into society as an adult, and soon a nurse, has required a lot of laser surgery.

"I really threw myself into the counterculture," he says. His adolescence was filled with all types of debauchery and overintel-lectualized temper tantrums. He received ninety-four write ups by the time he was in middle school and was expelled his fresh-man year of high school for placing a severed deer head on the school door.

"I was made to feel that there was something wrong with me because I didn't agree with my parents, my counselors, the cops, the teachers. I had to push the envelope. If having long hair pissed them off, I needed long green dreadlocks. If me stay-ing out all night pissed them off, then I had to be homeless. I'd rather be dead than alive on their terms. I delighted in my own self-destruction."

All of this is a bit extreme, though it takes intelligence and determination to stand against what everyone around you is telling you to think. The counterculture scenes that have been around for decades, as well as their current incarnations, are filled with people doing just that—and they proliferate some of the most exciting ideas happening in society.

Jason initially got into the punk rock scene as a way to find peers and a sense of affinity that he did not feel with the family he was born into and the culture at large. These were the same drives that compel young people to join gangs. It starts out inno-cent enough—we all want to feel like we're a part of something, and for those of us who are repeatedly failed by the authorities or the system, we often retreat to the counterculture, a place with different social norms where disaffected and creatively inspired youth can freely express themselves and declare their aim to live life in a different way.

There are reasons why we're congregating around alterna-tive political ideas, spirituality, and art. Millennials are having transcendental experiences at these gatherings and concerts. We get transported out of our rational minds by the magic of music and the almost religious experience of being immersed in it within the energy of a crowd. People are coming together to create alternative minisocieties for ourselves, where the goal is connection. We are attempting to party for a purpose. We want to explore ideas of collective love and social revolution.

But, so often, there's little revolution actually happening. It's more about consumerism. It's addiction. Bad things can go down when groups of people get together and decide to worship the same golden bean in an attempt to heal themselves. The same types of hierarchies emerge. People don't end up being who they portray themselves to be.

Because that subconscious mind is such a trickster. We can preach peace and love and unity all day, but if what we've always known is chaos, hate, and division, that's what we'll covertly recreate. If we aren't aware of the blind spots, the popular culture will find its way into the subculture.

VICE VS. VIRTUE

We're not done with Jason yet. Jason went as far down the rabbit hole of anarchy a person could possibly go, only to find himself, at the very end, wanting to be a part of the regular world after all. Now, he just wants to be normal.

Jason is a self-proclaimed shitty person, though he says he's improved over the years. He's gotten nicer. He's become more self-controlled. He's cleaned up his appearance. He refrains as best he can from acting out in chaos to relieve his internal stress because he believes it's easier to undo the impacts of inaction than wrong action.

Now that he's older, Jason realizes that all he ever wanted was love. This whole time, he had been rebelling against a loveless society and a loveless upbringing. He's had to realize this in order to make amends with the world so he can build a life for himself in it. At the end of it all, he still has a dream of finding love in his life.

Jason has found meaning in caring for others, which is why he enrolled in nursing school. It's the first time he's been back in school in over fifteen years. Academically, he's excelling, which is not surprising as he's always been hyper-intelligent. He just had to do things his way for awhile, the hard way, which led him to the best piece of advice he's ever heard: "You're an asshole, and all the stuff you blame others for is your fault."

"There is no one on this planet that can take responsibility for someone else," he says. "Get back on the horse. Just stop bitching. If I had approached life with that kind of discipline, then I would have been okay. I finally did. And the funny thing is, I feel better."

Is our contempt for the culture at large a sign of genius or stupidity? Jason doesn't view his years in the punk scene in total regret. There was a DIY ethos he found inspiring. He enjoyed the youthful rebellion, the sense of community people were building, the potlucks, the living room crowd surfing. He gets nostalgic for it, but his worldview has changed. What he sees now when he looks at the scene is an outlet for catharsis that didn't help him get to the root of his issues anyway. He has become too old to engage in it, though he hopes that future disaffected youth will continue to get their time pitting the graves of the oligarchs and stage-diving off cop cars.

There are people in the system who keep their heads down and live happy lives. Why then do some of us blame the system for our entire life experiences? I know I did. It was my personal traumas that first caused me to be at odds with the world.

Before he could accept himself as the creator of his own experience, Jason lived in blame mode.

"A lot of things I attributed my unhappiness to were external.

I always externalized my failures. It was my parents' fault that I had a shitty childhood. It was the school system's fault that I had a shitty experience. It was the town's fault for not being free-thinking enough. I always thought it was the universe's fault I was born at a time when there wasn't a more robust counterculture. If you asked me what my problem was, I would have told you: authority.

"It was all bullshit. There are people who have real issues that can't be fixed just by taking responsibility for them. People who lose limbs. People who are born into third-world problems. People born addicted to crack. There is a lot of fucked-up shit in this world, and I was just dead set on the fact that I was a victim. I don't know where that idea came from, but I latched onto it like a lifesaver. If you told me that's what I was doing, I would have cursed you out. It was a complete martyr complex. In my mind, my suffering was for a greater purpose. I'll be vegan. I'll only eat out of dumpsters. Take that, society."

Jason decided to put the bottle on the shelf. He gave up a life of crime, sleeping in gutters, and being different for the sake of being different in order to save himself. Initially, he thought the punk rock anarchist community was going to accomplish something politically, but he soon realized after years in the scene that nothing was going to happen. Moreover, how are a bunch of young people going to change the world if they can't even be good friends to one another?

Jason is what you might call a late bloomer. Rehabilitating himself has required high levels of self-awareness and mastery. He may not agree with what is going on in society, but he realizes he has to coexist with other people to survive. He remembers all the times nurses took care of him when he pushed himself to the point of near-death with his adrenaline-chasing antics. Today, he has decided to hang up his chef whites, put away his knives, and help others in the same way.

ACTIVISM IS A FULL-TIME JOB

Be uncomfortable now to live comfortably later. That's the prefrontal cortex talking. File your taxes now to avoid getting audited. Stand up to oppression today to avoid being swallowed by it in the future.

All this is sound logic. However, the only thing more exhausting than idly and self-righteously churning over injustice in your mind while numbing your misery with drugs and alcohol and pissing away your life alongside temporary, superficial compatriots is to organize and actually fight the hegemony. What millennials must do to create a hospitable planet is gut-wrenchingly terrifying to face and even more thankless to pursue.

And yet there are some of us who are giving up our lives to a different style of disobedience than the one Jason subscribed to—a civil kind. It's a widely used political tactic to partake in disruptive, socially negative behaviors in order to convey a positive, prosocial message.

Society likes to tell us that being an activist is just a hobby all good people need to participate in in their spare time. The truth is that, in order to make an impact, activists tend to be at it full-time, fighting for their lives. The average person barely has enough time to execute a downward facing dog and whip up a kale smoothie, let alone topple corporatism. There are, however, millennials who are making huge personal sacrifices to dedicate their lives—unpaid—to our most important causes.

Being a full-time activist requires sacrifices. You have to throw everything you've got into promoting very unsavory messages to the masses that the mainstream media often won't promote. Ignorance is the enemy, and pioneering a new world is an all-engulfing effort—especially when people are biased to view a new world as threatening.

It's 2014. Lee Stewart, twenty-six, is about to embark on the Great March for Climate Action, sponsored by 350.org.

He's planned to walk across the country for nine months, from California to Washington, DC, to bring awareness to global warming, perhaps the greatest social issue of a millennial's life. That year, climate change was already a familiar concept that many people insisted on sweeping under the rug. Four years later, today in 2018, it's becoming exponentially more dire. Icebergs are melting and breaking in the Arctic faster than scientists ever thought possible. Tropical storms and hurricanes are destroying islands and our coasts. The impact that our society is having on the fragile balance of the natural world is reaching a critical impasse.

Lee believes that if we want to mitigate the destruction that's forecasted, we've got to act now. We need to implement renewable energy and stop collectively profiting off the industries that are ravaging the earth. And if no one else would fight for this cause, he would. So Lee dropped out of graduate school at George Mason University to join the march.

"One of the reasons why I decided to come on this march was that I was able to. I don't have that much debt. I don't have any responsibilities yet; a lot of people do. They are trapped by these things. Even if they want to participate in movement building, they can't. I can. I'm leaving behind my master's degree."

Lee was studying education at George Mason, a career track he quickly found to be as confining as it was divisive. He was being trained to become part of what he identifies as "the problem," the problem being the industrialized system.

"Our education is factory-style, and it's becoming even more so," Lee says. "It's all about the economy, marketing, business, and so on. They ask us to get kids to work toward grades or some sort of success as defined by an institution as opposed to giving them the tools to find their own solutions."

It's not that material wealth equates to spiritual bankruptcy. What Lee is trying to say is that we're not meant to be mass-produced people. We're not meant to give our lives to someone else's paradigm. We're here to evolve it.

"Every person is unique," Lee says, "and they come from a different set of circumstances and a different perspective. Once you get into the school system, the teachers are not looking to the students for guidance on how to educate them. They are looking at a state-mandated curriculum that is operating in the interest of commercial society. They are trying to craft people who will make money and consume. You know, buying a house, all of that. It's designed to fit an industrial economy—a commercial society, very materialistic, growth- and money-focused."

He didn't want to be part of the problem so he left school—and now he's living with about sixty other marchers as they set up camp in cities across the country, marching across the highways of America holding signs. He's a part of his own counterculture, a community of people from all walks of life, and not just young ones. The impact of this all-encompassing demonstration at this time is unknown. Will it be worth the sacrifice?

By the end of a grueling nine months of walking across the country, the Great March for Climate Action received almost zero media coverage. There were no policies passed as a result of Lee's actions. This is a results-oriented society, but to be an activist and stay sane, you cannot expect the same. Hopelessness and despair are what activists eat for breakfast. Still, one of the reasons many activists do what they do knowing what they know is because swimming upstream feels like the right thing to do in the face of injustice—a spiritual feeling of transcendence is generated when you act in alignment with what you profess. Even if there are rarely worldly benefits to being an activist, there are existential rewards.

By the end of the march, Lee says his commitment to activism has only strengthened. It's remarkable. I'd see him again about a year later outside the Federal Energy Regulatory Commission in Washington, DC, at a protest against fracking, calling out the leaders of government agencies by name who are taking the money of oil lobbyists and corporations and refusing to implement renewable energy solutions into our infrastructures.

Lee says he has no plans of going back to school. He wants to stay on the frontlines of struggle to protect our earth and our people. He's finally satisfied with his life of rabble-rousing and pricking the consciences of those who are actively thwarting progress for humanity.

Because something has to change. The question is whether this change can be birthed from within this current system—or if our system will have to be destroyed for something better to emerge in its place.

CREATING AN INCLUSIVE CULTURE

The problem with countercultures, I've decided, is that they're ultimately conformist. I've loved my time partying my face off within them, but I've come to a conclusion they are not the only answer to our larger social issues.

I always dreamed about what would happen if the punks and the hippies and b-boys and b-girls and comic-con fans got together and had a giant celebration. It would be the best party ever; I have no doubts.

What I do doubt, however, is if people in these groups can get together to do more than that (though I'd love to be disproved). I've decided that it's truly up to individuals to wake up their consciousness (though having community in the process helps).

No matter what counterculture reigns supreme, I do know that one thing is for certain: alternative ideas are here to stay, and they can be adopted by the mainstream when, one by one, we put our energies toward solutions and rebel against that which is outdated and destructive. Don't rebel for rebellion's sake or the sake of being different; that's false individuation. Instead, resist the harmful notions culture has planted in our minds about who we are and what's possible.

So maybe it's not about a counterculture or the polarization of philosophies; it's not about fitting into a tribe where everyone is alike. It's about discovering our uniqueness. It's about getting our minds right so we can make space for differences and create a system that works in favor of what all humans have in common.

The pagan neo-hippies call it a "new paradigm"; the punks call it "not being an asshole." The question is: Can we manifest it instead of just speculating about it? Can we act in integrity when it seems like the rest are not?

Chapter 11

The Technological Revolution

I'VE HAD MANY DEBATES ABOUT WHETHER STEREOTYPING generations is productive. I've come to the conclusion that although the qualifiers so often used to describe millennials are not applicable in all cases all of the time, there are distinct patterns of a group that are a product of the particular evolutionary period and social environment and worth studying.

For millennials, the most important environmental factor contributing to our unique ethos is that we've grown up during the transition from analog to digital technology. Humans are more powerful than ever because of the design of our devices, and our minds and society have been fundamentally altered by the tech explosion.

Technology is transitioning us into a networked, globalized society. We can communicate with anyone in the world using a computer. Millennials connect with more people in one day than any other generation because of inventions like social media, dating websites, and text messaging—it's all part of our pursuit for love and connection (though, it's up for debate whether these gadgets are helping our relationships or if they are making them more shallow, opportunistic, and disposable).

We're living in the new nuclear age, and we have the technological power to both live and die en masse. In this time of infinite technological potential, we also carry heavier responsibilities. With each technological invention comes a cost. Now that we have the Internet and cell phones, our identities are catalogued, our phone messages are stored in government databases, and we have computers in our glasses. We can mourn the loss of our cassette tapes and Atari video games, but we can't go backward. Technology is either going to speed up our evolution and problem-solving or it's going to be make humanity obsolete. Whatever it is, it is here to stay. And we have to learn to harness our inventions in a good way.

THE ROBOTS TAKE OVER

I once had a vision in the middle of one of my mental doom spirals about the future of humanity. It was a dystopian scenario where humans had become brains stored in glass jars that were attached through wires into a virtual reality where we lived our lives as online avatars. The need for a body had ceased to exist. Tanks roamed the streets as our governments imposed martial law on the people, monitoring all of our activities, turning us into terrorists of one another.

Technology has allowed humans to become the dominant species on the planet, allowing certain factions of the human population to take control over other cultures. The places it could take us is terrifying, but it's also one of our greatest hopes for a global renaissance. Technology is the vehicle that can actualize our interconnected potential into a tangible reality. Technology will divide us or unite us.

Let's take automation, for example. Routine, lower-level jobs are now being performed by computers: self-checkouts at the store, automated customer service phone transactions, filing your taxes online instead of with an accountant. Google is making cars that drive themselves. House construction and cooking is forecasted to one day be done by robots. Part of this advancement is great—who wants to do the heavy lifting and perform mindless iterative tasks anyway? Humans have the capacity to do far more than back-breaking manual labor and scanning your groceries.

The drawbacks of this progress are that real people who've spent upwards of hundreds of thousands of dollars getting trained in professions that are getting automated will lose their jobs; they'll have to be reeducated to equip themselves with new skills to offer society. We're already experiencing a shortage of good jobs. Technology is transforming everything so rapidly that we can't predict the future of our economy. Everyone will have to learn adapt as we go. Perhaps, a few of us will use this opportunity to create our own jobs that realize our potential in more inspiring ways based around our true passions. If this happens, then human capital, regardless of automation, could flourish.

Something is being lost with all this fast-paced progress. We used to be creatures that lived in unison with the earth, animals who knew how to thrive and survive with the rhythms of nature. Now we're creatures of the computer, manipulating our environments to serve our own socially constructed value systems that often conflict with natural law. In manmade culture, productivity and efficiency rules. Humans are using their brains to construct brains made out of machines that may one day outperform their creators.

Artificial intelligence has created machines that think, act, and behave like humans. Scientists are teaching computers facial and pattern recognition. We've got sex robots that can go through the motions of love-making just as empathically as a real human—they can syncopate with your heartbeat and know when you're about to orgasm. We are teaching computers how to act with common sense, detect meaning and affect in words, and research and monitor outcomes in scientific studies. Computers can now do things that even humans can't.

The emerging field of AI is causing us to question what is human and what is a computer. We have yet to see where this will take us. But we always have to remember that machines have glitches—just like the humans who made them.

IDENTITY IN THE INFORMATION AGE

Our lives are fueled by information in this networked society. Data has become a form of currency. Millennials have these things called apps that have grown to govern many of our everyday decisions—from where we eat to how we invest; from what music we listen to to the roads we take while driving.

The information age is run by Big Data. For some reason, we're obsessed with trying to control the future. Even heart-centered pursuits with charity or nonprofit organizations are driven by left-brained analytics. If I angle my smile 45 degrees to the left, I'll get X amount more social media likes, which will better position me to receive funding from this rich person. We've got everything measured. We use big data in a race to obtain resources.

So, where does all this data go? Our every action—words, images, video and audio files—are stored online in this thing called a cloud, which is basically like an external hard drive that exists in the ether. The amount of information the cloud can hold is limitless. The interconnected networks of computers know *everything* about you.

Big data has caused the entire notion of privacy to become a national debate. Some people say: just surrender it. Privacy is gone. The NSA is tapping our phone lines. Instead, use your openness online to create an audience for your every move. Create a persona and capitalize on that shit. Others believe that keeping aspects of our personal lives private is a human right that should not be violated by any government or business. Openness makes us vulnerable in ways we don't have to be. And yet it is this very openness online that creates an interconnected humanity.

All this is happening because of an invention known as the Internet. As soon as computers were invented in the 1950s, people started to have ideas about creating networks where data could be shared. The Internet has become a fourth dimension of sorts in our three-dimensional world, an open-sourced, collaborative virtual system filled with information provided by billions of everyday citizens. It took what the telephone, radio, and telegraph did to help people in different locations communicate with one another, and it exploded our capacity for connection. The Internet is now such an integral part of everyday life that we become noticeably distressed without it. We compulsively check our iPhones. When you're used to busyness and constant stimulation, finding peace in deafening silence and idle moments becomes a challenge.

It's indeed a great blessing that everything you could possibly want to know about any topic in the world is available online. Millennials can start their own businesses, become online personalities, and tweet their every thought. The Internet is a worldwide collective brain full of scientific research, multimedia content, and citizen journalism, where you can shop for anything that exists. And yet, it is a double-edged sword: all of the information that you volunteer about yourself can be taken and used against you in an instant.

EVERYTHING THAT CAN BE HACKED WILL BE

Evan Saez knows why there's a virus on my computer. I met the nineteen-year-old computer hacker when he walked up to me on the corner of 1st Street and 1st Avenue in the East Village of New York City. I was surprised when he told me he already had a job at a giant corporation. Actually, Evan has more than one job. He has two, or three, if you include his status as a full-time student at St. John's University where he studies computer system securities. People with his level of computer expertise are in high demand. Because of his skill set, Evan now earns more income than almost 50 percent of Americans, and he's still in his teens.

The week I interviewed Evan, my computer came down with a little somethin' nasty. Porn ads were popping up on my Facebook showing yellow smiley faces superimposed on pictures of women with bubbly booties, bent over backwards. It turns out that people contract online viruses similar to how they catch them in real life—through exposure to other infected systems.

Evan agrees to help me fix the bug on my laptop as we sit together at a coffee shop. "This is actually not a virus," he tells me. "It's malware. Professional criminals go through extreme lengths to make sure malware cannot be removed."

The diagnosis is in. A Zeus Trojan has found its way into my laptop. Evan advises me to check my bank account, because if I've shared any credit card information online, this kind of bug can lift the data. He talks me through what he's doing to my computer with the bedside manner of a doctor who makes house calls.

"One of my teachers once told me that if your passwords aren't at least fourteen characters long, you're delusional," Evan says.

One of Evan's jobs is to search for cyber cons. Evan is what you would consider a "good" hacker—he hacks to fight crime. He explains to me that the word "hack" simply means that a computer system has been manipulated in a way it was not originally intended to be. Evan works to scam the scam artists.

"To succeed with a scam requires 80 percent human manipulation, 10 percent technical skills, 5 percent access to technology, and 5 percent luck," he says as he sips ice coffee through a straw. He's eager to talk about the craziness of his work, but he does so slyly, with a wandering eye that scans the room to survey who might hear him.

"The amount of people able to catch criminal hackers is dwarfed by the number of cons," he says. "If someone asked for my social security number online, I'd probably disconnect from the Internet and burn my computer."

Evan views the internet as a positive externality of capitalist innovation. One negative aspect is the amount of energy waste it produces, and the fact that our government—the NSA in particular—can subpoena all the information we input to prosecute everyday citizens without warrant. Whistleblowers like Michael Hastings and Edward Snowden were declared enemies of the state for leaking this reality.

And then there's the deep web, also known as the dark web. Some of the ugliest stuff humanity is capable of can be found here. It's the place where slaves, cocaine, AK-47s, and children are sold on the Silk Road, an online black market. In many ways, the deep web mirrors the shadowy side of humanity—the ways we violently profit off pain and addiction, lust, and the vulnerabilities of others. It is a virtual marketplace for sin, and it comprises most of the internet. The people who provide its content are anonymous. You can hire a hitman on the deep web or buy rob-to-order software. Evan explains to me that the Internet is like an onion. You can go deeper and deeper into it, peeling off the layers, only to find yourself in a dark hole of nothingness.

Now he's going show me how to do a gag hack, by phone fishing someone for their credit card information. To catch criminals, he has to know how they work. He pulls out his cell phone and presses *67 to block his number.

"Normally, a hacker would do this from a prepaid phone," Evan says. "This is reckless of me."

He's developed a special virus for this demonstration: he's made a fake Gmail account, from where he'll send an online form with a bank update labeled with a generic icon and a made-up 1-800 number, signed by the moniker James Holmes. Evan doesn't connect to public portals. He has "brought his own Internet" that he accesses from his smartphone. He has a software on his computer that masks his activity, so no one can see him logging onto a network. He opens a program called Gain, a password cracker he says the average person could learn to use in an hour after watching YouTube videos.

"Nothing is ever secure," he says.

Evan can now log onto the desktop of every single person connected to the public Wi-Fi in this coffee shop. I watch him infiltrate the computer of the man sitting next to us. His desktop screen shows up on Evan's monitor. He can now watch this person enter his credit card information to buy a Ninja blender on Amazon and copy it down. He can search through his documents. He can shut down his antivirus software, run a downloader, and give his computer malware—the same malware that's on my computer.

The Internet is a very interesting place.

THE ATTENTION ECONOMY

Of any invention that has shaped the lives of millennials, social media is perhaps the most predominant. When Mark Zuckerberg launched Facebook for college students back in 2004, it was just a fun way to meet new people at school, serving as a virtual yearbook. Who knew that it would become such an essential part of the average person's daily lifestyle?

When Facebook took off, it spread like wildfire. By 2016, the number of Facebook users reached 1.86 billion. Research by the International Data Corporation shows that the average smartphone user checks Facebook 13.8 times a day. Then there's also Twitter and Pinterest and Instagram—and Snapchat! Dopamine is released into our bodies with every like, comment, and message we receive. Nothing eases the banality of life like some validation from our peers. Social media has changed our values and the way we communicate.

Beyond ego gratification, Facebook and other social media platforms can also mobilize us. It's going to take a mob to fight the power, and these platforms have provided us with the means to rally together. With social media, every citizen can be a journalist. The positive work we're doing to make this world a more loving place can be broadcast and noticed. We all have a little brand of self that we can promote responsibly online to connect with others. We can create followers and an audience to listen and watch as we post about what's good and what's serious. We can shine hard—and document it.

So let's get back to democracy, social unrest, and Twitter. The Arab Spring of 2010, a popular uprising demanding more democratic systems from established regimes in the Middle East and North Africa, was also called the Twitter Revolution. Uncensored political information and photos were tweeted by users until they went viral. A surge of emotional reactions built up every day as violence against protestors spread. Pictures documenting these crimes inspired more users to organize protests and overthrow powerful elites. Because of this digitally enabled revolution, Tunisia has since successfully transitioned to a constitutional democracy. This is the power of social media.

If you need more convincing on the influence of social media, look no further than Donald Trump's Twitter page. Trump tweets every politically incorrect thought possible that would be better kept to himself—but it helped him win the 2016 US presidential election (not to mention the Russian-sponsored Facebook ads). Social media is where people are getting their news and how they are keeping themselves informed. Trump's supporters eat up his uncensored rhetoric. People share his tweets, whether they firmly support him or vehemently disagree. He is likely the most talked about person on the planet today, not because he leads with competence, but because he tweets, belligerently.

Social media can allow us to control what hits other people's brainwaves. It enables us to be the gatekeepers of news, even if we are spreading misinformation. Not all news sources are created equal, and there aren't too many fact checkers on the Internet. This powerful tool at our disposal can help us present our best face to the rest of the world and engage in a never-ending popularity contest. But if you become obsessed with it, social media can make you want to slit your wrists. It can either be a platform for celebrating the self or a black hole that sucks you into a pit of self-loathing and neurotic social comparison.

Millennials have been called the "ME ME ME" generation because social media has provided us with an outlet to express both our sacred thoughts and gifts as well as our self-obsessions. This fixation on impression management can consume a person. We anoint ourselves on the throne of virtual society; we use it to get famous and make money. There is an enormous pressure on young people to build an audience and market their image, and no amount of likes is ever enough.

Maybe all these vanity shots are just a distraction. Posting articles with angry sentiments about what's going on in the world might not change much, except give people the right to speak their opinions. But we have to start somewhere. It's taken me years of work to cultivate a healthy relationship with social media—to have fun with it, to use it as a way to celebrate myself, and to share media I find compelling and intelligent.

NATURE VS. TECHNOLOGY

I once thought that going off-grid was the answer to the horrors humans have created. That the best way to handle a world that has become so complex and out of control is to avoid it. I may not be participating in providing a solution by doing this, but at least, by living off-the-grid, I'm not hurting the planet in the same ways everyone else does—by driving in traffic, running my generator, and eating a bunch of food imported from other countries. Off-grid, my footprint is close to invisible. I'm practicing the art of doing no harm. The dirt will clean us all.

Caleb Bourg, twenty-four, works as a clam and oyster farmer in the marshlands of South Carolina. Caleb has an interesting passion—this young man loves trash. He loves finding old things and repurposing them—and he's certainly in the right space to do this. He's fixing up a house that's been abandoned for decades.

When he moved in, there was no running water. The house was infested with bugs and mice droppings. The other people on the island were using the front yard to store their junk. The windows were all smashed from a hurricane back in the 1980s. Neighborhood kids were growing pot inside the house. Caleb and his girlfriend's goal is to transform the property into a permaculture homestead. They are attempting to opt-out of the matrix and choosing the lives of a naturalist. They are experimenting to see if living away from technology and the economy is actually sustainable.

I've learned that leading the life of a naturalist is not an easier path per se. I spent so long glorifying it, and I learned after about a month of sleeping in a tent that perhaps I'd like some walls to make it through the winter. Technology, if nothing else, has provided humans with a way to survive in the wild. It has made our lives more comfortable. However, none of man's inventions can replace the wisdom we can learn from nature. Nature is a panacea and the master teacher.

It may seem like technology and nature are antitheses of one another because technology has made it possible for us to subdue nature. We've created tools to protect ourselves from and eliminate almost every natural predator. We've got central heating and air conditioning and can live at a consistent, hospitable temperature—73 degrees all day and night. Technology has allowed us to cultivate any food during any season. It's allowed us to travel across the world, to trade goods and services from our homes, and to have drones drop off Amazon purchases at our doorsteps.

Our current disconnect from nature is at the root of our sustainability issues. It all started with the philosophy that nature needed to be dominated. It makes sense that the colonists believed the wildness of the raw land was a threat to their survival—it was. Humans imposed their will onto nature so they could survive and flourish, creating tools to help them. But now, we are trapped in a society that revolves around these technologies that are rapidly endangering the world.

Partially because of the technocracy, the average person has no idea what goes into these computers, cell phones, and cars, items we think we can no longer survive without in contemporary society. We don't know about the electromagnetic frequencies produced; the impact of mining, manufacturing, and deforestation; and the volatile chemicals that are comingling in our air and water supplies as a result of these technologies. If we knew and viscerally felt these negative consequences, would we continue living the way we do?

Unfortunately, the answer seems to be yes, because we are dependent on these tools. Because of the Internet (ironically), all the information we need to inform ourselves is already out there, and anyone can educate themselves about the cause and effect of technology on the natural world if they go digging. We know the harm we do, and still, we do. Some of us view the destruction of nature as a necessary loss that cannot be avoided if we are to personally survive in an economic sense. The old paradigm says that for every win, there has to be a loss. And the winner in the old paradigm is man at the expense of everything else.

Most of us have learned to accept the way the system works. To resist is to struggle, and to struggle saps our energy and time, things people don't seem to have in excess. We are hooked into our machines of convenience. Without a car, we can't get a job. Without a cell phone, we can't keep friends.

Millennials have witnessed an industrialized society become a techno-industrialized society. The amount of technology and its capabilities are increasing exponentially as more of our natural world is plundered. Our savvy ingenuity and the constant drive to improve our surroundings has unfortunately become a slow form of suicide. But it doesn't have to stay this way.

COMBINING NATURAL WISDOM WITH TECHNOLOGY

Humans have been living our lives as if nature is the problem rather than our teacher. John Locke, Thomas Hobbes, and Jacques Rosseau—the social philosophers who created our current social system—questioned if nature is moral and if the human mind and logic can better determine what's right and wrong. Ultimately, they determined that the human ego knew better than natural intelligence, so they embarked on a crusade against the world that has led us into the situation we are now trying to get out of.

Luckily, we can use the very same technology to help us model our systems after nature. Look at the field of biomimicry, which operates under the assumption that nature is the most sustainable engineer around. If we emulate it in our own manmade processes, it will work for every living thing in the long term.

In Taos, New Mexico, some millennials are finding a middle ground between living off-the-grid and enjoying modern comforts. By investing in and developing technology that uses nature as a guide, they are learning to make a human life with less impact. Those who have peeked behind the veil—who care about climate change and biodiversity and investing in renewable resources—can no longer march alongside everyone else living a mainstream lifestyle. But it doesn't mean they want to live in a tent without a job or a cell phone, either.

Elizabeth Wolfe, thirty-one, is the manager of the Earthship Biotecture Visitors Center, where Briz, from chapter three, works. Earthships are "radically sustainable" buildings that fit within building codes. These houses, which look like spaceships, are made with earthen clay, old tires, and salvaged glass bottles, and they are equipped with solar panels, rain catchment systems, and more. The septic/sewage system is funneled into indoor food growing stations where the waste feeds the soil. An Earthship is an example of a whole-system design that repurposes waste instead of creating more of it—just like nature.

There were only a few moments on the road trip I took across America to interview people for this book when I felt the sky open and a surge of positive energy take over my body. I'm talking about the experience of true hope lighting a path to a different world that we not only envision but also see, taste, and smell—one we can build. Visiting the Earthships Center was one of those moments. I saw us coming together as a generation to create a new earth and redesign the way we live alongside others.

"Whether global warming is real or not isn't the issue," Elizabeth says when I ask for her opinion on climate change. "The point is that my lifestyle isn't causing any harm. Capitalism, communism, and socialism were all based on the assumption that we have unlimited resources. We're running out of coal and fossil fuels, and that's a fact. We know there's going to be no more at some point. Why don't we prepare ourselves and society for that switch? I'm happier living this way."

Elizabeth is not angry at the Man. She's not abandoning the system entirely or raging against the machine. She is simply choosing to live her domesticated life in a mindful way, using new, sustainable technologies. And in doing so, she is working to save what she loves. Preservation is her form of activism.

SACRED INNOVATION

Cliff DeBenedetto, thirty-two, calls himself a community developer. He travels the world living in permaculture communities funded by his internet business Solidworks Zen. Before he started the digital nomad lifestyle, he kept getting fired from his engineering jobs. Cliff had always wanted to be an inventor, and he says he was bored running someone else's business. Today, he runs his own, and his new goal is to invent the 3-D printing of organic material.

"Right now, 3-D printers are printing things made of plastic and metal," Cliff says. "I dream of making a 3-D printer that makes compostable products. I have a vision to 3-D print molecules."

His ideas may seem pie-in-the-sky, but the truth is there's no telling where this technology could go. We can already print 3-D print pizzas. Cliff thinks the future of 3-D printing will have people downloading programs as intellectual property that are available open source from a computer—and printing them at home. There will be no more shipping, no more strip malls. The entire world of industry will change. Manufacturing jobs will become obsolete. Income inequality will be eradicated. Everyone will have the right and access to property.

In the push and pull of evolution, the invention of one machine can cause a ripple effect that will cause all other inventions to become extinct. A single invention could eradicate all the problems that plague humanity and paralyze millennials in their existential crisis. There are mushrooms that eat plastic in the oceans and water filters that make ocean water drinkable. We just have to make these inventions legal. We have to incorporate them into our lives in an affordable way. And whatever technology millennials harness has to be used with mindfulness—for peace. We must remember that there will always be unintended consequences to whatever we bring into this reality.

"Imagine if you had a 3-D printer where you could print cocaine," Cliff says. "Right now, if you had a 3-D printer, you could print a gun. Imagine how threatening that could be if people misuse it. All of this could give everyone the craziest power on earth, the power of alchemy."

With great power comes great responsibility. That's why technological transformation and advancement is going to have occur alongside our own spiritual and emotional development. They are equally as important to each other.

"I really feel like I'm in the right place in the right time," Cliff says. He's not burdened by the problems of society. Instead, he's energized by the potential for solutions and what he can do to turn the tide. "I'm pretty pumped to be alive."

Chapter 12

The Environment Will Save Us

I F ALL SOCIAL JUSTICE ISSUES ARE TRULY INTERCONNECTED, then our relationship with the natural world resides at the core of any movement to restore balance to this each other and this planet.

I tried to interview a millennial plant for this chapter, one born between the years of 1980 to 2000, but I couldn't. Because it was a plant. D'oh! I tried in vain to use my psychic powers to ask the tree next to me what it felt about the US backing out of the Paris Climate Agreement, but it had no words.

Since the tree had no words, it definitely had no rights. No voice, no choice.

Once, I ran over a shrub while backing up my car in the middle of the road. I wasn't charged with plant-slaughter; however, I said a few apologies in passing because I realized I had just used speciesism to my advantage.

I'm a human, a careless asshole driving a two-thousand-pound piece of machinery that can demolish much in its path. That shrub will never be quite the same again because of my carelessness, and I got to drive away without any accountability.

But I believe that plant felt something. According to Daniel Chernovitz in his book *What a Plant Knows*, plants can recognize when they've been damaged. They just don't attach a bunch of judgments to it or call it suffering or need to talk about it with their psychologist for a year. Science is dispelling a lot of assumptions we've once had about what constitutes intelligent life here on Earth; and it's not just human.

I am learning to sympathize with all living things that don't speak the same language as me. Because if I pay attention, I can notice what I do that makes them grow and thrive and what I do that makes them wither and die. I can mind my impact. It's part of my responsibility to practice what people call a *biocentric system of ethics*.

THE INTRICATE CHAIN OF CAUSE AND EFFECT

One thing that makes humans different from any other species is our ability to significantly alter the environment using our highly advanced minds. For every cause there is an effect (at least when time is part of the equation and matter is vibrating below the speed of light).

The environmental problems humanity faces all began with agriculture. Yes, the many millennials who wish to get back to farming the land, like Tony Dee in chapter two, may believe that working on an organic farm is the best way to be a steward of the dying Earth—and in some ways this is correct. If every person grew their own food in their backyard on a rooftop garden, we would have no need for large-scale industrialized agriculture. Industrialized agriculture is one of the leading forces damaging our environment through the widespread use of pesticides and planting practices that overutilize subsidized crops like soy and corn, creating monocultures that strip the soil of its microbial content. Think Monsanto and their infamous pesticide product

Roundup, which includes a cocktail of chemicals so toxic that they have the power to kill human cells. It is sprayed all over the world.

Deforestation is also taking place across the planet to clear land to raise cattle and other livestock that require massive amounts of water and grain—so we can have our steak. It is important to keep trees, which absorb carbon dioxide in the atmosphere and convert it into oxygen, alive (especially since one of our biggest problems is an excess of carbon dioxide in our atmosphere). Industrialized agriculture is also an industry that's powered by fossil fuels, which are polluting the earth beyond measure.

It seems counterintuitive, but industrial agriculture creates food insecurities and shortages in the long term. We want tomatoes in the winter and avocados year round. We import and export goods from across the planet to meet the whims and fancies of culinary trends. All this takes a huge toll on the environment. Buying local and seasonal food is one alternative that has emerged as a solution the consumer can take part in—as well as eating less meat, in particular, beef.

What about waste? Our planet is trashed. According to the Environmental Protection Agency, the average American creates 4.4 pounds of trash a day. We're starting to recycle and compost a lot more, but there are still dumps overflowing with waste. We've got an ocean filled with plastic—an estimated 315 billion pounds of it. We wrap perishable goods in plastic, a synthetic compound that can be transformed into different shapes through recycling but that never naturally decomposes.

Despite our environmental woes, it seems the human population is thriving, at least in terms of numbers. Humans have become an invasive species that causes plants and animals to be endangered or go extinct. As the number of humans on the planet rises, biodiversity dwindles. Studies by Stanford biologist

Paul Ehrlich reveal that the planet hasn't seen this amount of species loss since the dinosaurs went extinct 66 million years ago. We are in the midst of an extinction period.

This die-off is also influenced by the constant development and perceived panacea of unlimited growth of our industrialized society. It's all our clever enterprising that is causing the depletion of the natural world, and it's going to take some clever enterprising to get us out. Estimations state that half of all plants, animals, and birds on the planet may die off before the year 2100 if we don't change our ways, according to a study published in *BioScience*. Most humans don't notice the impact of losing the Rabb's fringe-limbed tree frog, but the truth is we need biodiversity. There are keystone species that our survival is dependent on, such as bees, nature's pollinators, that will drastically alter our food production capacity if they go extinct.

As for our water, government-controlled tap water is filled with lead and copper, arsenic, germs, and tons of disinfectant byproducts. Levels of acid in the world's oceans are rising, which is killing coral reefs and marine life because these underwater changes are happening so quickly that ocean organisms don't have time to adapt. There is also the absence of water—droughts are occurring across the planet.

Finally, people in third world countries are watching their environments change due to the actions of the industrialized, developed world. Because of our excess of consumption and our insatiable need for the newest thing, the poorest and most vulnerable people will feel the effects of climate change the most.

WHEN THE SCIENCE SPEAKS, LISTEN

The earth is crying out louder and louder for us to alter our ways so we can continue this relationship with her, but on different terms. We can feel the temperatures changing and measure the sea levels rising. We see the earthquakes, the tsunamis, the forest fires. We've had a decade's worth of warning, and the economic costs of these environmental catastrophes are going to cost millennials billions of dollars that we don't have to repair. We can't simply support another GoFundMe campaign when entire communities are being blasted by wildfires, and especially since we can't afford health care to begin with.

A huge part of all of this has to do with fossil fuels. We started burning coal during the Industrial Revolution. Then we drilled into the Earth and found oil—petroleum, which could power cars and light candles. So we ran with it. In 1965, the world consumed 3.8 billion tons of oil; in 2007, our reliance on it has increased exponentially to a consumption of 11.1 billion tons.

Everything in our current economy revolves around fossil fuels. The majority of the stock market is invested in it, companies power their initiatives through oil, and even the value of the US dollar revolves around it.

Here's a bit of a history lesson. When Richard Nixon became president in the mid 1970s, he made an arrangement with Saudi Arabia to sell oil around the world in US dollars, in exchange for a military presence in the country to protect oil fields and US weapons. Gold was no longer the reference point for the value of our currency, as it had been until the Bretton Woods Agreement collapsed. Nixon then convinced the members of OPEC to also trade oil in US dollars as a way to stimulate the US economy and help make the US dollar the world's reserve currency. This contract became known as the petrodollar system.

If there's a conspiracy at play here that's keeping us from moving forward in the environmentalism movement, I believe that it starts and ends with oil. Currency is essentially energy, and right now the fossil fuel energy that powers the world revolves around US currency. And this wouldn't be a problem if oil didn't happen to be a nonrenewable, highly polluting resource that exists in a finite supply. And the constant burning of fossil fuels to power our society is releasing so much carbon dioxide into the atmosphere that it has created a phenomenon known as *climate change* or *global warming.*

According to climate scientists, a healthy amount of carbon dioxide in the Earth's atmosphere should not exceed 350 particles per million. Before the industrial revolution, there were an estimated 280 particles per million of carbon dioxide in the atmosphere; in 2017, there were over 400 particles, according to the environmental organization 350.org. Created by climate scientist Bill McKibben to raise awareness about carbon dioxide and how it contributes to climate change, the organization is named after the goal they hope to achieve.

It's a clever marketing tactic, but ultimately it's not the number of particles of carbon dioxide in our atmosphere that's going to emotionally compel people to take action; it's going to be the stories of how human lives will be affected and the devastation that will be caused. Empathy can compel us to employ our logic to do the right thing if we wish to continue prospering on the planet. We can change our system to address the reality of climate change in a way that will help average people to lead happier, more sustainable lives every day.

Ever increasing levels of carbon dioxide in our atmosphere affect everything. The ice in the Arctic is melting, causing sea levels to rise, which means coastal cities like Charleston and New York could go underwater. Wacky weather is going to be the norm. Monsoons and hurricanes will batter certain areas, while droughts will plague others. Meanwhile, animals will migrate to other ecosystems where they can survive, upsetting the delicate ecosystem and causing other species to perish.

We're going to see a similar imbalance in our human ecosystem as well. As certain terrains are rendered uninhabitable due to damages to the infrastructure caused by natural disasters—for example, Puerto Rico's loss of power in the aftermath of Hurricane Maria in 2017—humans are going to have to migrate to other locations. Refugees will flood already crowded cities that don't have the resources to support them.

We may temporarily enjoy the warmer (or colder) weather, but when food and water shortages transpire and farmers can't grow crops and wildfires spread and tropical storms wipe out cities and millions of people are displaced from their homes, our great reckoning will come. And it will come in the lifetime of the millennials if we don't act now.

IT'S ALL ABOUT POWER

There will be enormous profit losses if we divest from fossil fuels. Almost every industry, from construction to food and education, is invested in them, as well as every person who's spent decades accumulating wealth for their retirement through Roth IRAs and index funds. The captains of industry that rely on fossil fuels, many highly intelligent and powerful people, have a vested interest in continuing to profit off their industries staying the same, even if it negatively impacts everyone else in the long term. It's a risky experiment to try something new when there is financial security in a system that has "worked" for so long. We would have to revitalize and reorganize all of our systems, and few of us seem to be willing to risk our immediate safety net.

If there is an Achilles heel in humanity, it's our lack of foresight and our loyalty to old habits. By 2030, the Climate Vulnerability Monitor projects that damages caused by climate change will amount to seven hundred billion dollars annually. It's not necessarily cheaper for us to keep doing what we're doing in the long run. But the problem is that it's currently more expensive to invest in new, renewable biotechnologies because of issues of scalability. Here's the catch: the only thing that's going to reduce the prices of these technologies so they're affordable is an increased demand. Once we start hopping on the bandwagon, they'll become more affordable for everybody.

Ana Maria Quintero, twenty-seven, is a policy associate in Washington, DC, who works for the Nature Conservancy, an international conservation NGO that lobbies with the government to take into account the impact of a policy on natural habitats. Ana Maria fights for preservation, working specifically with hydropower, a form of renewable energy that she says isn't 100 percent "clean" but that is a lot better than oil and coal.

Ana Maria is working to implement renewable energy solutions across the planet. She says it's much easier for developing countries with weaker systems of governance to start transitioning to the various types of renewable power: wind, solar, geothermal, and hydropower. The more developed a country's economy and government is, the more bureaucratic red tape she faces. People on the inside of the government who are likely personally invested in petroleum products also have to be convinced that there's a better and safer way to power our planet, though it goes against their vested interests. She's got to find a way to meet eye-to-eye with these people in power and inspire them to try a different way.

There's not one kind of renewable energy source that fits all. Different situations require different action, and they take time to properly gauge. Ana Maria says the best practice is to survey a landscape before deciding how to power it. During a dry season, power a city off solar energy. During the wet season, fuel it with hydropower. The goal is to benefit people and nature at the same time by using the most appropriate energy source and as little of it as possible. Don't build five hydropower dams when one will suffice. The goal is symbiosis—letting our environment teach us what it needs and synchronizing it with what we need so we can support each other's goal of staying alive and thriving.

European countries are spearheading renewable energy movements, meeting their goals to reduce carbon emissions. Developing countries are growing their economies while learning from their neighbors about how to do it in a low carbon way. However, under the current Trump administration, the US is halting progress. Even under Obama, weaning ourselves off fossil fuels happened much slower than it could have if he had followed through on his campaign promises to truly prioritize environmental protection.

I believe that more wasn't done to make the US carbon-neutral and introduce renewable energies into our society because of the petrodollar—if we were to divest from fossil fuels, it makes sense that the value of the US dollar would decline. The more people divest from fossil fuels, the less power the dollar has as the world's reserve currency.

"How do you a give a voice to the environment instead of shareholders?" Ana Maria asks.

Fossil fuels and power companies like PEPCO are currently monopolies that keep raising their prices. It's even illegal to go off-grid in certain areas, and we don't have a choice but to pay these people whatever they demand for their services. Our government and antitrust laws need to support the creation and implementation of renewable energy sources. And if they won't, it is up to us to divest, one person at a time, and invest in more appropriate industries, no matter how small this contribution seems. If we each act, the economy of scale will grow and make alternative energy sources more affordable for us and future generations.

Right now, there is a lot of polarity surrounding the issue of climate change: the radical right wing conservatives deny its existence while liberal scientists spread apocalyptic messages of fear to get their point across. Neither seem to mobilize people—one side produces procrastination, and the other produces paralysis.

Millennials need to find a way to give the environmental movement a new, rousing message, because it's affecting our future. It's not about spreading more fear that freezes us from taking action or drowns us in guilt for contributing to the obliteration of the natural world. Facing the hard truths about climate change is like looking down the barrel of a gun, and somehow we've got to get the shooter to not pull the trigger.

It would be a David-and-Goliath battle to take down the fossil fuel industry. Luckily, there are alternative ways to reduce carbon dioxide emissions that don't have anything to do with eliminating the presence of fossil fuels. We can stop climate change by empowering and educating women and offering free birth control, which promotes family planning. We can eat plant-rich diets and use refrigeration chemicals other than hydrochloric carbon. We can plant trees in cattle pastures, create solar farms, and reduce our food waste. These solutions are a lot simpler and more accessible for the layman than dismantling energy titans and tycoons. We can make a huge difference if millions of people change their everyday behavior through a continuum of small choices.

And these choices can be reinforced by the design of our system as we change the values of our capitalist culture through the creation of social enterprises and litigious intervention. We can implement systemic rewards and penalties that promote pro-planet behaviors. There are counties that issue taxes and fees for using plastic bags and invest the collected money into education programs to teach the youth about environmental reform. Companies can also get subsidized or receive tax write-offs for converting factories to renewable energy resources in some places.

Climate change is teaching people to pay attention to the *externalities* of all our hustling and grinding, the hidden environmental and humanitarian costs of "business as usual." This level of mindfulness is very much a part of many indigenous traditions and how they learned to live in balance with the land. Now, we're creating the corporate version of this biocentric philosophy to transform the culture of industry. The UN calls this "green accounting" or "triple bottom line accounting," where corporations and industries take into consideration social, financial, and environmental costs—the impact on people, profits, and the planet—when they do business. Another thing we can also do is financially support businesses that operate in this way so they will prosper and demonstrate what is possible for such working models.

Healing our earth goes beyond acting out of altruism for altruism's sake. Humans are going to continue to want the creature comforts and conveniences they've grown used to; the promise of some far-off reward in heaven for denying a plastic straw at a restaurant isn't enough for most people to forgo the joy of drinking soda with one. In our most predominant expressions, we are selfish creatures, but because of this we will also act in our best interests. We can correct climate change without having to live in an off-grid, austere way.

STANDING UP TO BE PLOWED OVER

You could easily argue that our government's refusal to divest from fossil fuels is a civil rights violation. Because of this, people are suing the government for damages caused when fracking destroys their water supplies and climate change floods their homes—and I applaud them. Politicians are jeopardizing the future of humanity, and they have the world's most powerful military technology to support their moneyed interests. It's important to pick your battles in life, but there are times you cannot be a pacifist.

The Dakota Access Pipeline protest in 2016, also known as Standing Rock, was one of the most unique and galvanizing displays of environmental activism millennials had ever seen or participated in. The controversy began when the US government announced their plan to build the Dakota Access Pipeline that would move crude oil across the country. Besides the fact that this $3.8 billion project was a huge investment of tax dollars in an energy source we're supposed to be weaning ourselves off, the pipeline was being built right through a Lakota Sioux Native American Reservation—without permission.

Standing Rock was an indigenous people's movement first and foremost, led by teenage Native American activists whose protests soon attracted the attention of millennials all over America through social media. Young people from all over the country came to their support either online or in person, growing their efforts into a countrywide political movement.

Mack McTeer, thirty-two, is a visual artist and musician who works at a library. From August to September of 2016, he lived at Standing Rock along with the protestors.

"I still think about it," he says. "It was the most real situation I've ever been in in my life. I stopped myself when it was all said and done, and thought, *This is what it really means to be human—to see the ugliest sides of us and the most beautiful.* I hope it doesn't get forgotten."

According to the government website DAPLPipelineFacts. com, there were many misperceptions fueling the protests. The source states that the pipeline would be built entirely underground; that it would eliminate the need for shipping oil domestically through rail cars and trucks, which would cut down on emissions; and that it would be built using the safest and most technologically advanced methods to ensure no spills. But to the indigenous people, this was just another boundary violation of the scraps they'd been given in a long history of betrayals—this land had been set aside as a reservation for their culture to survive after their land was stolen, and the US government was taking it away again.

Mack says Standing Rock was an example of what happens when regular people decide to stand up to power. It was also a complicated and very dangerous place. He says people thought they were fighting in a clear-cut battle of good against evil, and some enlisted violence as a means to an end. There were points, Mack says, where no one could tell the difference between the attack and defense. The police had snipers and tanks and drones, and they burned down camps. Disorganized violence erupted from many protestors, especially from white millennials who had flocked to Standing Rock like it was Burning Man, hoping to find something that would bring peace and purpose to their soul. They quickly made it their place to let out their anti-authoritarian aggression. And sometimes, they did it in unintelligent and brash ways that incited more violence and threatened the peaceful protests held on the land by the indigenous groups. Mack, who is white, says the indigenous protestors needed people who were spiritually fit to show up and support them, not a bunch of young, reckless, naïve kids who can't keep their composure at the frontlines.

Unfortunately, the pipeline was built. While the Lakota Sioux lost the battle, their fight was not in vain. People across the world donated millions of dollars to the tribe so they could afford to be represented in court. They had to get money to fight the money; that's the way this world works.

THE SUSTAINOSCENE

We live in the ecological time period known as the Anthropocene, which is marked by human impact on the natural environment, predominantly through industrialization. Some scholars say the anthropocene started when we first lived in an agrarian society, though most of the measurable impacts began during the Industrial Revolution when humans created manufacturing tools to create goods on a massive scale in the mid-eighteenth century. Manufacturing led to the development of what is now our modern, global economy, so really, it hasn't taken us that long to do the damage we've done.

The environmental crisis we're inheriting, mainly in the form of climate change, is mother nature's way of kicking back after centuries of exploitation and maltreatment. We've created this society through the resources nature has provided us, but we haven't created it in a way that respects the needs of this Earth. The universe and its laws of cause and effect will either hit you with a feather or a frying pan, and right now, we're getting hit with a shit ton of deep fryers.

I believe the environmental crisis we are facing proves that we need to start recognizing as fact that everything is inextricably linked, that our every action matters, and that what we do to the living things outside our own flesh we ultimately do to ourselves. This spiritual truth is no longer up for debate. What is still up in the air is the verdict on human nature: are we selfish, untrustworthy, shortsighted slobs or bold, brilliant, caring, and innovative people capable of coming together in the last inning to save ourselves and each other from destruction?

There are a lot of unintended consequences that have accumulated due to our industrialized past and as the result of our unlimited growth in the name progress. But these effects are by no means irreversible. The earth is a self-correcting organism, and the solutions for how to bring our society back into a state of balance with the natural world already exist. We're nearing the end of the industrialized era, and we're about to harness new technologies to evolve what we've created into something else more sustainable. This is not just about stopping catastrophic consequences; it's about envisioning a new world, one where the solutions to all our environmental problems will help meet the many needs of everyday global citizens.

A group of scientists are calling this new epoch of humanity the Sustainocene—a time when humans will live in environmental and economic equilibrium, in a society powered by renewable energy, where all the nuts and bolts of the system will work in unison for all forms of life to thrive on earth.

For much of our history, our industries have been powered by finite energy sources like crude oil and coal. Industrialization has been about bottom lines, scaling businesses as large as they can grow, and producing as much crap in the shortest amount of time possible. The Sustainocene, on the other hand, knows that while nature is finite, it's also cyclical—it has an infinite capacity to regenerate itself. In the Sustainocene, humans will respect the cycles of life and death and harness renewable energies to fuel our economy from original, unlimited sources.

For the Sustainocene to happen, a transformation in governance will have to occur alongside the changes we make as individual people and as corporations. The technology to fix all this is here; we're just not implementing it. We're still doing things the way they've always been done before and expecting a different result. But we need to change now, or millions of innocent people and other creatures are going to die. We need to try something new. Any system that stops evolving eventually becomes tyrannical, and any science that stops advancing becomes hazardous to human progress. To heal our Earth and each other, we've got to find the balance between give and take.

MERGING THE FUTURE WITH THE PAST

Back to the future. Forward to the past. If we were to collectively manifest a Sustainocene era, what would it look like?

It's taken the developed world only two hundred years to use our industrialized technologies to colonize the planet and destroy the environment. On the other hand, indigenous people in every corner of the Earth knew how to live sustainably with the earth in small tribal systems. They lived without electricity. They subsisted by eating a few staple crops. They made shelters out of yak dung and palm fronds. They were eaten by predators from time to time and often lived shorter lives without modern medicine, but their impact on the environment was minimal. They lived in unison with nature. It's a place of privilege to be the dominant species on this planet.

If you're noticing a pattern in this book here, an underlying hypothesis, it's that almost all of our human issues can be addressed by coming into the right relationship with our surroundings. We're living in a time where our culture—western, individualistic culture—has evolved itself to a place of moral bankruptcy. We are faced with an existential dilemma about how to proceed. It makes sense to look to sustainable cultures elsewhere in the world, where every individual had a vital role and all phases of life were venerated, for guidance on how to heal our relationship with the earth and treat all life as sacrosanct.

Many of these nature-based societies worked with the elements, the directions, the plants, the seasons of time, and the spirit world. They knew that for every disease, there was a natural prevention or cure. Actions were taken in consideration of future generations. People belonged to the Earth, not the other way around.

Women were viewed as holy life-givers and the foundation of every family and were treated with dignity, respect, and understanding. Children were taught the values required to take on social roles responsibly. Elders carried the community's history and wisdom. No member of the tribe was isolated or abandoned. The pain of one person was viewed as the reflection of the pain of the entire community, and there was no reason to hide behind drugs and alcohol or be different from who you were and how you felt because you would always be supported in your truth.

Finally, these societies honored the presence of a mysterious, creative force they called the Great Spirit. There were designated days where people would come together to know this spirit through ceremonies and rituals and teachings about how to live in a good way. One of the main purposes of human life was to form a relationship with the invisible realms and harness them to find one's purpose in the interconnected web of life.

The environmental crisis we face is absolutely symbolic. Our industrialized society has deviated from ancient, universal codes of conduct in the name of human progress, and we have gone too far. We have raped the Earth. And now we are being called to look to the people we previously termed uncivilized to guide us toward the future. We can't go backward in time, but we can look to what worked in the past.

BRINGERS OF THE DAWN

Do we want to stop feeling so bad about our problems, or do we want to fix them? It's a serious question we have to ask ourselves. If you prefer the former, there are plenty of ways to do it—you can dope yourself or drown your conscience in a state of nihilistic hedonism; you can stop reading news reports and live inside your own bubble; you can carry around a magical talisman in your pocket to make you feel better. None of these coping mechanisms are going to do anything to fix the problem. And there are just as many proactive ways to devote your energy to manifesting large and small practical solutions to the very reasonable threat of danger that climate change poses.

To prevent our own victimization, we have to clean up the mess of what's been done by those who came before us. We have to pick up where human evolution has left us and be inspired by the possibility of what's to come.

The concept of critical mass conversion is a big one. If what we need is numbers, millennials have got them. If we need a cause to unite around, this is it. Mack says that one of the most beautiful displays of humanity he saw at Standing Rock was people huddling around one another for warmth during the icy cold nights. Humans can be selfish and shortsighted, but we also have an innately good nature that intimately feels the pain of others and ourselves and seeks to minimize it.

Miracles are happening every day. A millennial I interviewed named Michael Zambrano got his college, San Francisco State University, to divest two million dollars from the fossil fuel industry just by creating a petition and proposal and presenting it to the administration. If you listen to the call and do, you just might make magic.

Humans are creative and imaginative geniuses. Whatever situation we've found ourselves in, we can invent our way out of. We've come up with the concept of cradle-to-cradle design—resourcing packaging and other products sustainably so they biodegrade or are recycled into something else useful when their life cycle is complete. Coal companies are starting to use a "capture and storage" process, which removes carbon and pollution from the atmosphere. Legal actions are being taken to give animals and plants the rights currently offered to humans.

On this path of evolution, no effort is ever made in vain. Even if our efforts fail, they will create a spark of light that offers the world hope—and that hope is contagious, illuminating a trailblazing path that others can follow. It's hope that keeps people focused on what's possible. Following your hopes develops your faith, and faith opens us to the notion that the future doesn't have to hurt us as it has in the past. There's an intelligent design at play here that is too big for the human mind to fully comprehend.

Chapter 13

A Multicultural Movement for Unity

MILLENNIALS ARE THE MOST DIVERSE GENERATION IN HIS-tory. Diversity in representation and inclusion are two of our most important values. The majority of us want to be around people who come from different cultures and backgrounds. We know that surrounding ourselves with only those who pander to our worldview or who are similar to us is ultimately limiting. We value diversity in our workplaces and schools, in the media, and in politics. We believe it makes us stronger as a multicultural collective.

Celebrating diversity requires the ability to not just tolerate but also enjoy pluralism. It requires everyone to embrace our sameness and also our uniqueness no matter your in-group.

However, a totally multicultural, united movement is an uphill battle in a world where so much of our fate in life is determined by what we look like—our skin color, gender, and physical appearance—and what we identify with—our sexuality, religion, and culture. It's said that we're born colorblind and that we become color-coded over time as we are socialized into society. If race and color is a cultural construct, then our identities can be dismantled just as easily as they can be built.

We are worthy of acceptance and celebration; we have a say in how we allow others to perceive us in a world full of stereotypes and discrimination.

IT TAKES ALL KINDS

Charles Revard, twenty-two, was born in Tokyo, Japan. He moved to America when his mother married his father, a US citizen. Charles is mixed race (like all of us, if we go back far enough!). His mother is Japanese and his father is a white American; he also has a little Native American blood. However, his sense of identity was predominantly influenced by his mother, who taught him Japanese customs and the language.

There were no other Asians in his immediate community in Washington state. Charles says he always felt part of two worlds. He watched his mother struggle to assimilate in the US, and he couldn't help her do what he was learning to do himself as a child. He says she never figured it out.

"We need to be able to hold the entire paradoxical nature of culture within ourselves," says Charles. "From a higher consciousness perspective, we are one human race. We all physically experience life through the same human body. We all have a certain way of breathing. We all experience sadness around death. We appreciate laughter and enjoyment. We may experience different things, but how we experience them is very similar."

But while we are all made of the same light—the same "starstuff," as Carl Sagan would say—we are not the same. We are unique, and somewhere in our uniqueness resides the codes to our purpose and the part we will play in evolving our collective culture—by embodying and preserving the wisdoms of our individual cultures. Millennials, more so than any other generation before, are embarking on the quest to consciously engage with our identity and be at peace with it. This quest can border on self-obsession, but ultimately our liberation lies within our sense of self.

Our cultural identity is in the songs we sing, the clothes we wear, and the food we eat; we see it in the god/s we pray to, the ways we move our bodies, and the languages we speak. Culture orients us, gives us a sense of self, and allows us to feel like we belong to something bigger than ourselves.

"Our histories and cultures alter our worldview, and because of this, we're always going to be different," Charles says. "The most important thing is to be humble enough to recognize that when we do see major differences between my culture and yours, we should not make it a reason for conflict. Be curious, and use these differences to understand ourselves and others more deeply. It's all just another part of achieving oneness."

Conflict is the dilemma piercing the heart of humanity. For some reason, differences consume us. They cause war. They create slavery. We seem to have an innate desire to assert our cultural dominance over others.

Conformity might seem like the easy answer to avoiding conflict, but it's not an appropriate solution. Even if everyone on the planet decided to wear the same clothes, listen to the same music, chant to the same god, and get the same tattoo on their right thigh, we would still have to deal with differences. People would still see the world through their own subjective filters. We are still individuals. I've learned in my life that there are some differences that cannot be overcome if we honor our innate individuality, but that doesn't mean we can't coexist.

Humans are a species of multiplicities—we're made up of introverts and extroverts, empaths and left-brained thinkers, leaders and followers, queers and straights. No one person is identical to another, and yet our DNA is about 99 to 99.9

percent the same. There is much paradox in the concept of diversity. And I think Charles is right—for us to attain peace on the planet, we have to catch and stop ourselves whenever we start to harp on our differences before we can connect over what makes us the same.

EXAMINING WHITE MALE PRIVILEGE

It's no secret: white men rule the world.

When we look at the CEOs of large corporations and political leaders, we see, overwhelmingly, white men. Over the course of history, white men have colonized and homogenized cultures and economies all over the world, and their legacy of imperialism continues today as they continue to remove other, disparate identities that challenge their dominance. It's clear that the current system we've inherited is by their design, and it causes the suffering of other social groups who have been overlooked, unfairly treated, and discriminated against in sometimes life-or-death cases of enslavement and abuse.

It's true that not *all* white men are consciously and directly creating oppressive institutions, but they are living in a system where patriarchy is already entrenched and from which they benefit. If you pick any average, well-intentioned white man off the street and blame him for all society's woes, and he will look at you in bewilderment and say, "Who, me?"

Yes, that random man probably isn't directly responsible for the racial profiling of African Americans or the existence of the KKK. However, what he likely doesn't realize is that his life experience is inherently privileged, at the expense of others, because he's a white male. Time and time again, white men receive free get-out-of-jail passes; they are provided better opportunities than others and their voices dominate the conversation. And all of this is normalized in our world.

To not have to deal with, or even see, the hardships others experience daily because of your skin color or gender or sexual orientation or degree of your physical and mental abilities is the definition of privilege. It's important that each one of us examines it, because once you recognize your privilege, you can make the first steps toward changing this status quo.

Plus, having privilege doesn't make a person happy. Many white men live in misery. According to American Foundation for Suicide Prevention, white middle-aged men have the highest suicide rates of any population, accounting for seven of the ten suicides in 2016 (however, females attempt suicide twice as often as males). Men are socialized to be aggressive and desensitized. They are sent to war. They are pressured to be providers. Instead of being encouraged to express and be true to their emotions, men are shamed for doing so, which prevents them from being self-aware, conscious of their impact, and the creator of their own happiness. If you can't feel your own pain, you can't have true empathy for others. Behind it all is trauma that is perpetuated by the very same system of white male supremacy.

This is why dismantling white male supremacy will help everyone—of every color, gender, and cultural background. In this age of identity politics, the task at hand is to create a multicultural movement of unity, where everyone exercises their right to exist, so we can cocreate a culture where everyone has the resources to live as a human being with dignity.

EXPLAINING WHITE FRAGILITY

"I'm white, damn it. Don't shame me for it! Your problems are not of my making. I don't want to hear about them."

You'll often hear words like these coming from the mouths of white people. As a white woman, it took me a while to realize that I'm a member of the race every other race is measured against. While not all white people are wealthy, whiteness is inextricably linked to the possession and inheritance of property and power in this country.

Some say that whiteness is somewhat devoid of its own culture other than its inherent privilege. There's not much that defines my whiteness except for the fact that I picked the winning lottery ticket that makes it easier for me to get a job, a boyfriend of any race, a house, and an education. I was born "the right" color, grew up with "the right" networks, and went to "the right" schools. My white life was so insulated that had I not taken the time to discover how nonwhite "lower class" citizens lived in this country, I might not even have known that some people have it way differently.

There's a term going around called "white fragility." It describes how uppity, uncompassionate, and emotionally frail white people can get when someone from a different culture tries to have a conversation with us about race in an effort to show us that we're blind to how good we have it, and how often we use that blindness as an excuse to continue to assert our own superiority. White fragility is the privilege card that ends conversations whenever the topic of racism is brought to the table, because it makes us uncomfortable. White fragility doesn't want to see that racism still exists. White fragility wants to tell black people how to protest. White fragility doesn't want to admit all the ways in which we benefit from white supremacy, even though we say we don't support it. We may claim to be morally against it, because we want to be seen as good people, but that doesn't mean we are actually willing to go out of our way to stop the injustices experienced by others. White fragility doesn't want to see that our own complicity cocreates a culture of oppression.

It's easiest to talk about whiteness in the negative, in terms of what we don't have to experience. Most of us don't know what it's like to be stopped and frisked. We don't know what it's like to be refused service or to see people express shock when they realize we're well-read and well-spoken. White fragility doesn't want to have conversations about all this because we don't want to feel like we are bad people because of what we don't go through. But as news commentator Van Jones once said, "If you want unity, you have to hear the pain first." I believe this statement is very true.

Tyquan Morton, twenty-three, works as an English teacher for Teach for America in Jacksonville, Florida. Tyquan has a unique perspective on the culture of whiteness that I was not aware of before I interviewed him. He says black people have the burden of having to act white in order to prosper in a white man's society.

"I care about education," says Tyquan. "I speak 'proper' English. I have good grades. In black communities, all of those things are attributed to being white. To some people, they're viewed as betraying my race. There are three ways of being black in America. You can reject everything that represents whiteness: school, money, status. Then you can straddle the lines of that, doing well in school and work, but not leaving your people behind. Then there are the people who just reject blackness completely and only hang out with white people."

Tyquan's experiences opened me to the reality that "whiteness" is also a cultural code of behaviors. And while "blackness," too, is ultimately a fluid, culturally constructed identity, at the end of the day it is still seen as a biological trait and fixed onto people with a certain skin color, regardless of what they do. Blackness means a lot of different things to Tyquan, but according to him, it's always viewed through a negative lens in the US, no matter what kind of blackness is being personified.

And therein lies the problem with cultural appropriation, a widespread phenomenon in which white people freely adopt the very cultural trends of marginalized populations that minorities are so often discredited for. We wear Native American head-dresses during Halloween when indigenous peoples have been chased out of their lands and prevented from practicing their traditions; we sport cornrows that are called "fashionable," when the African Americans with this hairstyle are told it's unprofessional; we attempt to cleanse our souls by placing little Buddha sculptures all over our bedrooms; meanwhile the Buddhist mindfulness and meditation practices that we have transformed into a profitable industry for our own consumption is too expensive for the average immigrant.

Why are we so attracted to these other cultures? Despite not wanting to hear what life is like for marginalized people, we still seem to deeply crave connection to the cultures that white supremacy actively oppresses. There's a difference between cultural appropriation and cultural appreciation. Perhaps the better of us adopt customs from other cultures to connect with the depth of self, community, and spirituality we're missing in our whiteness. I actually think it's a way some of us are saying, however misplaced the sentiment, "I appreciate this, and I want to learn from it. I want to learn from you."

So take off the dream catcher earrings, acknowledge your white privilege instead of entertaining your white fragility, and be humble and listen to a minority who is open and willing to educating you.

FIRST STEP: ADMIT THAT WE'RE ALL RACIST

Millennials get triggered easily by any kind of pejorative reference to our identity. These days, everyone's triggered by everyone. We're even triggered by the word *trigger*.

It can get a little extreme, but I think it's a sign of progress that millennials are demanding safety in the moments when people from previous generations would have swallowed their pride and internalized someone's projections. We need places where we can be whoever we choose to be and rock out the identities that are inextricably linked to our history, biology, and personal preferences without having to deal with intimidation and uneducated judgments imposed upon us that strip us of our humanity—in school, at home, or in the workplace. When we are not accepted, we will get political about it. Some of us even make our identities about our politics.

But ultimately, we have to do more than correcting someone's language or walking away when faced with triggers. We also need to understand that just because an emotion is activated in us doesn't mean we're physically unsafe, unwanted, or that the other person deliberately said something offensive. Many times, it's just that damn ego that's getting jabbed, and all of the psycho-emotional baggage that attaches to it.

First and foremost, we have to stop the war within ourselves and stop burning every bridge that could help us access a different world away from the safety of our own in-group. We also need tools to talk about these kinds of trauma. We need to open ourselves to conversations with others who express ignorant views so that we can take organized, deliberate actions to ensure that these histories of oppression and genocide never repeat themselves.

Racism is still prevalent in the US. African Americans face incarceration more than other race. Efforts to integrate, especially in the South, have proven inadequate. There is still an underclass of minorities who don't have access to the same resources and sense of safety and agency that others have. And today, with the culture of terrorism, we've caught Islamophobia, too.

We still live in a day and age when wearing a headscarf at a job interview won't get you hired and when being black and wearing a hoodie can get you shot by the police. We have to recognize and admit that we all discriminate, and we have to catch ourselves every time we do so. Our ingrained racist tendencies can come out at any moment, and it will have an impact on others.

"You have to identify the biases inside of you," says Tyquan. "You have to be aware when one pops up. Psychologically, you have to know yourself. And socially, you have to understand the landscape of identity."

Tyquan is black. He's queer. He identifies as male. He has a college education. He's an only child. He comes from a working-class family.

"Some of these identities have privilege and power attached to them," he explains. "I also have identities that are oppressed. We all have the best of a few worlds. I try to let those identities interact with each other and grow. I use the identities that have privilege to advocate for people who are oppressed. People are more likely to pay attention to people who aren't being oppressed."

However, you can't advocate for a population if you don't understand the other person's perspective and all the ways you don't experience the same vulnerabilities. That's why the process of emotionally and intellectually understanding the effects of oppression can empower everyone involved—the privileged and the oppressed. At the end of the day, we all have the same goal—to connect.

I believe we can only end racism by first acknowledging the ways in which we're all racist. Admitting your racist predispositions doesn't make you a "bad" person; it just makes you a human who has been subject to social conditioning, as we all have. This first step of acceptance demonstrates that you are someone who is capable of respecting the experiences of others. From there, you can start to address the ways racism is reflected in your own behavior and in the behaviors of others. And you just have to keep correcting yourself until all of the notions of superiority and inferiority that we attach to different identities become eradicated.

Every single social justice issue ultimately intersects. We can't eliminate racism and homophobia before we eliminate sexism. And beyond this, our civil rights will cease to matter if we're all dead due to an environmental apocalypse. We have to work together to address the problems our brothers and sisters face; ultimately, they all stem from the same white, supremacist, colonial system that keeps us living at just a fraction of our potential for happiness.

We've got to shred all of the stereotypes within us. There's a lot of unlearning we have to do. We have to take stances against oppression. We have to befriend those we have been taught to fear. We have to get over the idea that there's a superior race or culture. We've got to come to know, on an inherent level, that we are equal though we are different. It's going to take a shift in consciousness.

IT'S ABOUT AGENCY

Agency can be defined as the capacity each person has to act independently within a given system and make choices, the kind that lead to a happy, safe, and healthy life. What cultural, systemic violence ultimately does is strip people of their agency. When your very survival is at risk because the authorities of the system you live in want to kill you because you look a certain way, your welfare and safety are on the line.

When you struggle to find housing and work because people assume that you're inept as soon as they see that you have a certain name, that's an issue of agency. These microaggressions add up and often alter our beliefs in our own abilities to survive and thrive. They are a reminder of just how much harder it is for us to make it in the world compared to others because of an identity we were born with. They corrode our self-worth and our ability to declare, "I have a right to exist."

Discrimination, displacement, and cultural genocide leaves a person with emotional scars that often take longer to heal than any type of physical injury. And it's the covert microaggressions that harm us the most—because they are so subtle and implicit, they are the hardest to unravel. And understand that these are the failings of a culture; they have nothing to do with who you are.

"Oh absolutely, I've experienced discrimination," says Bryan Serrano, twenty-three, a first-generation Mexican-American. "We went on a school trip in high school, and we stopped by a Chili's. The waitress told us that she doesn't serve Mexicans. A few months ago, I was walking down King Street and someone from across the sidewalk, yelled at me 'Go back to your country!' It happens more often than I'd like. It's not a pretty thing to have to experience, especially since I serve in the Navy. I'm just like, what makes a person American?"

In a rigged system, we have to find our own ways to deal with institutional racism, homophobia, xenophobia, misogyny, or any other form of bigotry without letting it affect our self-esteem. We also have to find a way to prevent the sometimes violent uprising of identity politics from dividing and conquering and keeping us from uniting over common humanitarian goals. Our self-esteem is what determines how many times we get back up after we've been knocked down, and we can't stop until we find our people who will judge us only by the content of our character.

"I have yet to learn a way to cope with it," Bryan says. "My first impulse is to fight them, but I won't fight them because I don't know how to. I haven't learned any decent coping mechanisms. I try to educate people through my poetry. A lot of my poems are about immigration."

It's worth noting that there are some minorities I've interviewed who do not feel the effects of racism to the same extent. Evan Saez, the computer hacker from chapter eleven, is a sandy-skinned Puerto Rican living in Alphabet City in Manhattan who doesn't feel affected in the same way as Bryan.

"My experience has shown me that if you're a relatively decent person, the world is colorblind," Evan says. Evan believes that some of us experience more adversity than others, but if you refuse to internalize these projections of inferiority and work hard, you can make it in this country, no matter what you look like. It is why so many people risk their lives to immigrate to this country.

GO WHERE YOU ARE WANTED

Charles remembers the first time his Japanese-ness was referenced in conjunction with the bombing of Hiroshima.

"In first grade, I was sitting at a table with some girl, and she said to me that we were the losers. That was the first time I recognized that I wasn't like the other white people in my town. I have a piece of pie in me that no one else has here. I remember watching some Japanese animations that took place during the time of World War Two. It was a graphic representation of what happened when the bombs hit. I recognized as a child that this was part of my genetic history. And then to have someone joke about having bombs dropped on me has created some kind of rift within myself. My people were mass murdered by the government of the country where I live. It's in the past but still present within me. And yet it's also very much hidden."

Bryan is a poet, a waiter, and a fire dancer performer; and he serves in the Navy. He also happens to be raised by two illegal immigrants. When he was sixteen, he watched his mother get arrested for identity theft—she had used a social security number from a cousin who had married a US citizen but no longer wanted to live in the country in order to find a job working for the government. She was imprisoned and eventually deported.

The US made it clear that she was not wanted here. Bryan's father no longer lived with them, so he and his brother lived alone and raised themselves.

"If you're here in the States illegally, you don't tell people," says Bryan. "You don't ask people if they're here legally. It's not a common question we think to ask each other."

The history of the United States is a story about immigration. from over two hundred countries have made many sacrifices to come to these shores, whether to find refuge from war or to lift themselves out of poverty, from modern-day immigrants to the early pilgrims. In cities like New York City and other major metropolitan districts, there are neighborhoods representative of every community: Chinatown, Little Italy, Spanish Harlem—the list goes on.

"Ninety percent of El Paso, where I grew up, is Hispanic," Bryan says. My parents specifically moved to a town that's good for immigrants. Everyone speaks Spanish. They did this so they could blend in. Bringing attention to themselves would only create trouble. They needed solidarity."

For a culture to survive, there has to be an amount of uniformity. Each generation keeps their ancestral traditions alive. Tradition may seem antiquated when compared to the trends of modernity, but cultural practices are a beautiful thing to be preserved.

It's said that everyone needs a tribe, and millennials, in the stage of emerging adulthood, will roam the ends of the continent looking for a place and people to whom they belong. If you don't like what they do in Rome (Georgia), you don't have to hang out with the Romans. The way this country operates—with fifty states divided by different laws, demographics, and geographies—allows for many unique microcultures to exist within one place. People in the US have an opportunity to find their very own cultural ecosystem that fits with their values, personality, and traditions. The liberal hipsters go to Portland. The rich conservatives congregate in Fort Worth, Texas. There is safety in numbers among likeminded people and danger in standing out.

And it's a function of evolutionary psychology, if nothing else. As hunter-gatherers, when we saw color on a tree, it meant there was fruit for us to eat. When you're different in today's world, you can easily become a target for negative attention—people may want to eat you (really). But, being different also makes you valuable. In this world of paradox, the answer is always *both*. As valuable as it is to stick with your tribe and preserve your culture, it is also important, in this day and age, to venture out as an ambassador and have other cultural experiences, meet new people, and learn from differences.

Bryan's parents came to America for more economic opportunities, but they didn't necessarily want to leave behind what made them Mexican. Today, Bryan considers himself both Mexican and American. He says this means he doesn't really belong in either country.

"I don't even think I'd want to belong solely to either side," he says. "I like having bits and pieces of both. I like to celebrate the Fourth of July and Deiz y Sies de Septembre (Mexican Independence Day); I want all of it. I don't want to "belong"; I just want it not to matter. I'm just a little bit Mexican and a little bit American, and I want to be a little bit of both. I just wish it didn't matter where I came from. I come from Texas!"

Empathy. That's what Bryan thinks people need more of. He thinks others should educate themselves on what being an immigrant is actually like before they declare that they should all leave. When his mother was deported, she was dropped at the Mexican border in the middle of the night, an area where women are raped, trafficked, and murdered regularly. She managed to make it back to her parents' house by banding with the other women on the bus and hauling ass to the nearest terminal.

What happened next for Bryan's mother is actually a success story. Because of her work experience with the US government, when she returned to Mexico she ran for office twice and won both times. Now, she overlooks the mayor's spending. She returned to school and received her high school diploma, and today she is about to graduate college with a degree in political science and public administration.

"It's not just about being more sensitive or aware or politically correct," Bryan muses aloud. "It's about celebrating, being open, and learning. In America, immigrants are taught to ignore who they are and become American. It hurts people to lose part of their identity just to fit in if they don't have a community that supports where they come from. These things make me human. There are aspects of my culture that make me who I am."

CAN WE COEXIST?

No group of people has ever been immune to invasion. The Ottoman Turks conquered the Byzantine Greeks in 1453. The Chinese hijacked the Tibetans in 1950. The US took over Iraq in 2003. The Israelis invaded the Palestinians in 1948.

What is left in the aftermath of conquest is thousands of people who have to live with the traumas that come when the land and people you love dearly and that you depend on for your survival is stolen from you. So often your identity and culture are also seized, not just a territory. Sometimes entire populations undergo brutal ethnic cleansing—from the Jews and the Bosnians to the Armenians and the Sudanese. Forces like colonization and imperialism decide that spreading nationalist agendas would be easier if a certain group of people didn't stand in their way. So, these locals are displaced from their homes and forced to live in camps. Often, religions and others forms of thought control are imposed onto them by the invading powers so that cultural differences are eliminated. Throughout history, the names and cultures change, but the story is the same, and the aftermath is horrific.

This leads back to the question: Will we ever learn to get along? If humans are so deeply frightened by difference as an ingrained survival mechanism, if humans are so deeply tribal that we use "the other" as a way to consolidate our tribe and overpower others, then does it make sense to stay in our separate corners and surround ourselves with our own kind to avoid conflicts?

Bryan spent a bit of time living in Utica, New York, a refugee city filled with Bosnian and Serbian immigrants who had left their countries to escape the war. According to Bryan, even though the two communities were in a safe space, they brought their conflict to the US; they would even fight in the grocery store.

"And I was like, 'I'm just here for cereal!'" Bryan says.

The sum total of everyone on this planet may never be able to fully unite in harmony. Some of us will not stand in a circle with people of different ethnicities, ages, or sexual orientations and sing "Kumbaya, My Lord." And we can't force them. But that doesn't mean we don't have it in us to come together in a far more profound way than we do currently.

There's a well-studied phenomenon in quantum mechanics that proves that some forces have destructive influences on each other while others are harmonious, by virtue of the different wavelengths in which they operate. The harmonious interferences propel the organism forward; the destructive interferences stop it dead in its tracks. This issue of compatibility also occurs in the natural world. Not every kind of plant will survive growing next to each other. So keep your black walnuts and cherry tomatoes separate.

We see these issues of compatibility play out in our interpersonal relationships on a micro level as well as among communities and countries on the world stage. Some people make easy allies, and others become easy enemies. To some people, I'm a poison. To others, I'm energetic lubricant. Being successful in life is very much about finding synergistic connections—dynamics that move you forward. But, just because someone clashes with you doesn't mean you have to make your life about destroying them. Just stay in your corner. There is enough to go around, alright?

There are seemingly unsolvable and stalemated conflicts that still exist between communities that date back centuries, and the transgressions are so deep and painful that no one can cut their losses and move forward to live together with new eyes. But we don't have to start a war; we just have to find a place of our own and respect the right of others to claim and keep such a place.

I used to be distraught over these issues of war and violence, and obsessed over ways to create world peace. One day, my father told me, "People have been clubbing themselves over the head since the dawn of time. You've got to get over it!"

Now I've come to terms with the reality that I probably can't solve the unsolvable problem of human war and violence. I can make my peace with the fact that violence exists. I can make peace with the fact that all humans are capable of it when pushed to the edge. And I can avoid it at all costs. I've found that the best and easiest answer to promote peace with the people in my immediate sphere is to empower and support others to be exactly who they are, as we all work on evolving into the expression of our best selves.

THE MOST SACRED WORDS ARE *I AM*

Ultimately, millennials believe in what you could call an "ideal" culture, one where we unite around values before individual cultural identities derived from customs, religions, and ethnicities. For diversity and multiculturalism to thrive, we have to come together around a meme of deep caring and understanding before nationalism and ethnic pride.

There are so many labels we could place behind the words "I am." Whatever we choose gives shape to our powerful identities. I try not to get too attached to any of them anymore because I've found that I'm most peaceful when I don't give a shit about my identity—I just am it. My self-image is positive, and that's what counts.

I also know now that my identity can be a conscious creation. I'll never be able to pin down one or three or twelve words to define myself, because I know that I'll keep changing. The best part about life is I get to decide a lot about who I can become.

Am I an agrarian demi-sexual anarchist, a libertarian Jewish-American Buddhist princess? At one point in time, I thought I was, but now I' not so sure. Because I'm all of it. I'm none of it. I am. And we are.

How do you like the sound of that?

Chapter 14

Sex, Sex, Sex—and Some Queer Stuff

"I found myself deep in that rabbit hole of realizing that it's kind of an illusion to think that you're this or that or associating with male or female, gay or straight. Because then there's a pressure to be and become it. I don't try to intellectualize the process too much anymore because it creates a weird debate in one's mind. Male and female are connected. They are the same thing in different ways."

—John Pericles, thirty-two,
cosmic jester, music producer, and actor

MMM, SEX. NOW WE'RE TALKING ONE OF MY FAVORITE SUB-jects. Not because I'm a sex-pert in any way. I've had scary sex, the kind that takes a few years to recover from. I've had sex that sent me straight up the stairway to heaven, relishing in angelic expressions of ecstasy as I was cherished and honored by another person. I've had sex that felt *meh*—could have done without it, but we wore a condom so #noregrets. Most millennials have had a ton of sex that falls on many different points of the spectrum.

This is a sexy planet; there's no way around it. Our sexuality is a powerful force that we don't always know how to harness in the best ways. It can be healing, creative, and self-expressive; it can also be highly destructive and can alter our nervous systems forever. Sex is how everything got here—and we owe it to ourselves and each other to contemplate what it means to enjoy pleasure in mutuality and manage the insatiable urge we have to unite with that which is outside of us. We have to want to procreate and fornicate from a space of love. And if love is too big of a pill for you to swallow, then show respect, at least.

Sex—it's about gender, it's about reproduction, it's about bonding, and it's also about power politics. It's about the roles we buy into, impulses that are shameful and hard to understand, stereotypes about masculinity and femininity that we both revere and deplore. Sex, ideally, is an act that helps us connect with each other to experience the capacity for bliss that exists within our own body. Magic is created when people come together to explore the many levels of human intimacy and connection.

However, there are many other reasons why people have sex, and often the more crude motivations seem to dominate the mainstream cultural landscape, at least since the sexual revolution of the sixties that loosened our puritanical mores in positive and negative ways. People use sex to manipulate others, to feed their own egos, to hide from their inner emptiness, and to self-medicate from stress and other forms of relational trauma in a splurge of orgiastic tension release. Sex and aggression are linked, as are fear and arousal and pleasure and pain. This stuff gets messy, and because we're not all equipped with the right tools to practice responsible sex and manage our sexual energies, people's boundaries are violated, so much so, that some of us shut down from letting in pleasure at all.

At its truest essence, sex is a deeply vulnerable act that requires trust to fully enjoy. But because of birth control, porn, all of our new communication tools, and more, sex for millennials can be far more mindless and impersonal. When it comes to figuring out an authentic relationship with sex, we've got to battle tons of mixed messaging. This is a conservative Christian country that has long deemed lust as a sin and sex as sacred only in the context of marriage (to make babies). By and large, millennials don't really believe in all that.

Our generation is striving to be sex-positive. However, a truly healthy sex-positive culture would look a lot different than how the media currently portrays it.

FROM PROFANE TO SACRED

Sex can be the most degrading experience in the world or the most healing and uplifting. The quality of the kind of sex we have is highly dependent on the quality of the presence of all parties involved. We can always practice safer sex, by knowing the risks involved and setting the appropriate boundaries that will allow you to enjoy the act. It's a concept called informed consent. And to practice true informed consent, our integrity has to come before the race to an orgasm. There are far too many casualties created when sex becomes just about that. The sole prerogative of sex is not to get our rocks off, feel wanted, or view each other as conquests. That's just what this culture teaches us.

Combining sex with the heart and soul to be a fantastic lover requires practice. When we're in an egoistic state, sex becomes about performance. You've got to get out of your head and drop into the ripening potential of the present moment. When we're in our soul, it becomes about merging with the divine through the art of making love to another. You can set intentions and focus your energy on visualizing fulfillment. Why shouldn't we explore the multidimensionality of touch, communication, intimacy, and psychic revelations?

Learning how to pleasurably, respectfully, consensually, and sensually relate to one another can do a lot to heal our planet. To achieve this, we have to move beyond sexual and shaming or hating ourselves because this desire inside of us exists. Instead, we can accept that we are sexual beings and learn how to channel our sexual energy for the highest potentiality.

To become masters at sex while doing no harm, we have to become masters of our own energy. We have to know our boundaries—and be able to respect other's. We have to have enough empathy to stay in the mindset that anything that feels good to me but not to someone else is a space I will not go to. The beauty of sensuality, when fully explored, is the realization that sex does not have to revolve around penetration or orgasm. We've got to give up goal-orientation in sex and be grateful for all the different types of connections we can have with each other.

Seduction, on the other hand, according to my definition, is the use of false pretenses to get something from someone else without honoring what they want or caring for their experience. People are conned into sex all the time. All it takes is a few ego strokes coerce people to give the most intimate part of themselves over to another in a way that they wouldn't have if the truth of the other person's intentions were fully exposed. Seduction comes from the culture of sexual objectification. Seduction is ultimately cowardly. If you can't tell someone outright that you want a one-night stand and nothing else, it's because you fear hearing the word *no*. In the realm of informed consent, both *no* and *yes* are considered sacred, and using deception compromises that.

Conscious sex requires honest communication and deep listening. It's about savoring the spaces where we can meet and agree on how close we'd like to be. It's about relishing in mutuality, exploring your edges, and learning to become acutely aware of your senses, moving toward what supports your vitality and what drains it. Conscious sex is about giving and receiving, containing, regulating, and releasing. I believe that if you can figure out how to master sex, you will figure out how to rock out life as the epic creators we are designed to be. Once we understand that sex is sacred, we'll be able to see that all life is sacred, too.

Our sexual drives are part of our vital life force. If we learn to harness it and strip away all of the conditionings of the mind and our culture, bliss is accessible to all. You just have to train your mind to tap into it—through breath, movement or sound, as the ancient practice of Tantra teaches. And the more I get into it, the more I realize that my pleasure does not depend on someone else doing what I want. I can make my own bliss, and there is no need to take advantage of anyone else.

"It's about using the body as a meditation object," says Alice Hart (a pseudonym), an independent sex worker living in New York City. Alice explores all the taboo realms of sexuality for a living. There are no pimps or drugs involved in Alice's business. She's chosen this profession of her own volition.

She says what she does is highly specialized work. She has to live on the fringes because our society still isn't ready to study and take seriously the efficacy of what she does. Prostitution may be one of the oldest professions in history, but the erotic healing arts, under her terms, are only just starting to poke their nose out into the mainstream. Alice wants to change that.

"Healthy sexuality and tantric practice are about using the body and eroticism to reach beyond the body, to go deeper into yourself and intimacy," says Alice. "It's about sharing a self-intimate journey with another and creating a mindful union of energy, of loving energy."

It's always been about love. Our ability to connect healthfully in a sexual way with others is a direct reflection of the depth of our own self-partnering, our relationship with ourselves. As far as I've seen, we've got to know how to love ourselves before we can fully express love with someone else.

In one session, Alice says she repaired an early sexual trauma in her client that decades of talk therapy never could. By pouring pleasure into a place where an emotional wound is stored in the body, she reprogrammed the way the trauma was wired in her client's memory and nervous system, so the fear of it could stop controlling their reality.

"I provided my client with a corrective experience. In the process, I'm paying attention to everything—their body, the temperature of the room, their emotional landscape."

Alice also does BDSM in her practice, which can also be a very healing experience. "The submissive is surrendering and the dominant is taking care. BDSM is not meant to hurt. It's not meant to be abusive. When a person chooses to put themselves in my care, it's a mindful, self-loving thing to do. I'm deliberately entering spaces where pain is stuck so it can be expressed in a healthy way and reimagined."

And it doesn't matter what that edge for you is, Alice says. It's just about expanding into new experiences and steadily moving out of a place of fear when it comes to our bodies and connecting with others.

"For some people, it's keeping handcuffs on the table; that's enough for them to go somewhere they wouldn't normally."

THE SERIOUS CONSEQUENCES TO SPORT FUCKING

Oscar Wilde once said, "Everything in the world is about sex except sex—sex is about power." Thoughts of sex consume so much of our mental space and are the driving force of so many of our pursuits—from our desire to hone our physicality to our choice of friends to our career ambitions. It's all a subconscious way to get sex and attention, to be considered desirable, and to feel power in a world where many of us walk around with a great deal of disempowerment and loneliness. What's crazier is that for as much mental energy sex occupies in the average person, as soon as actual sex becomes a part of an interaction, it transforms into something else entirely—it becomes about birth control, STDs, marriage, and who's paying for dinner.

Part of this is because most of us didn't get much of a sexual education in school beyond the preaching of abstinence, which is a lofty ideal for hormone-filled teens and twenty-somethings to do. The kids these days are sending each other naked pictures as young as age twelve. This is one dark symptom of the sex-positive movement. As much as we'd like to view sex through a positive lens, these are very tender times, early in our lives, when we're too young to understand the sensitivity of our sexuality or exercise our voice and choice. There are times and places where it's very important that we're not sexualized—and there can be devastating consequences if boundaries we didn't know we even had are violated when we're young.

Maybe this is why puritanical Christian cultures deem sex profane. It's all the more reason why we should prioritize teaching others how to have a healthy and conscious relationship with sex in a society where rape, unwanted pregnancy, pedophilia, sex slavery, STDs, and more make up the underbelly of a society driven by sex, money, gender roles, codependence, and power politics.

Just because you stick a penis into a vagina (in a heteronormative scenario) doesn't mean it's going to feel good for everyone; in fact, it can do a world of harm (especially to women). To be sex-positive, you've got to make sure the sex you are having is fulfilling for all involved. It doesn't require a lifetime commitment to the person either, just a commitment to care and offer full transparency during the course of your intimacy.

Personally, as I've gotten older, I've come to realize that without chemistry or emotional connection, sex usually feels pretty vapid. And if casual sex is what I'm after, I have to make a conscious effort to remember not to feel abandoned when the person I just had a one-night-stand with doesn't ask me out for brunch the next day. I've also learned that a casual hookup is not worth the price of an STD check.

I am striving instead to use sex as a vehicle to understand my capacity for connection. And as I've gotten older, I've become more cautious about who I get involved with if my heart can't be in it 100 percent.

Woody Allen said, "Love is the answer, but while you're waiting for the answer, sex raises some interesting questions."

Questions like:

- Are we really designed to be monogamous creatures?
- Can no-strings-attached sex still be healthy?
- Can I really stay sexually attracted to the same person for an entire lifetime?
- What should I do if I have fantasies about people of the same gender?

Millennials are experimenting with options as a way to avoid replicating the loveless, sexless marriages many of us see in our parents. What all of us want is more love and connection.

OUTWITTING BIOLOGY

In terms of biology, sex is ultimately about making babies. Humans, however, are one of the few species that have sex for pleasure—and lots of it. Very rarely do we think about sex as a means to creating another human with someone, unless we're already in a harmonious partnership and have decided to start a family.

The standards of beauty we find ourselves drawn to are deeply rooted in both biological and social constructs. Most heterosexual women are instinctively attracted to men with physiques that signal to us that he can kill and bring home the mastodon for supper. In the modern world, that translates into men with big muscles and a fat wallet. Meanwhile, heterosexual men instinctively like women with smaller waists, larger hips, and perky breasts—the indicators of fertility. To complicate things, within our society's construct of race and white supremacy, white partners are often seen as more desirable than others, perhaps because to breed with one would elevate your social standing.

Our current gender roles and patriarchal structures stem from our days as hunter-gatherers. Women in most societies didn't work in the same capacity as men due to monthly menstruation taboos or pregnancy. Many died during labor. Women were physically more vulnerable to predators—naturally amassing less muscle mass than men and more fat. Emotionally, our hormones cycled with our period, and this natural sensitivity made us fit to care for children. Children also needed to nurse, so women stayed in the camp while the men went out and brought home the bacon. It makes sense how we somehow inherited the notion that men can do all these things that women can't.

While our differences are biologically rooted, we are held to the same gender roles and cultural norms of what is considered "masculine" and "feminine," which are no longer useful in a modernized society. Instead, many of these ideals have become oppressive. What began as biology has now become politicized. The sex or gender you're born with relates to the roles, cultural conditioning, and stereotypes that are assigned to you, and the politics emerge because, in our modern patriarchal world, one set of gender qualities are still perceived as more powerful and more valuable than the other. Our society seems to value logic (male) over emotion (female) and physical strength and the use of force (male) over nurturance and empathic intelligence (female). Not only is that an ineffective and unhelpful way of thinking, but the other truth is that *all* genders have an extraordinary capacity to embody any of these traits, which, together, create a balanced individual. And what about queer folk, who embody gender roles and sexual preferences that don't fit neatly into society's predetermined categories? Queerness is biologically based, too.

In Simone de Beauvoir's *The Second Sex*, she describes with the utmost detail the social evolution of the relationship between man and woman and all the cultural constructs and associations that created the concept of femininity. Evolution exists because duality exists, and when opposites merge, they create a world of diversity. Even our reproductive anatomies function in terms of opposites—the egg rests in passivity and the sperm competes to penetrate the zygote. Masculinity is associated with action; femininity is associated with submission and passive enveloping.

These associations may be predominant patterns in nature, but they don't fully reflect our true capacity. I believe we're here to transcend the limiting and often maddening concept of duality. We're here to revel in our uniqueness, which gender roles suppress and violate.

Our evolutionary impulses and biological differences as men and women lead to misunderstandings, though our needs as humans are very much the same. When people meet in the heart, I often find that while our biology differs, we all yearn for love and connection. Oh, and also the desire to hump like rabbits on Discovery Channel (or not, if you're asexual).

GENDER ROLES DON'T MEAN A THING

"There is no one in my generation who has been raised without gender. Why do we have to celebrate what type of genitals a person has? It's a thing we do when kids are born. We don't stop to think about how strange it is. Why does anyone need to know what genitals you have when you're in the womb as if that has any bearing on who you'll become? We start decorating nurseries in the color blue, because it's so fucking manly! Really, all of it is so fucking arbitrary . . . and yet here we are . . ."

—Lenaya Leeds, twenty-three, permaculturist

For most of human history, women were treated as lesser-class citizens than men. They weren't allowed to work in the kind of jobs that made money. Back in the day, they were purchased as brides—in fact, this still happens today. For a long time in western civilization—and even now in developing countries around the world like India, Pakistan, Cambodia, and Nepal—women aren't offered a right to an education. If a woman is illiterate, she wouldn't understand what is going on in society enough to take a stance, which helps the agendas of men. For centuries, their domestic labor was unpaid. They cooked and cleaned and raised children and had to ask their husbands for permission to go outside or buy anything. As long as they stayed obedient, they could keep a roof over their head. Even the word *vagina* translates into "sheath or scabbard"; women were thought of as a decoration to the man's sword.

Today, these centuries of programming still lurk behind the division of who does what in our society and how much they get paid for it. It's why sex and money are inextricably linked. Traditionally, "masculine" attributes have always been given more prominence and rewarded with more monetary value in our culture, to the point that it has thrown our entire economy off-kilter. What about equal pay for equal work?

According to an article in Fast Company, the top two highest paid male CEOs make more than the top ten highest paid female CEOs combined. The difference in salary amounts to hundreds of millions of dollars each year. This means men have hundreds of millions of dollars more say in the making of our society than women. This is how much we've made gender matter, when it ideally shouldn't.

The women's liberation movement has been an attempt to shatter these unhealthy gender roles. Women want to work and become stakeholders in society; we want to have economic power and to not rely on men for our survival. At first, the jobs women held were in mostly caretaking professions—a secretary, a nurse, or a teacher. Now, we have more female CEOs, fighter pilots, and Olympic athletes than ever. Women can do everything that a man can do if given the opportunity. But can we do it as women and not as men?

In the past, the women who fought for empowerment in a man's world often took on "masculine" traits to compete with men. They believed they had to toughen up to be independent. They, too, pretended that the emotional sensitivity and proclivity to nurture that makes a woman didn't exist, so they could fight in a dog-eat-dog world. They suppressed their sexuality and sensuality so they wouldn't be a distraction to men. If they were assaulted, it was their fault for looking stereotypically feminine.

This version of feminism, despite the economic freedom it has given women, has not challenged our gender roles—in fact, it continues to feed into them in a way that demonizes the feminine. The key to dismantling the patriarchy is not in continuing to assimilate into patriarchal roles. We should allow our natural energies to flow and play their important role in balancing out the other without condemnation.

We're the midst of one of the most overt backlashes in history to the patriarchy—the social revolt of the Women's March and the #MeToo sexual harassment movement. People are looking for a way to end harmful gender roles and sexual predation. Everyone is hurting from the violence and excess of ego in both the bedroom and the boardroom. And one of the ways we can shatter these cultural norms is to challenge "socially accepted" sexual mores.

Women are taught from a young age to view ourselves as sex objects. Our worth is in our looks, and so is our financial security. We are conditioned to feel so insecure that we mutilate ourselves with surgery to look as desirable as possible. We starve ourselves to be symbols of fertility gone mad with balloon tits, dick-sucking lips, skin as tight as cellophane, and liposuction at the waist.

The idealized feminine in current popular culture is an unrealistic standard of beauty, designed for men in a way that destroys women. It also goes both ways—men get their penises enlarged, they kill themselves at work for the biggest paycheck, and they compete to be the king at the top of the pyramid. Some might say men do this to get any woman they want, but they also do so to be validated and respected by other men; after all, it is men who hold the power and who determine who to share it with.

The reckless and power-hungry male is as insecure as the superficial, helpless female. Every gender archetype has its shadow and wounds, putting too heavy an emphasis on sex as the root of identity. So much of sexual violence can be attributed to the mindset of colonization, where The penis is a phallic weapon used to penetrate one's surroundings at will, whether it is another person or an entire civilization, and the vagina is supposed to just keel over and take it. None of this will get us to where we really want to be, regardless of our gender—and that is love and connection.

"There's a great deal of mental and emotional violence on men," says Taylor Clark Johnson, thirty-two, a professional photographer who is in training to become a sex educator. "One of the deepest woundings of men in our culture is that it's not okay to be an open-hearted person. Don't cry around other men. You don't want to be too open or soft."

All of this has a huge toll on the quality of our sexual relations. Taylor adds astutely, "You can't help a woman orgasm if your heart isn't open. You have to be tapped into her."

So, open up, dudes. Let the floodgates of emotion pour until your false ego is shattered. The female orgasm demands it.

CELEBRATING GLOBAL QUEERNESS

While language traditionally described people in highly dualistic ways, it has begun to adapt to include those who cannot be labeled as one or the other. Queer and trans people are challenging the dichotomy of gender and sexual orientation, and it's causing us all to accept that there could be a different paradigm to view sex and gender.

Attitudes toward queerness have evolved considerably. Most millennials believe, even if we're as straight as a wooden board, that everyone has the right to be attracted to any gender and that our gender identity can be fluid. Ninety percent of millennials are in favor of LBGTQ rights.

While there haven't been many progressive political reforms passed in the US during a millennial's lifetime, gay marriage is one success. Congress finally decided that being gay is okay and that married gay couples should be able to get tax benefits. Homosexuality was once considered a mental illness in the Diagnostic and Statistical Manual of Mental Disorders until it was removed in 1987; now, 20 percent of millennials openly identify as gay, according to a study by GLAAD. Twelve percent of us identify as transgender.

Jackson John Taylor, twenty-four, is bisexual. He works as a psychologist in the military. Being gay in the military has had a long, controversial history. The fact that Jackson gets to do what he does shows how far we've come.

"I didn't anticipate that I would be in the military," Jackson says. "In response to the really high need for mental health care with soldiers, the military is paying for me to get my PhD. I only have to work for them for three years."

At the time of our interview, Jackson is counseling survivors of torture. His job has forced him to think deeply about the ethics of war. Every day, he sees the way acts of brutality debilitate the human psyche. He says he believes there is nothing heroic about war. The psychological price is not worth it, ever.

Jackson says that his journey to become comfortable with his identity and his sexuality, as well as his struggle to "come out," has been a long one. It started with being willing to be who he is regardless of what other people think. Back in the 1700s, there was such rampant homophobia in society alone that anal sex was considered "a crime against nature." Flash forward to 2017, and Jackson is experimenting with anal plugs to break through his psychological and somatic blocks in that area of his body. We are, without a doubt, growing more tolerant and open to experimentation. We are also recognizing that there's a little queerness in us all.

There's something so amazing about the word *queer*—it encompasses the entire spectrum of sexuality outside of heteronormativity. It acknowledges that while labels are useful in helping us understand how to appropriately interact with each other, there is a large chunk of the population that can't definitively label themselves according to society's definitions of sex. Basically, queerness allows for the open exploration of sex and gender without the burden of assigning a label. You have the freedom to decide who you are and what you want.

This has always been a big debate inside John Pericles's head. When I ask him what his sexual orientation is, he laughs.

"Can you call me pansexual?"

John has changed identities many times in his millennial life. On the surface, he looks like a prototypical tough guy. He's six-foot-two. He has a highly muscular physique. In 2009, he started cross-dressing.

"My girlfriend at the time would dress me up," he says. "I wasn't doing it to be funny. I just felt super good dressed like a woman. I discovered that there's a side of me that felt horribly mistreated my whole life. A boy in Southern culture is told, 'Be tough, don't cry.' Girls were treated gently and more carefully. And I was like, why not me? Why am I forced to play sports?"

In 2012, he came out as gay and trans and moved to Oakland, California, where he changed his name to Ella. He says the spirit inside of him wanted to express itself as female.

"It was such an amazing feeling to be with people who had never met anyone other than Ella," John says. "It felt great to be seen and respected. The people in Oakland are very diverse, and I loved that after spending so much time in the South. The way I was treated wasn't based on anything other than how I acted. That was just so freaking refreshing."

Since then, Ella has become John again. He dresses like a guy and is now professionally acting in a variety of male roles. John says he identifies his gender with the indigenous term called "two spirits." The nature of a two spirit is to shapeshift and change. It's an ancient archetype that has helped put John's mind at rest a bit, because he has needed a label to understand himself and explain himself to others. Effectively, he labels himself as someone constantly in flux, and that's definitive enough.

Whit Anicelli, age twenty-seven, formerly Whitney, is transgender. Whit sports a brownish-red beard and tattoos on his large bicep. He says that he spent his entire time in high school feeling disconnected from his body. While John craved to be treated with gentleness, Whit enjoyed the personal space and social respect that comes with being a man. Today, he takes testosterone.

"When I learned that I was queer and trans, I realized the person I was," Whit says. "Before then, I felt like I was living underwater because I had become the amalgamations of all these people's perceptions. People were holding me to this way of living as a female. None of it was my decision; it was different people making those decisions for me. It was all just the inertia of my upbringing."

People often question whether transgender people are simply experiencing body dysmorphia. They ask, wouldn't it just be easier to accept the gender you were assigned at birth? Whit says it wasn't a choice. His body simply knew it would feel more comfortable in a male form. Still, he seriously questioned his motives before taking testosterone.

"If I was on a desert island with no one else around me, would I take this? I would ask myself that every day. And the answer was always fuck yes, I would."

Lenaya Leeds agrees that it's not a choice. She prefers the term *nonbinary* when describing her gender.

"I've known I was nonbinary since I was a child," Lenaya says. "I never felt like I was suited to anything of either being a boy or a girl. It didn't matter to me, but it mattered so much to other people. I eventually fell into the role of what was comfortable for the people around me."

Leneya didn't hear about transgender people until she was in college.

"At the time, I was incredibly insecure. I made fun of trans people for a while. I was fighting against it because I knew it was what I am, and it scared me."

For too long in our society, indulging in homosexual fantasies or identifying as trans were considered social death sentences. Even now, it's incredibly challenging for people to come out as gay or transgender. They have to deal with a lot of resistance. It helps to know that you're not the only one—and you're not alone one bit.

The Kinsey Scale, created in 1948, was the first scientific and psychological barometer of sexual orientation. It stated that all human beings fall somewhere along a spectrum that ranges from heterosexual to homosexual. The Kinsey Scale made queerness natural and did much to make it a bit safer for one to "come out" with queer tendencies.

Other ways of measuring sexuality have emerged since the Kinsey Scale. The Purple-Red Scale of Attraction combines sexual orientation with other types of "attraction," recognizing that sexuality can range from aromantic and asexual (someone who feels no romantic or sexual attraction) to hypersexual. Not everyone has lustful desires, and not everyone needs companionship to accompany their lust. The Genderbread Person encompasses a scale of your biological sex characteristics as well as your preferred archetypal expression of gender identity. Teachers use the Genderbread Person to talk with young students about the trans movement and why it's important to use the gendered pronouns someone requests.

"If you want to be an ally, understand that people just want to feel respected," says Lenaya. "Isn't that what we're aiming for? To make people feel like they're safe so we can really and truly learn from each other?"

Leneya believes that one of our big issues is spending so much time as a society trying to differentiate between masculinity and femininity and how to fit into the boxes of what constitutes a woman or a man, when we are a rainbow of sexual constitutions.

"We should just drop the subject completely and empower each other," she says.

SEXUAL REWIRING

In this alpha–beta culture, we are taught that there are leaders and there are followers. There are abusers and the abused. There are submissives and dominants. We've all been hurt by the opposite sex in some way or another—whether by a harsh and controlling mother or a possessive and jealous boyfriend—and for some people, these past abuses play out in how we relate to our gender roles in the bedroom.

BDSM and kink are becoming mainstream for many who are simply curious about how to make sex with a stable partner more exciting; but for others, BDSM can create a safe container to express our darker sides and fetishes that we wish to transmute. It's a way to turn our past experiences of abuse into graphic expressions of vulnerability, power, and ecstasy without actually hurting someone or being hurt in the process.

There's so much to reprogram. We have to find ways to release the trauma caused by sexual violence and the perversions that develop when our sexuality is shunned by predominant moral codes. And as long as it's consensual, I personally don't care what's goes down behind closed doors.

In my personal life, I've found that the most healing approach to connecting intimately with others is to go slow. You wouldn't try to bench press two thousand pounds your first time at the gym; you have to build up to it or you'd get hurt. Hopping into bed with another human being can be seen in the same way.

"I've enjoyed not rushing into physical intimacy with women," says Taylor, who has embarked on his own very deliberate voyage to rewire all his beliefs, assumptions, and expectations around sex. "If it's clear that I'm not going to try to fuck them without their consent, trust is built. If there's hesitation or fear, it's not as enjoyable for me."

He adds, "It's important for men to become aware of their urges or else they can project their sexual needs onto other people. They think 'Oh, it's my partner's job to get me off.' Or, 'Hey! I'm horny, and I need to go fuck someone.' Come to a meeting point with people and don't force yourself on them, even energetically."

It takes self-mastery. We often fall out of balance with our own energy and with other's from time to time. It can start out innocent enough, but sometimes it becomes pathological, and the damage done is criminal.

One in five women will be sexually assaulted in college,

according to the Bureau of Justice Statistics. According to RAINN, one out of every six women in America has been the victim of an attempted or completed rape. Nine out of every ten assault victims are women. According to the same study by RAINN, the number of cases of sexual violence has fallen in half since 1993, and that's wonderful. However, I still think that the best way to proceed in a sexual encounter is to assume that every woman you know, within her lifetime, has had her body touched by a man in a sexual way without permission.

It all boils down to voice and choice. In a culture where we've been silenced for so long, women need to learn to speak up, and men need to learn to ask and listen. Check in with your partner about STDs, partnership status, and what having sex will mean for each person involved. If you can't be transparent about that and get laid, you shouldn't go ahead.

If you do get the green light, keep asking your partner how they feel throughout, especially if they start sending you mixed messages. Talk to them the next day to see how they are feeling and how you can make the experience better for both of you the next time—if there is a next time.

Pay attention to nonverbal communication. It's more important than you think. When you're alone in a room with someone, the misinterpretation of body language can mean the difference between having passionate, wild, willing sex and rape. Be wary of sleeping with someone if there's tons of alcohol involved. Also, know that most women freeze when they experience a man using force to take physical intimacy at a pace faster than what feels comfortable. To an excited person high on sex-brain, this might appear as normal submission. The key in any of these encounters is not just asking to touch or speaking and listening to the word "no," but also checking in to see if your partner expresses a resounding "yes." If the answer is a "meh," take a step back. If things are hot and heavy and then all of sudden the other person stops, you should stop, too. It takes a lot of self-restraint and control, but do you really want to have sex with someone who's acting like a dead, sad fish? Is that the idea of lovemaking to you?

These are the lessons I've learned the hard way. There's a lot of gray in the realm of sex—about fifty shades of it. Fortunately, there are many easy solutions. Use a goddamn condom until you're with a steady partner. Wait for enthusiastic consent. Women, know your ovulation patterns and use hormonal birth control when prescribed. Get checked regularly for STDS. Protecting yourself and others from the consequences of sex will create an environment of trust where human sexuality can thrive as it is meant to.

The sex-positive movement is a most rational one. We're figuring out how to move beyond our relational traumas to become a pleasure-positive culture through trial and error, and it's often a messy, neurotic process for young adults. Luckily, more and more people are realizing that simple honesty is what works best. Getting to know someone before exchanging bodily fluids is the best way to involve our entire essence in the act. After all, this is what conscious sensuality requires.

Chapter 15

Relationships Are the Journey

OR BETTER OR WORSE, HUMANS ARE CREATURES WHO NEED to bond. We're pack animals, and we associate our relationships with survival. To truly love someone—even though we know we're all going to die in the end and we might eventually lose them—takes courage. And to keep choosing to love someone day after day, making the commitment to fall deeper and deeper in love with them instead of tiring as time goes by or turning away in times of conflict and strife, is a conscious act of devotion that builds resilient emotional muscles.

We will have many relationships over the course of our lives—from casual acquaintances to partnerships forged under legally binding agreements. When the entirety of you is fully known to a person who chooses to love and be loyal to you anyway—that's gold. It's one of life's greatest gifts, a treasure that can't be taken for granted in this often hostile world.

Humans are also capable of what I call transpersonal love—an affinity for all of life. We have the ability to extend and receive love and compassion to everything and anything. I am full of love for the trees! I am brimming with love for the sun! When we're in a state of transpersonal love, we don't need any commitment or promises of permanence to express the joy inside us. Transpersonal love goes beyond an attachment to outcomes. When we're in its space, there's no need to seek love, because love is already what we are.

In the university of life, relationships are by far our greatest teachers. If peace is the journey, then relationships help us get there, most often by revealing to us the parts of our personalities that stand in the way. I believe that's why we're here: to learn to love by seeing the reflections of ourselves in others (both good and bad traits) and making the decision to evolve.

Relationships reveal to us the core of our intimate selves and force us to understand the issues of humanity that afflict us. They can bring all our unhealed wounds to the surface, but they can also make us instantly feel like we don't have any pain at all. They make us recognize the needs we have and challenge us to treat another's as equal to our own. They train us to stabilize ourselves whenever our emotional triggers are set off.

The question is: Are you willing to face the repressed parts of yourself that you might resent or deny through the mirror of your relationships? And will that attract you more to them, as you consciously attempt to improve yourself, or will that make you turn away and run?

PICKING WISELY

First, a disclaimer: I'm no relationship guru. I've had some great relationships, and I've had some debilitatingly painful ones. Here, I speak from my experience and theories that I'm compelled by. As of this writing, I'm not currently in a committed romantic relationship and I'm not married; I'm still not sure if I'm ever cut out for marriage, though I highly respect the sanctity of the concept. When I'm ready and with the right person, I'd do it.

A 2014 survey by Gallup found that only 27 percent of millennials are married, compared to the 36 percent of generation Xers and 48 percent of baby boomers at the same age. We're in no rush. As much as we value community, we like to roll solo. We're experimenting with the concept of being alone, together. Some of us are highly skeptical of the institution of marriage because we look at our parents' relationships and they don't seem happy. We see marriages that seem born out of duty and obligation that have become stagnant.

Some people think our hesitancy to commit to one person is because we're extending our adolescence to an unreasonable length or because we've become cynical and no longer believe in love; we're commitment-phobes and only interested in casually relating. I don't think that's the main reason. Marriage may be the foundation of a capitalist society, but the millennials who resist this social norm are more rational than they appear. I believe this generation is smart enough to know that if we don't know ourselves well enough and work through our deepest personal hang-ups prior to marriage, we won't be able to make a good, conscious choice about our mate—or discern if whether we even want one in the first place comes from an authentic space. Choosing (or not choosing) a life partner is one of the most important decisions we'll ever make. This person with whom we choose to build a family and share assets will hold 50 percent of our creative potential.

From playful dalliances of free love; to stormy, star-crossed, traumatic unions; to those rare, effortless soul mates that instantly put you at ease and whom you can't imagine your life without— each relationship has its purpose and place. Each relationship serves as a stepping stone that helps us figure out who we are and what we want. Some of the best relationship advice I've ever been given is: love who loves you. It seems simple enough. But the catch is: it takes true self-esteem.

There's this idea that marriage is the end goal for all romantic relating, and it's a strange, heavy one. It's irrational to think that one person is going to be able to meet all your needs. I've found that until I learn how to energetically fill my own cup instead of placing that responsibility on one or more flawed persons, I'll end up trying to control them in an attempt to regulate myself. This is a subtle form of relationship violence that can quickly spiral out of control. If that's how you see relationships, as a means to a selfish end, you can never be in a healthy partnership. There's a huge difference between caring for someone and needing to be cared for—and the nuance between the two makes all the difference in the quality and equanimity of our connections.

In my own personal process of learning to love myself to more authentically love others, I've become very curious about my own hypocrisies—all the ways I say I want love only to push it away. Culture tells us that the answer to life's problems is love. Love is all you need—but *how* do we do it?

Many of us have learned the hard way that not everyone is suited to play the role you want them to in your life. Not everyone is capable of treating the people they're close to with kindness and consistency. Relationship dynamics vary—two professional rivals can be passionate lovers; a great friend could make an awful domestic partner. The biggest problem occurs when we demand someone to be who we want them to be, ignoring who they actually are. That's when love becomes a game of distancing and pursuing, punishing and forgiving, making up and breaking up.

THE ART OF ATTACHING

The world of relating is riddled with various types of faulty templates for what love is supposed to be. Some psychologists theorize that our very first relationships within our family during the first few years of our lives influence the rest of our serious relationships—and whether we'll be secure in them or not. This burgeoning field of study is known as attachment theory.

Children are dependent on adults and form attachments to family members. Regardless of the quality of their care, they will come to associate love with the particular traits of their caretaking adults. If your definition of love was tinged with pain as a child, as an adult the prospect of loving might bring up the same feelings of desperate longing. Whatever our parents modeled for us as love is what we tend to later be attracted to—not because it's necessarily loving in actuality, but because it's so damn familiar.

There's a common myth that's been propagated in our culture—that love is what happens when two people come together and complete each other. We see it in the romances of Disney movies and Jerry Maguire. There is usually the hero and the damsel in distress, and almost always, someone is in crisis. Somehow screenwriters and storytellers have convinced us that love is about rescuing a person from their awful lives or about needing another person so badly that it's impossible to survive without them.

This myth of a fairytale romance has created a culture of codependency—where we stay in relationships that cause us pain because we're afraid to be alone. We are looking to fulfill our identities and find happiness outside of ourselves through someone else—but it never works. Because a healthy relationship isn't fifty-fifty; it's hundred-hundred. It's two whole, healthy people coming together to support each other through life's inevitable joys and sorrows, and doing things together that they could never accomplish by themselves. Oh yes, and it helps if they actually like one another.

I believe that true, attached, bonded love is a very mature undertaking and that good, stable relationships are grown over long periods of time. I used to get high off the intensity and chemical rush of romance, but now I know that our hearts are breakable, and that it's unwise to trust them with just anyone. There's more that matters than feelings if you want a partnership to go well.

THE MAGIC OF CHEMISTRY

Humans are made of a periodic table of chemicals. When we combine forces, a transformation inevitably occurs.

Call them your twin flames, your hell mates, or karmic relationships. I don't quite know what happens when we feel the intense zing of electricity with certain people. Maybe you've had a past life together; maybe you come from the same soul group. I don't fully understand the workings of the universe, but I have experienced the magic of chemistry. I know it can be intoxicating.

However, all this said, it would be totally irresponsible for me to tell you that every time you feel that sort of instant affinity or love-at-first-sight with a person, it's a cosmic synchronicity to be explored. Psychopaths have pretty mesmerizing stares, too, and sometimes our karma is a story that our lives depend on us to never repeat. When we're under chemistry's spell, who we fall in love with doesn't seem like a choice. It helps to discern whether you're in a relationship with chemistry, rather than the actual person themselves.

Love at first sight doesn't always mean that the person you've set your sights on is meant to be a soul mate for forever. It can, however, mean that you've just met someone you're about to learn a lot from. There is a science behind attraction that starts in the neural networks of the brain. What people call *love at first sight* happens when two people's mental and emotional dysfunctions match up with each other. It's for this reason that a shit-ton of chemistry is so often a recipe for drama. What we've found is someone who activates a pattern of relating that has been stored in our implicit memory, attached to the neural networks we've encoded as love. Feelings of euphoria and fantasy and irrational desire take over. We fall under a spell, a chemical rush of dopamine, cytotoxic, and norepinephrine that distracts us from the pain and boredom of everyday life. Because it feels so good, it's easy to think that we can somehow be healed by this person—when so often we end up rewounding ourselves. Our subconscious patterns take over as we dance the only dysfunctional dance we've ever known.

With diligent effort, self-control, and awareness, we can sometimes turn these dramatic, chemistry-filled relationships into something sustainable. However, I've often found that it's the next person who comes along after a relationship like this who benefits the most from what we've learned about ourselves.

All this might make you want to run away from the spark when you feel it, but a little chemistry is also a necessary ingredient that keeps a relationship compelling. There are billions of people in this world to spend time with, and something has to keep us returning to a single person every day. Chemistry is the emotional glue that compels us to keep investing in this person, because they hold the ticket to our spiritual transformation.

THE PRACTICALITY OF COMPATIBILITY

It's possible to have chemistry with a person with whom you also get along easily. It's not just about finding a person who makes you crazed and horny; you also need that person to be your partner and companion as you raise your children and share finances. Someone who will remain by your side if you get sick. Someone who, like you, prefers to live in the mountains rather than the city. Someone who is ready for an adult relationship in their life—to commit to someone.

Chemistry cannot work without compatibility. You have to be able to get along with your partner and make some pretty big decisions together without compromising the core essence of who you are and what makes you happy. The goal of partnership, as far as I'm concerned, is to learn how to achieve harmony with another human being in a way that adds value. Without compatibility, you'll end up miserable and resent your partner for the things they made you give up to stay together at the expense of yourself.

How do you find the right partner? Some people think it's by working on yourself until you become the best version of who you are—when you're so happy in yourself that you don't need anyone else, that's when, out of nowhere, they show up. As for knowing when you've met the right one, some people say that sometimes you just *know*. You joyfully give your life to them because when you're together, you become a better version of yourself.

So, just cross your fingers, pray to the stars, and enroll in a Tony Robbins course—and if that fails, hop online and create a badass profile that makes you look better than you actually are. Online dating can reduce compatibility to an algorithm. There are websites that match Christians and Jews, farmers and science fiction geeks, queers and sugar daddies, and even people with similar STIs. You no longer have to wait for Cupid to find a potential match; just hunt for someone to love online.

Justin Blackburn, thirty-four, a writer and poet, met the love his life, Gianna Rackham, twenty-two, online.

"We met on Facebook," says Justin. "That's millennial as fuck."

Justin used to Facebook message a thousand women a day and wait for a response. On the twenty-fourth day, he met Gianna. Okay, I'm kidding. He had some mutual Facebook friends with Gianna, which was how he found her profile. He says he wasn't looking for a romantic relationship at the time, but her work as a love coach inspired him. He wanted to connect with a light-hearted person.

"I couldn't tell if he was a creep at first," Gianna says.

All it took was talking about the Abraham-Hicks Law of Attraction for Gianna to let down her guard. "I started spouting the universe's advice to her online," says Justin. "And she thought that was cool." Gianna says she knew she could trust Justin immediately.

According to Abraham's teachings, interpreted by authors Esther and Jerry Hicks in the book *The Law of Attraction,* everything you experience in your reality is a reflection of your emotional reality and belief systems. You attract that which you are. Different emotions vibrate in denser or lighter frequencies. By focusing on what you want and changing the beliefs that keep you settling for less and living in emotional pain, you can consciously manifest your wildest dreams in the real world. You can live in a state of happiness.

Before meeting Justin, Gianna had a series of failed relationships with unavailable men who treated her poorly. "If you're attracted to difficult things all the time, you have to reflect on that," she says. "I started becoming more receptive as I got over my own issues in my love life that were attracting me to unavailable people. I think love can be easy. Love is pain when you're in pain."

Justin agrees. "Everything is a reflection of you. If she's acting distant, I ask myself how I'm being distant, and boom, it disappears. Everything between us is a cocreation. Think you're cool until you get into a relationship, and then all of a sudden you're crazy? No, you're just crazy. Relationships open your heart to all the things that you haven't loved about yourself yet."

"My last girlfriend had a lot of issues," adds Justin. "I wrote down on a piece of paper who my ideal mate would be. I realized that I wanted the opposite of her."

Compatibility is not always about finding the person who is exactly like you. Often, it's about finding someone who energetically balances you. A healthy relationship includes differences—because as much as we crave connection, we also need to retain our own sense of self to stay sane in a relationship.

There is quite an age difference between Gianna and Justin, but Gianna says it doesn't affect their compatibility levels. They've been together for three years. They live together and rarely fight. When they do have a hiccup, it's quickly resolved. They have found a love that is inspired, peaceful, and always deepening, no matter what insecurities pop up.

Vikki Matsis, thirty-one, is a hostel manager, founder of an independent radio station, musician, published book author, and mother. She has been with her partner, Lee, for over seven years.

"I was attracted to Lee's passion and intensity," she says. "Also his blue eyes! We were interested in the same things: media consolidation, natural living, vegetarianism, music, and travel, so we had a lot in common."

However, what strikes me most about my interview with Vikki is how she emphasizes the importance of their separateness.

"I have learned that I am on a journey, and so is my husband," she says. "We walk it together, and it is sacred to share that experience with someone. He watches my life, and I watch his. We are interconnected, yet separate, beings. I've learned that having a compassionate mirror has helped my growth and development tremendously."

Vikki uses the modality of nonviolent communication to convey her unmet needs to Lee in a way that doesn't alienate him. They have a weekly meeting where they talk about finances, other practical matters, and also any kind of emotional triggers that came up for each other throughout the last few days. They take time to process these triggers on their own before impulsively lashing out when they're emotionally activated. Meeting weekly allows them to mentally prepare and formally discuss sensitive topics, so their issues can be better received.

Vikki and Lee spent time and energy to create a working system for their relationship before deciding to have a child. They formed a deep, committed bond so they could raise a family in a loving home. They are monogamous, which Vikki defines as not extending sexual energy to anyone else with thoughts, words, or actions. She has trained her mind to only focus on her relationship with Lee and to not fantasize about seeking romance or sex outside of it. A lot of people might think this is unnatural, but it's completely possible if you are disciplined with your thoughts. They are a Jedi couple.

EVOLVING TOGETHER TO STAY TOGETHER

When you're on a date with a potential mate, you have one job only: observe the person as objectively as possible. Pay attention to how they treat people. Do they keep their word? Do they behave like they're capable of partnership, or are they a selfish prick? Do you even like who they are? Or are you too busy projecting your fantasies onto them because you so badly want "love" in your life?

While people do change—we really can with consistent effort—it's your safest bet to assume that who a person is when you first meet them is the person they will continue to be. You may be able to convince them to get a haircut, but if they're emotionally unavailable now, they'll probably still be emotionally unavailable next week. If they're an alcoholic now, don't expect them to start recovery next Tuesday. When someone shows you their true colors, believe them the first time around. Protect that heart and the life you've worked your ass off to create for yourself.

People are able to change, because change is the only constant, though we change at different rates. Some of us love growing. We dive into every opportunity and are constantly working toward becoming the highest versions of ourselves, while others

are more content with routine. Some people are just more accept-
ing or avoidant of themselves and the world. It helps to find
someone you can grow at a similar pace with, or you'll probably
grow apart.

True compatibility takes time to figure out. As we date, let's
try to let each other down gently when we realize things aren't
meant to work out. Whenever I date someone, I make a vow that
even if it's not a long-term fit, I'll try to leave them better than
how I found them.

EXPERIMENTS IN NONMONOGAMY

Oh, love. It's said that is love the energy behind the matter of the
universe. Love is infinite. Love is unconditional. So why must
we only love just one, when there is so much love to go around?

"We're moving out of constricting forms of relating," says
Steve Tourma (not a millennial), director of the REAL Center in
Asheville, North Carolina, an educational institute with a mis-
sion to give people tools for awakened relating.

"Polyamory is a course correction to the imposed moralisms
we've inherited around monogamy. Dominator cultures create
nice, dead people who are willing to go along with empire, the
war machine, consumer culture, and pathological insanity. Our
wildness and ecstasy have been so beaten down. We're looking
for ways to reclaim that."

Polyamory, or nonmonogamy, is the call of the wild. Steve
says humans are awakening from delusion consciousness into
connection consciousness.

At the REAL Center, Steve teaches a tool called nonviolent
communication (NVC), what Vikki uses in her weekly meet-
ings with Lee. Steve believes nonviolent communication can
solve 90 percent of the conflicts in human relating. He thinks
that what causes conflict between most couples and people

in general is an outdated evolutionary survival mechanism. When humans feel like we're about to lose a connection or we experience an uncomfortable emotion in response to someone else, we go into fight or flight mode, and those impulses are what end up sabotaging most of our connections, not the initial conflict. Nonviolent communication helps us talk about the things that go on inside of us in a way that brings us closer together, instead of shaming and blaming the other for not being a mind-reader or letting our primitive fears of abandonment take over.

Here is the NVC process:

- Make objective observations about your perspective.
- State the feelings that arise for you when you witness someone do certain things.
- Use compassionate questioning to inquire about the reason why people are doing what they do from their point of view—perhaps they are trying to meet a need they have. Don't automatically assume that they are trying to hurt you.
- Then, state the unmet needs you have.
- Make a request for a behavioral change the next time the same situation presents itself.

Nonviolent communication provides a framework to relate to others from a place of deep honesty and vulnerability without forcing our will onto another to make our weird feelings disappear, sometimes in ways that only create more.

Humans are taught to use manipulation, demands, and punishment to get others to do the things we want them to; that's how our dominator culture operates. The opposite of this is what Steve calls a partnership culture. How can we make life more wonderful together?

"Deprogramming takes work. It's like a spiritual practice. It's self-directed neuroplasticity," he says. "All the great spiritual teachers like Jesus and Buddha have said that if you want heaven, there are practices that you have to do over and over again."

In no other form of relationship is the element of practice more prominent (and these communication tools more important) than a polyamorous one. One of our most honored social moral codes is monogamy, which builds the foundation of the traditional nuclear family. But for so many millennials, making this model the end-all-be-all goal to our every interaction just creates a bunch of forced awkwardness. The marriage-and-babies paradigm forces us to size up every potential partner to see if they can provide this one utility for us in our lives. It makes things heavy and keeps us from appreciating the person for who they are and the many unique connections we'll have in our lives, regardless of if they last forever.

Many millennials are having multiple love affairs in a society that shames it. The people crusading nonmonogamy are striking new ground so we can all find a way to love the people we want to without sabotaging the connections we've previously built. Some might think that nonmonogamy quickly gets way too complicated, but for DJ (last name omitted by request), thirty-four, his experiments with nonmonogamy have been easy.

"Everybody knows what's going on and consents to it," DJ says about his multiple partnerships. "Details of how everything is navigated are negotiated."

There is a sense of wonder and joy that comes with discovering someone new and what a connection with them is about. DJ thinks nonmonogamy can be really healthy when it's done for the right reasons. Sometimes it can be a cover-up for sex addiction or the fear of really bonding with someone, so we have to be careful and conscious of our reasons. Safe sex is key to keep things functional and safe, as is communication and time management.

DJ goes to support groups with other practicing nonmonogamists to work through challenges that come up. DJ has a "no surprises" rule with his partners. If he feels a desire to do something that might stir up negative feelings with someone, he prepares them first and emotionally supports them through their own feeling process so they don't feel abandoned when he seeks connection outside of their relationship.

Nonmonogamy can be a far more freeing relationship style for those who are not prone to intense jealousy. Because, at the end of the day, people aren't property. The desire to share energy with someone else doesn't have to be the end of a committed relationship. We should be free to celebrate the beauty of love. Every person we meet brings out a different side of our personality and teaches us a different lesson about ourselves. There is enough to go around. Love can be like the light of a candle, multiplying when shared so it doesn't burn out.

AVOIDING CODEPENDENCY

Do you want your relationships to be based in abundance or depravity? Do you want people in your life that give you energy or take it away? There are many emotional vampires out there, people who are so insecure and oblivious to their own issues that they'll try to use you and call it love. I, too, have been sucked dry in a way that's left me bedridden for months, and the experiences led me to the conclusion that the most important relationship I have in life is with myself. I want people in my life who are attracted to my empowerment, not my pain.

Abandonment is one of the core issues that plague us. The fear of abandonment can manifest itself in two ways—it can make you super guarded or clingy as hell. But when you love who you are, when you've learned the lessons of your own lone-liness and grow to enjoy your time alone, and when you are able to meet your own needs independent of a primary partner, then you know you can never be abandoned.

The opposite of abandonment is engulfment—and we fear them both. If you feel suffocated and consumed by another person in a relationship, like an evil octopus is stuck to your face, you're being engulfed. When you're in a relationship with someone who can't self-source their own well-being, they usually end up consuming more and more of your energy to fill a void inside them that simply can't be filled by someone else. Relationships should expand your life, not make it smaller. You should not be your partner's caretaker.

Codependency, also known as "relationship addiction," is a behavioral phenomenon in which a person compulsively chooses unhealthy, one-sided, and emotionally destructive relationships. A codependent typically sacrifices their needs for others and loses their sense of self in them. Psychologists still aren't really sure what keeps codependent people addicted to miserable relationships. Some think that relationship/love addiction is really just an addiction to the inconsistent back-and-forth dynamic of love and abuse.

A codependent person will often do anything to avoid ending a relationship, because they need those chemicals to distract them from whatever they're avoiding within themselves. No matter how excruciating the dynamic becomes, they have no bottom lines. They'll go down with the ship. Sometimes they're the parasite; other times, they're the host. From an outsider's view, these toxic relationships don't make sense. But when you understand that codependency is a by-product of person's upbringing, the obsessive and pathological relationships we sometimes find ourselves in start to make sense.

Some researchers believe that codependency is not necessarily a disorder or even a negative trait; instead, it is simply a matter of good traits demonstrated in excess. Codependent people like to fix and rescue others. They are extremely loyal, especially to the people who don't deserve it. They confuse love with sympathy. They settle for being needed. They are people pleasers. Codependents live in a state of self-denial, and they often have no idea how to communicate their feelings. Their addiction to unhealthy people keeps them from being happy, but they continue to look to others as a source of their happiness. It's quite the vicious cycle.

"Avoiding codependency has been my biggest challenge," says Corey Harvey, twenty-five. Corey got pregnant during her senior year in college and walked down the aisle with a baby bump, about to throw up. "It's better than *Teen Mom*," she kids.

She and her boyfriend had only been together for a few months when she became pregnant. She decided to have the baby even though everyone in her family told her not to, because love is like walking down a cobblestone road with an ice cream cone. True love would find a way. At least, that's what she thought. Unfortunately, love isn't always enough to make a relationship work.

Corey's love affair began in an instant—with that spark of electricity. They met at a bar, and he asked if he could snuggle with her—just snuggle. She had seen him riding his bike around town years before and thought he looked like a hunky Jesus. After that, they hung out every second they could. They were young and enmeshed in adolescent love, the kind of love that thinks your partner is there to make you feel good, instead of one conducted with the intention to live in integrity as you walk beside and support someone else.

When she decided to have the baby, Corey didn't realize that her soon-to-be husband was struggling with drug addiction. He became distant and would go through mood fluctuations. On her end, it was easy for her to feel needy and make his suffering about her.

"You marry someone, and they're your best friend—and then you watch them deal with their struggles. It's hard to make their struggles not your own. That's where the spiritual understanding comes in. I could sit there and feel forgotten in this world of chaos or view all this as a lesson in patience. It's something I can use to grow. With patience and unconditional love, things come around."

To make it through the hard times, Corey has had to become resilient. She's had to deny her needs in the relationship and has tried to use this as fuel for growth. She had to first be completely emptied and exhausted spiritually before she could learn to be present with it and love herself.

At the time of this interview, Corey and her daughter Mila are living with her husband's family in Nashville, Tennessee. There have been many ebbs and flows in their dynamic, but throughout it all, there is one thing she never regrets: having her child. The one thing she's sure of in her life is that her relationship with Mila will always be strong.

Corey decided to burn and love fiercely in the relationship crucible instead of leaving when times got tough. She learned how to set internal boundaries with her husband. She now has two children with the same man, who eventually became sober, went to law school, and set up a private practice as a lawyer. But while many struggles were overcome, the dynamic never really changed. After the honeymoon period was over, Corey filed for a divorce. She knows she did all that she could, but the relationship never became a truly adult, loving one. She decided it was more important to be happy and on her own as a single mom than miserable with someone else.

On this path to learning self-love, we'll have to walk away from everyone who treats us in a way that's less than we deserve. It takes great faith to trust that you'll meet that special person if you just don't give up. And it helps to know that whether you're in a relationship or not, no one can solve your problems. Relationships often just give you a whole set of new ones. But are they worth it? Yes. They are what give life meaning and purpose more than anything else.

After all, we're just walking each other home. (You can thank Ram Dass for that one.)

Chapter 16

The Energetic Art of Changing the World

THERE HAVE BEEN MANY TIMES WHEN IT SEEMS THE BIGGEST mistake I've made is betting my chips on a changing world (and putting my faith in the people who claim to be leaders in that movement). This whole time, I've focused my attention outward. *When the world changes, I'll be happy.* That's what I've thought.

I've had to burn my idols and learn to stand on common ground with the sinners and the saints. I've had to stay optimistic in the midst of opposition—to ignore the voices of reason that believe all is lost for the human race because of dismal facts and figures. And I've found that the real work of changing the world starts within—because if I'm able to address my own suffering, then there's one less person suffering on the planet.

I've got to be the change I want to see. Damn it, because if I can't figure out happiness and peace and contentment with all of the opportunities I've been given, how the hell can I preach to anyone else about it? As I sit here typing these words, I am proud of the person that the five-year process of writing this book has helped me become.

I'd convinced myself for so long that this pursuit was about others, when really, it's been mainly about me. It's been about overcoming my paranoid apocalyptic visions, my dichotomous black-and-white thinking, my delusions (and illuminations) of grandeur, my self-sabotaging insecurities, and the voices of authority over the years that said I would never amount to anything. To write this book, I've had to confront it all to create something that would benefit someone else.

I hope that it does.

THE NEW PARADIGM ARISING

I know what it's like to be at a choice point when I have only three options: die, go insane, or grow. I speculate that we're now at this same choice point as a species. We could all just give up and die in a natural disaster or at the hands of a tyrannical leader—but that would be lame. We could deny the obvious and keep doing things the way we have done in the past, but then you're right where you started. The only worthy option is growth—to change our lives and our beliefs about it and what's possible.

Everything that's currently happening is a cause-and-effect reaction to what humans have been doing throughout the ages. But if evolution is fact, then through the accumulation of our efforts, everything that ails us personally and socio-politically can be resolved. Each one of us has a karmic code to crack, self-defeating familial and intergenerational patterns to liberate ourselves from, and a mission rooted in play and service that we can find if we dare to be brave. We're at a time in history when our systems need to transform drastically for humans to survive. We need what people call "a new paradigm," which can only come from people who operate from an ever-changing mindset.

I've heard the phrase "change the world" plenty of times to the point that it's become cliché. Because what does it even mean?

I think what we mean when we say we want to change the world is to change our inner worlds first, so we can then change our outer lives. It's a two-step process, in the following order. It can be ugly, but rebirth comes from dismemberment. As we shatter our limiting concepts of self and burn away the darkness one by one, a new paradigm will rise from the ashes.

Change is intriguing. It happens a little at a time, all of the time. And when we make a lifestyle out of turning negativity into positivity, we'll witness that even the smallest energetic and emotional shifts in our inner landscape will affect what we are capable of in the external world. The human mind is that powerful.

EMERGING FIELDS OF SCIENCE CAN HELP

Remember that guy named Isaac Newton? He discovered the concept of gravity when he saw an apple fall from a tree and developed. Newtonian physics (also known as classical mechanics), a system that measures how physical matter interacts. Physical matter is defined as anything vibrating below the speed of light. If we want to become light beings who can defy the laws of classical mechanics, we have to find a way to make our cells vibrate faster than all the dysfunction and emotional turmoil of the cause-and-effect duality that plagues the physical world.

Piece of cake. No big deal.

Newton's first law of physics very much explains the philosophy of the dominator mindset that governs human civilization: objects remain at rest until there is outside interference or applied external force. Another one of the most commonly held beliefs in the physical paradigm of science says that objects in the world exist separately from one another. This belief has led us to think that our actions don't have consequences that someone else can feel halfway across the world.

Now science is exploring quantum mechanics—what happens on the subatomic level of reality where matter and energy converge and are indivisible from one another. On the quantum level, nothing behaves the way it does in the physical. On the quantum plane, time isn't linear, but rather relative. Objects are found to exist in different states of matter at the same time. They are both wavelengths and particles. Every atom in the universe is communicating with one another through networks of information. Matter changes when it's observed.

Quantum physics also proves the existence of what mystics throughout the ages have called "god"—that, like the wind, there is something ruling the material world that we cannot see but that we can feel. And that force is energy. Call it consciousness, call it god, call it whatever you want; you are a part of it and the whole world is made from it. "It" exists.

Quantum physics proves that this consciousness affects matter. Quantum physics demonstrates what studies on psychological healing are now confirming—that our perceptions of our experience determine our experiences of it. Change our perceptions, and we drastically change our experience of reality. When we look at the world through a different lens, the world around us changes. What was once your trash can become treasure. A shift in perception is all that it takes, and the physical particles within and around you will respond to that change in your vibration, rearranging themselves around your shifting awareness. This means that no matter what hardship we've endured in the past, we can be free from it as long as we visualize and actualize a different life. Power and awareness can burst through all that's dense and dead inside us until we are born anew. True healing happens on the quantum realm.

The quantum paradigm also reflects the principles of interconnectivity long touted by ancient spirituality. Scientists call this interconnectivity *quantum entanglement*. It shows that even when particles are separated by long distances, they know what's happening to the other and have a measurable correlated reaction. In the same way, some of us find ourselves psychically connected to people—we know when they're about to pick up the phone to call us; we know when they're hurting. The actions of one person, while perhaps initially undetectable by the naked eye, are having a cumulative effect on everyone else. Just as we are seeing that what we do in the developed world affects the developing world, what we teach our kids through our behavior will become part of their inheritance. We are all creating this collective experience.

Everything has its own intelligence and is evolving at its own pace in this perfect, self-correcting universe. A seed doesn't need any instruction to turn into a tree, just like you don't need to do anything to ripen into your fullest expression, except to breathe.

However, when you understand that consciousness affects matter, you realize that life is no longer happening to you; *you* are happening to life. Everything that we envision collectively can come to fruition. As we start to use the power of our conscious intent, we can manifest our visions in a quicker and well-orchestrated way.

This is the difference between needing others to adhere to your point of view and being content with the evolution of everyone's personal philosophies. It's the difference between believing what others tell you about who you are and creating your own identity. It's the difference between thinking you need more resources to be empowered and appreciating the ones you already have. This shift from the internal to the external means everything. It means we can do without being attached to the results and stay content regardless of if we fail or lose. It means we can take joyful and inspired action instead of being consumed by worldly pursuits in order to fulfill ourselves.

There is much to be concerned about, but our life doesn't have to be consumed by fear and suffering. It's also about pleasure, joy, connection, health, and growth. I used to find myself so inundated by our problems—the war and the interpersonal strife and the scarcity—that I couldn't see the safety, beauty, and nurturance that was also there. I thought that fixing these problems first would lead me to that positive space, when I could have tapped into it all along.

FIELDS OF AWARENESS

It might sound crazy, but scientists are starting to study the possibility that perhaps every thought, belief, action, and emotion that humans have ever felt throughout generations of history is stored in a universal energy center called the morphic or morphogenetic field.

Rupert Sheldrake is one such researcher who believes that memory is implicit in nature and that all of the observable phenomena we currently think of as laws are really just habits. Sheldrake may be bashed in some communities for pushing pseudoscience. But in his book *Morphic Resonance*, he describes a study in the 1920s where rats learned to escape a maze in Harvard. Over time, their subsequent generations learned it ten times faster. Intelligence progresses as generations progress.

Sheldrake's ideas are iconoclastic because they point to the limits of scientific method, which assumes that the nature of phenomena is law. But maybe, just maybe, these repeating patterns that have defined human history don't have to stay the way things are. Our habits can be broken. Scientists can observe how things behave on repeat in controlled environments, and then study how to break these patterns in more unpredictable containers. Just as science evolves, so do Earth's self-organizing systems. Theories that were once thought of us as ironclad are disproven decades later.

Inside every human is an electromagnetic field. Our nervous system is like the electrical wiring that lights up a house. We are magnetic beings that attract and repel. And the most powerful electromagnetic field in the human body stems from the first organ created in the womb: the heart. A study by the HeartMath Institute called "Science of the Heart" shows that the state of our emotions influences our intelligence, our awareness, all of our perceptions, and our entire quality of life. The heart is a brain in and of itself. And it has an electromagnetic field sixty times stronger than that of our actual brain. Maybe that's why evolution for humans is, at its core, an emotional process.

Emerging fields of developmental biology and quantum theory are helping us in this pursuit, and perhaps the scientific method won't be regaled as the only way we can understand how life on Earth operates. Instead of studying the science of repetition in a controlled environment, let's study the science of what it takes to break cycles of suffering on a planet that is becoming increasingly unpredictable.

MOVING AWAY FROM RELIGION

It's funny—millennials care so deeply about finding meaning and purpose, but they are also rejecting religion. Millennials are one of the least religiously inclined generations in history. We don't think that our goodness is determined by adherence to dogmatic rules and literal translations of holy books. We don't believe our awakenings should be forced upon another human.

We've seen the sex scandals in the Catholic Church. We've heard the LGBTQ hate broadcast in the name of a Christian god. We know the bloody war led by Islamic Fundamentalists. We're aware of the ethnic cleansing of the Rohingya led by Buddhist monks. We don't trust religion that has been set in stone by fallible human devotees, especially when we see its destructive consequences.

Plus, millennials don't like to choose a single thing. Why settle for one religion when there are so many rich spiritual traditions to contemplate? Why can't I read the teachings of Rumi and Adyashanti and the Dalai Lama while praying at sweat lodges and going to yoga—while declaring myself as nothing? By in large, we don't believe in a heaven and hell in the afterlife as much as we believe that we create our own heavens and hells on Earth. We're a create-your-own-way generation, and many of us are defining our spirituality experientially, based on our own experiences of personal transformation. We may have been raised in a culture of secularism, where acknowledged truths don't have the word *god* attached to them. But we still want to be free to contemplate what happens on the invisible planes.

There are many paths that can lead us to the mystical states and divine visions religions have pointed to over the years. Meditation, consciousness psychology, and mindfulness studies are taking what religions described through mythopoetic allegories of gods and demons and interpreting these principles through the framework of science. When we're high on god, we're tapping into specific regions of the brain that all humans have the power to reach. We can now uncover the secrets to becoming our highest selves through empirically proven and applicable wisdom.

And when all seems lost, we can pray. Mother Teresa once said, "Prayer changes us, and we change things." Prayer itself may not end climate change and racism, but it can prepare the mental space within us to go out there to make a difference.

THE IRREPLACEABLE ROLE YOU PLAY

"Be moved forward by the hand of the universe, the creative fuel toward unlimited love. The path doesn't need to be clear. Respond to the people who are sent you. Make choices based on meaning rather than economics.

At some point, the violence and emptiness of our culture will bottom out."

—Dr. Steven Post, positive psychologist

We are all biologically, economically, ecologically, psychologically, and cosmically intertwined. And you have an irreplaceable part to play in the collective epiphany waiting to transpire. You absolutely matter because the evolution of your consciousness can affect everyone else's.

I believe that our ideas choose us. I invite you to answer when you hear the call. I invite you to take action.

The world of matter takes on three forms: creation, destruction, and preservation.

So:

What must we create?

What must we destroy?

What must we preserve to make a world that works for everyone?

Notes

Chapter 1: What Are You Going to Do with Your Life?!

American Psychological Association, "Stress by Generations: 2012," *Stress in America*, http://www.apa.org/news/press/releases/stress/2012/generation.pdf.

Hope Yen, "Half of new grads are jobless or underemployed," Associated Press, last modified April 24, 2012, http://www.nbcnews.com/id/47141463/ns/business-stocks_and_economy/#.Wnywreg-fHp.

Jackie Burell, "College and Teen Suicide Statistics," *The Spruce,* last modified February 18, 2017, https://www.thespruce.com/college-and-teen-suicide-statistics-3570768.

Jeffery Arnett, *Emerging Adulthood: The Winding Road from the Late Teens Through the Twenties* (Oxford: Oxford University Press, 2014).

PayScale and Millennial Branding, "3rd Annual Study on the State of Gen Y, Gen X and Baby Boomer Workers," November 19, 2014, http://millennialbranding.com/2014/3rd-annual-study-state-gen-gen-baby-boomer-workers/.

Pew Research Center, "MILLENNIALS: Confident, Connected, Open to Change," *Social and Demographic Trends*, February 24, 2010, http://ww.pewsocialtrends.org/2010/02/24/millennials-confident-connected-open-to-change/.

The Substance Abuse and Mental Health Services Administration (SAMHSA), "Key Substance Use and Mental Health Indicators in the United States: Results from the 2016 National Survey on Drug Use and Health," 2016, https://www.samhsa.gov/data/sites/default/files/NSDUH-FFR1-2016/NSDUH-FFR1-2016.htm.

United States Census, "Young Adults Then and Now," 2014, https://census.socialexplorer.com/young-adults/#/.

Chapter 2: The Anatomy of an Adult

BF Skinner, *About Behaviorism* (New York: Vintage, 1976).

"Consumption by the United States," *The Associated Press*, 2008, https://public.wsu.edu/~mreed/380American%20Consumption.htm.

Erin Grinshteyn, David Hemenway, "Violent Death Rates: The US Compared with Other High-income OECD Countries," *The American Journal of Medicine* (March 2016), doi: 10.1016/j.amjmed.2015.10.025.

James E. Cote, "Emerging Adulthood as an Institutionalized Moratorium: Risks and Benefits to Identity Formation," in Arnett and Tanner, *Emerging adults in America: Coming of age in the 21st century* (Washington, DC: American Psychological Association, 2006).

Jonathan Chew, "Half of Millennials Believe the American Dream is Dead," *Fortune,* December 11, 2015, http://fortune.com/2015/12/11/american-dream-millennials-dead/.

William D. Mosher, Jo Jones, and Joyce C. Abma, "Intended and Unintended Births in the United States: 1982-2010," *National Health Statistics Report* (2012).

OECD, "PISA 2015 Results in Focus," 2015, https://www.oecd.org/pisa/pisa-2015-results-in-focus.pdf.

Reporters without Borders, "2017 World Press Freedom Index," 2017, https://rsf.org/en/ranking.

Shelby Livingston, "Americans are sicker, skip care more than citizens of other high-income nations," *Modern Healthcare,* last modified November 16, 2016, http://www.modernhealthcare.com/article/20161116/NEWS/161119930.

The Pell Institute, "Indicators of Higher Education Equity in the United States," 2017, http://pellinstitute.org/downloads/publications -Indicators_of_Higher_Education_Equity_in_the_US_2017 _Historical_Trend_Report.pdf.

United Health Foundation, "America's Health Rankings: Comparison with Other Nations," 2016, https://www.americashealthrankings .org/learn/reports/2016-annual-report/comparison-with-other -nations.

Chapter 3: The Many Different Expressions of Success

Arianna Huffington, *Thrive: The Third Metric to Redefining Success and Creating a Life of Wellbeing, Wonder, and Wisdom* (New York: Harmony, 2015).

Carolyn Gregoire, "Finding Happiness: Americans Care More About Pursuing Personal Passions Than Wealth, Survey Finds," *Huffington Post*, last modified May 15, 2013, https://www.huffing tonpost.com/2013/05/15/redefining-success-americ_n_3279718 .html.

Emily Smith and Jennifer Aaker, "Millennial Searchers," *The New York Times*, last modified November 30, 2013, http://www.nytimes .com/2013/12/01/opinion/sunday/millennial-searchers.html.

Harvard Institute of Politics, "Survey of Young Americans' Attitudes Toward Politics and Public Service—27th Edition," 2015, http://iop.harvard.edu/sites/default/files_new/IOPSpring15%20 PollTopline.pdf.

Leonard E. Egede, Kinfe G. Bishu, Rebekah J. Walker, and Clara E. Dismuke, "Impact of diagnosed depression on healthcare costs in adults with and without diabetes: United States, 2004–2011," *PubMed Central* (February 9, 2016), doi: 10.1016/j.jad.2016.02.011.

American Express, "The LifeTwist Study," 2013.

Martin Seligman, *Flourish* (New York: Atria Books, 2012).

Peter Temin, *The Vanishing Middle Class* (Boston: The MIT Press, 2017).

Chapter 4: Reinventing the Quarter-Life Crisis

Colin Fernandez, "You may think you're grown up at 18, but our brains don't fully mature until after we hit 30," *Daily Mail,* last

modified December 21, 2016, http://www.dailymail.co.uk/sciencetech
/article-4055490/You-think-grown-18-brains-don-t-fully-mature-
hit-30.html.

Sarah Clark, "4 Ways Millennials are Changing the Face of Travel," *The Huffington Post*, last modified June 18, 2017, https://www.huffing
tonpost.com/sarah-clark/4-ways-millennials-are-ch_b_10503146
.html.

Chapter 5: To School or Not to School

Gallup, "How Millennials Want to Work and Live," 2018.

Kasia Kovacs, "The State of Undergraduate Education," *Inside Higher Ed*, last modified September 22, 2016, https://www.insidehighered
.com/news/2016/09/22/more-people-enroll-college-even-rising
-price-tag-report-finds.

Student Loan Hero, "A Look at the Shocking Student Loan Debt Statistic for 2018" (2018), https://studentloanhero.com/student-loan
-debt-statistics/.

William Deresiewicz, *Excellent Sheep: This Miseducation of the American Elite* (New York: Free Press, 2015).

Chapter 6: Entering a World of Working

Bentley University, "Millennials at Work" (2014), https://www.bentley
.edu/newsroom/latest-headlines/mind-of-millennial.

Edelman Intelligence, "Freelancing in America: 2017," *Upwork* (2017), https://www.upwork.com/i/freelancing-in-america/2017/.

Greg Schoofs, "These Charts Show How Much College A Minimum Wage Job Paid For, Then And Now," *BuzzFeed*, last modified September 14, 2014, https://www.buzzfeed.com/gregschoofs/how-
much-college-did-your-summer-job-pay-for?utm_term=.qrYwoB-
bJM#.dxr4Ekw7O.

The Status of Women in the States, "Spotlight on Millennials," 2013, https://statusofwomendata.org/millennials/.

Jamelle Bouie, "The Wealth Gap between Whites and Blacks is Widening," *Slate*, last modified September 17, 2017, http://www
.slate.com/news-and-politics/2018/02/cpac-was-a-window-into
-the-staying-power-of-trumpism.html.

Jennifer Robison, "Happiness is Love—and $75,000," *Gallup News*, November 17, 2011, http://news.gallup.com/businessjournal/150671/happiness-is-love-and-75k.aspx.

United States Census, "Young Adults Then and Now," 2014, https://census.socialexplorer.com/young-adults/#/.

Valerie Wilson, Janelle Jones, Kayla Blado, and Elise Gould, "Black women have to work 7 months into 2017 to be paid the same as white men in 2016," *Economic Policy Institute*, July 28, 2017, https://www.epi.org/blog/black-women-have-to-work-7-months-into-2017-to-be-paid-the-same-as-white-men-in-2016/.

Chapter 7: The Ritalin Kids (Try to) Grow Up

Arielle Eiser, "The crisis on campus," *American Psychological Association* 42, no. 8 (2011), http://www.apa.org/monitor/2011/09/crisis-campus.aspx.

Center for Disease Control, "Adverse Childhood Experiences," https://www.cdc.gov/violenceprevention/acestudy/.

Charles Ornstein, Lena Groeger, Mike Tigas, and Ryann Grochowski Jones, "Dollars for Docs: How Industry Dollars Reach Your Doctors," *Propublica*, last modified December 13, 2016, https://projects.propublica.org/docdollars/.

David J. Morris, *The Evil Hours* (New York: Eamon Dolan/Houghton Mifflin Harcourt: 2015).

Jackson MacKenzie, *Psychopath Free: Recovering from Emotionally Abusive Relationships with Narcissists, Sociopaths, and other Toxic People* (New York: Penguin, 2015).

Kaitlin Bell Barnett, *Dosed: The Medication Generation Grows Up* (New York: Beacon Press, 2012).

National Institutes of Mental Health, "National Survey Tracks Prevalence of Personality Disorders in U.S. Population," October 18, 2007, https://www.nimh.nih.gov/news/science-news/2007/national-survey-tracks-prevalence-of-personality-disorders-in-us-population.shtml.

National Center for Victims of Crime, "Child Sexual Abuse Statistics," http://victimsofcrime.org/media/reporting-on-child-sexual-abuse/child-sexual-abuse-statistics.

Sigmund Freud, *Beyond the Pleasure Principle* (New York: W. W. Norton & Company: 1990).

Chapter 8: Cutting the Apron Strings
Karl Alexander, *The Long Shadow: Family Background, Disadvantaged Urban Youth, and the Transition to Adulthood* (New York: Russell Sage Foundation: 2014).

Marion Woodman, *Leaving My Father's House: A Journey to Conscious Femininity* (Boulder: Shambhala, 1992).

Tyler Durden, "Why Are Half Of All 25-Year-Olds Living With Their Parents? The Federal Reserve Answers?", *ZeroHedge,* last modified October 27, 2015, https://www.zerohedge.com/news/2015-10-27/why-are-half-all-25-year-olds-still-living-their-parents-federal-reserve-answers.

Chapter 9: The Corporate Socialist Oligarchy
Harvard IOP, "Harvard IOP Spring 2016 Poll," April 25, 2016, http://iop.harvard.edu/youth-poll/past/harvard-iop-spring-2016-poll.

Steve Schaefer, "Five Biggest U.S. Banks Control Nearly Half Industry's $15 Trillion In Assets," *Forbes,* last modified December 3, 2014 https://www.forbes.com/sites/steveschaefer/2014/12/03/five-biggest-banks-trillion-jpmorgan-citi-bankamerica/#7bbf339bb539.

Chapter 10: Retreating to the Counterculture
Amy Adkins, "Brands Aren't Winning Millennial Consumers" *Gallup News Business Journal,* June 15, 2016, http://news.gallup.com/businessjournal/192710/brands-aren-winning-millennial-consumers.aspx.

Robert W. McChesney, *Rich Media, Poor Democracy: Communication Politics in Dubious Times* (New York: The New Press: 2000).

Chapter 11: The Technological Revolution
Chris Taylor, "Smartphone users check Facebook 14 times a day," *CNN,* last modified March 28, 2013, https://www.cnn.com/2013/03/28/tech/mobile/survey-phones-facebook/index.html.